Shaping Higher Education with Students

Ways to Connect Research and Teaching

Edited by

Vincent C. H. Tong
Alex Standen
Mina Sotiriou

First published in 2018 by
UCL Press
University College London
Gower Street
London WC1E 6BT

Acknowledgements

Our biggest thanks go to everyone in the student author and editorial teams. Coupled with a tremendous team spirit, their desire to make a difference in higher education is deeply moving. Our heartfelt gratitude also goes to all the academics who have served as our R=T Professors in the project. We thank them for their infectious passion for research-based education and unyielding support to our student authors. Their exemplary approaches to student education are celebrated by their partner students in Section 2 of the book – as they have undeniably inspired our next generation of research-based educators.

Apart from the R=T team, we would not have got to where we are without the support from other colleagues and students at UCL. We would like to thank Professor Dilly Fung for supporting the R=T initiative as part of the UCL Connected Curriculum and for her inspiring leadership of the UCL Arena Centre for Research-based Education. Other colleagues from the Arena Centre, particularly those from the Connected Curriculum and ChangeMakers teams, have given us their invaluable support throughout the project. Our special thanks go to Dr Paul Walker, who has given us some great advice on student–staff partnerships. We would also like to thank Howard Gossington and Kim Allen for their copy-editing of the manuscripts, and to Patrick Robinson for his filming and editing of R=T video materials. The students and staff who participated in the Masterclasses, discussion events and focus groups have made the project a success by sharing their valuable experience and ideas. We are very grateful for their contribution to the initiative.

Our gratitude goes to Dr Asma Buanz, who has kindly allowed us to use her beautifully created image for our book cover. The image shows crystals forming colourful chain link patterns on glass. The crystals themselves are the result of a mixture of two metastable polymorphs. Our book is all about connections – between students and staff *and* between research and teaching – and it is our hope that it will inspire many more such linkages at microscopic and macroscopic scales. Asma is herself a researcher and educator in the School of Pharmacy at UCL.

Last but not least, we would like to thank Wahida Samie (Education & Campaigns Officer, Chair of the UCLU Board of Trustees, UCL Union, 2015–16), Professor Anthony Smith (UCL Vice-Provost for Education and Student Affairs), Professor David Price (UCL Vice-Provost for Research) and Professor Michael Arthur (UCL President and Provost) for their support for the R=T initiative. Their presence and sharing of precious ideas at the R=T Launch Event in November 2015 was not just a show of support to the initiative but also sent an all-too-important message to the institution and beyond that research-based education is indeed a truly cross-community student–staff partnership effort.

Contents

List of figures and table

List of contributors

Peter Abrahams
Warwick Medical School, University of Warwick

K. M. Nabiul Alam
UCL Institute of Education

Mariya Badeva
The UCL Bartlett Faculty of the Built Environment

Harry Begg
Department of Political Science, UCL

Isabelle Blackmore
BASc Programme, UCL

Jacopo Blumberg
BASc Programme, UCL

Yekatherina Bobrova
The UCL Bartlett Faculty of the Built Environment

Frazina S. Botelho
Department of Physics and Astronomy, UCL

Frances Brill
Department of Geography, UCL

Tobias Buschel
Department of Computer Science, UCL

Lauren Clark
UCL Institute of Education

James Claxton
Department of Physics and Astronomy, UCL

Rebecca L. Coates
Department of Physics and Astronomy, UCL

Charlotte Collins
Department of Geography, UCL

Alison Cook-Sather
Bryn Mawr College

Elisabetta Costa
Department of Anthropology, UCL

Emily Cox
BASc Programme, UCL

Cosette Crisan
UCL Institute of Education

James Davenport
Department of Computer Science and Department of Mathematical Sciences, University of Bath

David d'Avray
Department of History, UCL

Robert Eaglestone
Department of English, Royal Holloway, University of London

Julie Evans
Faculty of Brain Sciences, UCL

Pedro I. O. Filho
Department of Chemical Engineering, UCL

Lora Fleming
Medical School, University of Exeter

Eirini Gallou
UCL Institute for Sustainable Heritage, and The UCL Bartlett Faculty of the Built Environment

Danny Garside
Department of Civil, Environmental and Geomatic Engineering, UCL

Eirini Geraniou
UCL Institute of Education

Carl Gombrich
BASc Programme, UCL

Arnaldo Griffin
UCL Institute of Education

Laura Haapio-Kirk
Department of Anthropology, UCL

Yu Hao
UCL Institute of Education

Nell Haynes
Department of Anthropology, UCL

Mick Healey
Healey HE Consultants, University of Gloucestershire, UCL

Graham Hodges-Smikle
BASc Programme, UCL

Tejas Joshi
UCL Institute of Education

Neema Kotonya
Department of Computer Science, UCL

Alvina Kuhai
Department of Physics and Astronomy, UCL

Jeremy Levesley
Department of Mathematics, University of Leicester

Jiaqi Lin
BASc Programme, UCL

Tika Malla
Department of Biochemistry, UCL

Jenny Marie
UCL Arena Centre for Research-based Education

Maria Margeti
UCL Knowledge Lab

Ljiljana Marjanovic-Halburd
The UCL Bartlett Faculty of the Built Environment

Katherine V.C. Marshall
Department of Physics and Astronomy, UCL

Kelly E. Matthews
Institute for Teaching and Learning Innovation, The University of Queensland

Manolis Mavrikis
UCL Knowledge Lab

Alastair McClelland
Faculty of Brain Sciences, UCL

Rachel McCrindle
School of Systems Engineering, University of Reading

Tom McDonald
Department of Anthropology, UCL

Laura K. McKemmish
Department of Physics and Astronomy, UCL

Daniel Miller
Department of Anthropology, UCL

Mark Miodownik
Institute of Making and Department of Mechanical Engineering, UCL

Preeti Vivek Mishra
UCL Institute of Education; now at Department of Education, University of Delhi

Masuma Pervin Mishu
Department of Epidemiology and Public Health, UCL

Jawiria Naseem
UCL Institute of Education, now at University of Birmingham

Virginia Alonso Navarro
BASc Programme, UCL

Razvan Nicolescu
Department of Anthropology, UCL

Martin Oliver
UCL Institute of Education

Charles Orr
BASc Programme, UCL

Francesca Peruzzo
UCL Institute of Education

Sabrina Jean Peters
Department of Civil, Environmental and Geomatic Engineering & The Centre for Urban Sustainability and Resilience, UCL

Ellen Pilsworth
Department of German, UCL; now at University of Bristol

Christine Plastow
Department of Greek and Latin, UCL

Siân Preece
UCL Institute of Education

Agathe Ribéreau-Gayon
Department of Security and Crime Science and Institute of Archaeology, UCL

Dallas Roulston
Department of Microbial Diseases, UCL Eastman Dental Institute; now at Middlesex University

Sayara Saliyeva
Department of Chemical Engineering, UCL

Ran Sing Saw
School of Pharmacy, UCL

Siir Saydam
Faculty of Brain Sciences, UCL

Sebastian Seriani
Deptartment of Civil, Environmental & Geomatic Engineering, UCL

Elizabeth Shephard
Department of Structural and Molecular Biology, UCL

Jolynna Sinanan
Department of Anthropology, UCL

Mina Sotiriou
UCL Arena Centre for Research-based Education

Juliano Spyer
Department of Anthropology, UCL

Alex Standen
UCL Arena Centre for Research-based Education

Joseph Telfer
School of Management, UCL

Joe Thorogood
Department of Geography, UCL

Vincent C. H. Tong
UCL Arena Centre for Research-based Education

Ahmet Alptekin Topcu
Department of Mechanical Engineering, UCL

Adam Townsend
Department of Mathematics, UCL

Laurence Z. J. Turlej
Department of Physics and Astronomy, UCL

Gozzal Utemuratova
UCL Institute of Education

Shriram Venkatraman
Department of Anthropology, UCL

Xinyuan Wang
Department of Anthropology, UCL

Introduction

Shaping higher education pedagogy with students in a consortium setting

Vincent C. H. Tong
UCL Arena Centre for Research-based Education

Can students, like professional educationalists, shape higher education pedagogy? Can they put forward their ideas about the method and practice of teaching in the form of scholarly writing for a wide audience?

Students have of course always played a role in influencing how their lecturers teach. Academics are inspired by their students' questions and fresh ideas on their subject. Through reflecting on their interactions with students, lecturers refine their teaching approaches. Students also give specific feedback, formally and informally, on their learning experience, thereby providing valuable information that can be used to make teaching more effective. While students in higher education are increasingly encouraged to work with both academic and non-academic staff to improve the quality of their education, they are by and large addressing issues in their own learning contexts. In other words, students' contributions to their lecturers' development as educators have hitherto been indirect, and their impact is likely to remain local. Given the many common challenges and opportunities across higher education, there is a strong case for students to exert collective influence by sharing their unique perspectives on learning and teaching beyond their classrooms and institutions. Writing scholarly materials on teaching for academics from the student perspective would be a radical but compelling way to inspire pedagogical innovations – by challenging the very core of the conventional roles taken by students and teachers. This is what our book project is all about.

Research-based education . . .

It takes some creative thinking to accomplish this seemingly impossible task of asking students to inspire not only their own lecturers but also other teachers in higher education to teach differently. After all, higher education pedagogy encompasses a diverse range of topics – what should the theme of the book be? We clearly needed to identify and focus on a theme that academics (and students) from different educational contexts, institutions and countries would find relevant and interesting. Connecting research and teaching for student learning is one such theme. Among different approaches to research–teaching synergy (e.g. Brew 2006), research-based teaching is a model that emphasises students' active participation in the research process (Healey and Jenkins 2009). As an institutional framework for enhancing student education through research and inquiry in academic programmes of study, the UCL Connected Curriculum goes beyond the research-based teaching model to research-based education (Carnell and Fung 2017; Fung 2017):

> The Connected Curriculum framework is built around a core proposition: that curriculum should be 'research-based'. That is, the predominant mode of student learning on contemporary degree programmes should reflect the kinds of active, critical and analytic enquiry undertaken by researchers. Where possible, students should engage in activities associated with research and thereby develop their abilities to think like researchers, both in groups and independently. These activities may include not only undertaking investigations and formulating related critical arguments and findings, but also peer review, dissemination of knowledge and public engagement. Such approaches can apply at all levels of study, from the first undergraduate year. (Fung 2017, 20)

The research-based education approach provides the ideal subject for our students to focus on. The following paragraph sets out the reasons why this is so.

First, research-based education requires continuing development of closer links between research and teaching to enhance the quality of student learning. Although it enjoys widespread support across the higher education sector, making research-based education a reality for all students at all stages of their studies remains a formidable challenge. For research-based education to be more than mere rhetoric, we need to change the institutional culture and promote the exchange of ideas about education at all levels in a university. Research-based education is therefore a current topic in higher education development and likely to remain so for some time to come. Second, research-based education, by its very nature, cannot be separated from active learning. As active learning is linked to a wide spectrum of best practices in teaching and assessments (Prince 2004 and references therein), research-based education is a useful unifying theme for discussing effective teaching practices, as it gives them a higher-order purpose. Third, advancing research-based education is a matter that concerns students as much as academics, and it transcends disciplinary traditions. Research-based education therefore serves as a platform for forging new links between different communities. In this way, students are encouraged to present their unique perspectives, as everyone has something valuable to offer to this collective endeavour in research–education synergy. As research-based education has become an institutional approach to student education at UCL, perhaps it is a good time to ask what our students really think of it, within and beyond their classroom settings?

. . . through student–staff partnership . . .

Apart from identifying research-based education as the unifying theme for our book project, it is important to help our student authors develop a broad understanding of the emerging trends, complexity and perspectives in research-based education. After all, it is important to engage our students with their curricula (Barnett and Coate 2005). We need to empower our students, allowing them to develop and present *their* ideas about research-based education in the form of scholarly writing with confidence. Student–staff partnership (e.g. Little 2010; Cook-Sather et al. 2014; Healey et al. 2014) is an effective way to help our students in this regard. In fact, student–staff partnership has been increasingly promoted by universities as a way of students collaborating with staff – both academic and non-academic – in taking forward agendas in research and education. Student–staff partnership is different from other forms of student engagement in that students and staff are working collaboratively as partners towards a collective goal, with power and opportunities distributed more evenly between students and staff members than established conventions might dictate. The scholarship of teaching and learning is one emerging way in which students and staff work together (Healey et al. 2014), and our book project is an example of this new type of student–staff partnership.

While it is encouraging to see that students and academics are beginning to work on the scholarship of teaching and learning together, it is challenging to undertake studies beyond small-scale work that addresses learning in local contexts. Our book project was conceived with the idea that students work with academics and other staff in a consortium of partnerships to widen the impact of scholarship of teaching and learning. We launched our R=T (Research equals Teaching) initiative at UCL in November 2015 to advance research-based education through student–staff partnership, and this book project is a key output of the initiative to date. It is part of the UCL Connected Curriculum initiative (Fung 2017). Apart from promoting research-based education across UCL, the activities jointly led by the students and staff in the R=T initiative were designed to help the student teams prepare, write and edit their chapters on connecting research and education through learning. The student author and editorial teams have worked with the R=T core staff team (i.e. the three editors of this volume) throughout the book project, adding another dimension to the student–staff partnership.

Student and staff teams in the consortium conducted student–staff partnership activities in six stages:

1. Student author team co-hosting university-wide discussion events on research-based education with a team of invited researcher–educators (the 'R=T Professors')
2. Student author team conducting focus groups, and writing up their findings and critical reflections with their partner R=T Professors and the R=T core staff team
3. Student author team peer reviewing their book chapters using the guidelines from R=T core staff team
4. Student editorial team co-developing a common framework on research-based education through student–staff partnership (the 'R=T Framework') with the R=T core staff team
5. Student editorial team working with the R=T core staff team on writing editorial commentaries based on the R=T Framework
6. Lead of the student editorial team working with the R=T core staff team to write the lead introductory pieces for the three sections of the book

The first stage of activities involved 15 UCL student authors from different disciplines co-hosting five R=T Masterclasses and two discussion events (R=T Launch Event and R=T Tech event on learning technology in research-based education) with the R=T Professors on a range of research-based education topics for staff and students across the university. The R=T Professors comprise a team of 12 UCL and non-UCL research professors with a track record in educational leadership and innovations, many of whom are also recipients of national teaching prizes. Student authors developed their own questions for interviewing their partner R=T Professors, drawing on their own experience and background research and reading. The R=T Professors, who represented a diverse range of academic disciplines, mentored the student authors on broader issues and trends in education, including research-based education, and shared their ideas and passion for making innovative connections between research and teaching for student learning. The following pedagogical themes, which are closely associated with research-based education, were featured in the R=T Masterclasses:

- Connecting students with staff research activities and real-world outputs
- Transcending disciplinary boundaries in student research activities
- Connecting students with the workplace
- Involving teachers and teaching assistants more actively in large-group teaching
- Peer-assisted learning and assessment

The first two themes are explicitly linked to research-based education with reference to the UCL Connected Curriculum Framework (Fung 2017), whereas the last three are explored in the context of how research-based education can be effectively implemented. Staff members attending the events had the rare chance to reflect on any mismatches between any of the presumed student-centred approaches to teaching and the students' views on a broad range of issues on research-based education. Students, both attending and leading the events, had the opportunity to interact with larger groups of staff (and other students) with different academic backgrounds and roles. The staff and students benefited from these activities as they shared their experience with passionate colleagues. By working with staff as partners, the student author team therefore had opportunities to develop ideas on research-based education beyond their own learning contexts – a prerequisite to ensure that their scholarly writing would appeal to a broad readership.

After co-hosting the events, the student authors continued to work with their partner R=T Professors in the second stage of the book project. Their work in this stage resulted in two types of outputs. Five UCL undergraduate and graduate students conducted their focus groups with students and staff across the institution based on the five aforementioned themes on research-based education. They wrote up their work and findings (**1.5–1.9**). The second group of 10 students – all research/

postgraduate students also taking on the role of teaching assistants in their departments (or having significant teaching experience) – went beyond the five themes. By drawing from their unique experience and perspectives as young researcher–teacher–students, as well as the ongoing discussions with their partner R=T Professors, they wrote up their critical reflections in partnership with their professors (**2.1–2.10**). We are very pleased that a young UCL teaching fellow with a track record in entrepreneurship joined the student author team in the first two stages of the work and presented his critical reflections (**2.11**). Each chapter in this section starts with a quote from their partner R=T Professor on the significance of the research-based education topics discussed in the critical reflections. The 11 chapters in Section 2 together showcase the students' pedagogical ideas in three broad areas of research-based education:

- Learning as the connector between research and teaching (**2.1–2.4**)
- Research-based education within the university (**2.5–2.8**)
- Research-based education beyond the university (**2.9–2.11**)

The third stage was centred on students peer reviewing each other's chapters, generating constructive discussions on topics beyond the one they focused on in their writing and further enhancing their own writing as a result. The final three stages of the book project involved a different team of 11 UCL undergraduate and postgraduate students serving as editors, again from a diverse range of disciplines. Their goal was to draw out the underpinning themes emerging from this student–staff partnership project on research-based education. More specifically, in the fourth stage of the project, the student editorial team studied the detailed reports on the five themes informed by the focus groups (with key ideas presented in Chapters **1.5** to **1.9**). Working with the R=T core staff team, the students co-produced the R=T Framework (Figure 1) summarising:

- Key challenges in research-based education through student–staff partnership
- Key opportunities in research-based education through student–staff partnership
- Key principles in research-based education through student–staff partnership

The fifth stage of the book project involved applying the R=T Framework to the 11 critical reflection chapters in Section 2. Each student editor

Key challenges

- Inadequate resources and individual prioritisation of research over teaching activities
- Academic and student resistance to curriculum change
- Perceived differences in knowledge and experience between academics and students
- Inadequate institutional communication systems
- Tensions between external pressures and the innovations required

Key principles

1. The traditional relationship between academics and students needs to change.

2. There must be equal and reciprocal effort from students and academics.

3. Practices should be embedded from the beginning of degrees.

4. There must be robust evaluation processes and opportunities for reflection.

5. There is no 'one size fits all' solution.

Key opportunities

- Promotes interdisciplinarity and cross-departmental working
- Provides a space for staff to be recognised for excellence in teaching and offers developmental opportunities to early-career academics
- Promotes active learning, independent learning and the acquisition of transferrable skills
- Promotes equality between academics and students
- Creates opportunities for real-world links to make learning relevant and engaging

Figure 1 The R=T Framework (co-developed by Tong, Standen and the R=T Student editorial team)

wrote a commentary on one of the critical reflection chapters using the framework they co-produced in Stage 4 of the project. Their commentaries, which form a very important part of the editorial work, are presented after the respective chapters in Section 2, giving the book another layer of coherence on the unifying theme of research-based education through student–staff partnership. In the final stage, the lead of the student editorial team wrote the introductory piece for Section 2 of the book, using all the work developed by the student author and editorial teams. The other introductory pieces for the book were written by the R=T core staff team.

Apart from the pieces from the student author and editorial teams, staff also contributed to the book project as chapter authors, making the book truly an example of student–staff partnership at all levels. Leading academics in student–staff partnership and research-based education set the scene by presenting a chapter on the international trends and contexts for the R=T initiative and the book project (**1.1**). The interplay between the institutional and international contexts for R=T is analysed in Chapter **1.2**, bringing the UCL Connected Curriculum (Fung 2017) and UCL ChangeMakers (Marie et al. 2016) initiatives together. These introductory pieces were followed by a chapter expounding on the significance of the prominent roles played by the graduate teaching assistants in R=T (**1.3**) and a study on the students' perception of student–staff partnership in the initiative (**1.4**). These four chapters written by academics provide the background for the students' work on research-based education in the rest of Section 1. Featuring a different kind of student–staff partnership, the eight short chapters in Section 3 of the book, which focus on staff-initiated projects on research-based education at UCL, are each explained with students as co-authors.

. . . for a new form of higher education pedagogy

Student–staff partnership has underpinned this book project at multiple levels. The three sections of the book showcase three distinct types of student–staff partnership for advancing the scholarship of teaching and learning in a consortium setting. The consortium approach is consistent with the true sense of the word, as more than 50 students from 24 departments (10 UCL faculties) were involved as authors/editors in the book project. But how does this book on research-based education come together to shape higher education pedagogy, given all these different contributions from academics and students? What has been explained so far is from the point of view of the book *project* itself as a student–staff partnership on research-based education. Now we should look at the *book* from a different angle – the overarching themes of the three sections and how they are connected. Do the themes of the book, taken together, constitute a new way to approach higher education pedagogy?

In the first section of the book, the focus is on the context and scope of research-based education through student–staff partnership, which is highlighted by the R=T Framework. It is the 'what' section – recognising the international and institutional contexts, with an overview of the opportunities, challenges and general principles. The theme of the second section is showing how research-based education can be conceptualised as praxis, or a cycle of theory, action and reflection, for both students and staff. It is the 'how' section – learning as praxis is how research and teaching can be connected within a university and beyond. The final section of the book features case studies of research-based education through student–staff partnership in a diverse range of settings, for enhancing transition phases and fostering the formation of communities of practice. It is the 'why' section – not only showing the key benefits to students and staff but also highlighting the wide applicability of research-based education through student–staff partnership in real learning, research and teaching scenarios.

The critical reflection chapters in Section 2 feature a diverse range of writing styles as the authors, many of whom do not have any formal background or training in education studies, were encouraged to explore their chosen topics of research-based education. Their writing reflects the partnership work with their R=T Professors, including their co-hosted R=T events and Masterclasses, as well as their experience as a teacher–researcher–student. Some pieces were accompanied by comprehensive lists of references in education, while other chapters were more akin to topical essays written by practitioners. The research findings from the student-led focus groups (**1.5–1.9**) contrast with the practical case studies co-written by staff and students (**3.1–3.8**). The student authors and editors represent a fantastically wide range of cultural backgrounds, from Bulgarian to Malaysian, and from Kazakh to Kenyan, to name but a few. Their perspectives, which are rooted in a full range of academic disciplines, are united by their passion for research-based education. We are celebrating these diversities in student–staff partnerships through their synthesised thoughts, presented in formats that are not dictated by those found in a conventional edited research volume.

We therefore have an answer to one of the questions put forward at the beginning of this piece. Yes, students can, and indeed have, put forward their ideas about the method and practice of teaching (or 'pedagogy' as defined by the *Oxford English Dictionary*) in the form of scholarly writing. They have done it collectively and collaboratively with staff in a consortium, with a wide audience in mind. But what about the very first question – are students shaping higher education pedagogy? The students have certainly given us, the academics, a wide range of inspiring ideas and views on research-based education through student–staff partnership in the book. Perhaps more importantly, the students have given us an approach to pedagogy: working with them closely as an important part of our development as teachers in a *learning community*. This goes beyond taking student feedback on board as we design and refine our teaching as individuals or in small peer groups. It goes beyond engaging with evidence-based, student-centred approaches as documented in studies published by academics. It goes beyond students working with staff on education matters in committee meetings. It is the collectiveness and connectedness in the consortium setting that allows us to see the commonalities in, and passion for, inspiring pedagogy in higher education. In this way, the students have shown us that they too can shape pedagogy.

Working with students closely in these learning communities for our own development as teachers – asking students to help 'teach' us as a group how to teach, to put it in a somewhat provocative way – can be radical. This involves challenging the very core of the roles of teachers and students, and pushing the frontier of student–staff partnership. Given that the R=T initiative and the book project are mostly based in the UCL setting (albeit with direct input from the non-UCL R=T Professors), how relevant is it to academics and students in other institutional contexts? Different institutions necessarily mean that there are different local priorities across the higher education sector. But, as we have seen in the book, 'learning' is a way to connect research and teaching and to link students and staff, so involving students collectively in our development as teachers may not be such an alien idea after all. With online communities and staff development programmes featuring students' voices, shaping our pedagogy with students may not be an insurmountable challenge. Radical as it may seem, getting students and staff together to discuss teaching methods and practice in a community setting should not be dependent on institutional priorities. In fact, it should help to address and advance institutional priorities together. The benefits to both students and staff can be transformational – as we have seen in the book chapters.

The book chapters are organised in three sections and can be read in different orders. We would, however, suggest starting with the Section Introductions (**1.0**, **2.0**, **3.0**), which put forward unifying perspectives on the book chapters. The **Epilogue** looks at the theme of emerging relationships between research-based education and student–staff partnership in the light of the R=T initiative, and argues how the initiative itself may be viewed as a form of research-based education. For multimedia contents and ongoing developments linked to the book, please visit us at:

www.RequalsT.org

I would like to end this piece with a quote from one of the undergraduate student applications for a place on the student author team co-hosting one of the R=T Masterclasses. She wrote in her application:

> Academia has historically been a space where there is no hierarchy separating knowledge creators and knowledge consumers. There is an understanding that even researchers and senior academics are still learning, and thus bringing together research and teaching continues in this strong tradition of community.

She has subsequently made an enormous contribution to the project. This quote epitomises the significance of R=T in approaching higher education pedagogy with a community spirit. That spirit, together with the passion shown by colleagues and students, has given us the inspiration to take forward the initiative.

References

Barnett, R. and Coate, K. 2005. *Engaging the Curriculum in Higher Education*. Milton Keynes: Open University Press.

Brew, A. 2006. *Research and Teaching: Beyond the Divide*. Basingstoke: Palgrave Macmillan.

Carnell, B. and Fung, D. 2017. *Developing the Higher Education Curriculum: Research-based Education in Practice*. London: UCL Press.

Cook-Sather, A., Bovill, C. and Felten, P. 2014. *Engaging Students as Partners in Learning and Teaching: A Guide for Faculty*. San Francisco: Jossey-Bass.

Fung, D. 2017. *A Connected Curriculum for Higher Education*. London: UCL Press.

Healey, M. and A. Jenkins. 2009. *Developing Undergraduate Research and Inquiry*. Heslington, York: The Higher Education Academy.

Healey, M., A. Flint and K. Harrington. 2014. *Engagement through Partnership: Students as Partners in Learning and Teaching in Higher Education*. Heslington, York: The Higher Education Academy.

Little, S. 2010. *Staff–Student Partnerships in Higher Education*. London: Bloomsbury.

Marie, J., Arif, M. and Joshi, T. 2016. UCL ChangeMakers projects: Supporting staff/student partnership on educational enhancement projects. *Student Engagement in Higher Education Journal* 1(1).

Prince, M. 2004. Does active learning work? A review of the research. *Journal of Engineering Education* 93, 223–31.

Section 1
The Context

1.0
Student–staff partnerships

Setting the contexts for shaping higher education with students

Alex Standen
UCL Arena Centre for Research-based Education

In his introduction to the volume, Vincent Tong sets you, the reader, a challenge. He asks you to place your trust in us; to navigate with us what can, at times, seem a complex and ambitious journey. Our project, R=T, was comparatively small when it started: we invited postgraduate research students to interview leading academics and educators in a workshop setting as part of UCL's institution-wide Connected Curriculum initiative (Fung 2017). We then invited other students, undergraduate and postgraduate, to lead follow-up focus groups with staff and students to explore the issues raised in the workshops in greater depth. From there our project expanded exponentially – eventually to result in this volume, which aims to position UCL as a case study for what can be achieved when students and staff work together to disrupt traditional relationships between research and teaching and to reconceptualise partnership working in a higher education setting.

Tong's introduction asks the 'big questions', setting the scene for the rest of the volume. In this, and subsequent section introductions, my co-authors and I intend to guide readers through the volume in more depth, highlighting recurring themes and signposting individual chapters within each section. The chapters in this first section aim to set the contexts for the remainder of the volume. The first four chapters situate the R=T initiative and the book project within current developments in higher education, particularly in light of burgeoning debates around student–staff partnership activity and research-based education (see the **Introduction** for a discussion of the relevant background to the latter). Then it is the students' turn to explain how they have actually approached research-based education through student–staff partnership in **1.5–1.9**, drawing together their experience of the R=T activities and the findings from their focus groups (which, as described in the **Introduction**, led to the development of our 'R=T Framework'). Read together, the nine chapters present a persuasive response to Tong's question, 'can students, like professional educationalists, shape higher education pedagogy?': the answer is a resounding yes. Section 2 responds to his second question, by offering postgraduate students (and early career academics) the opportunity to 'put forward *their* ideas about the method and practice of teaching in the form of scholarly writing for a wide audience' (emphasis added). Section 3, meanwhile, presents a range of short case studies which highlight the diverse ways in which our ambitious aims around student–staff partnership have been put into practice.

The idea of students and staff working in partnership to enhance higher education has gained increasing traction in recent years; indeed Healey et al. (2014) venture that it is, 'arguably one of the most important issues facing higher education in the 21st century' (2014, 7), traversing, as it does, many interrelated areas of key debate, including assessment and feedback, employability, and retention. Student–staff partnership work spans a wide range of activity, taking place in a variety of contexts; Cook-Sather et al. (2014) advise staff considering engaging in student–staff partnership that processes and programmes are not to be adopted uncritically, and that there is no 'one-size-fits-all model' (2014, xxi) (interestingly, our student editorial team came to the same conclusion, as highlighted in the R=T Framework). Nonetheless, scholars and policy makers have increasingly sought to conceptualise partnership activity and develop a language with which to discuss it (Bovill and Bulley 2011; NUS 2012; QAA 2012; Cook-Sather et al. 2014; Healey et al. 2014, 2016; HEA 2015; Healey et al. 2015).

For the purposes of this brief introduction to Section 1, I wish to focus in greater detail on a model for student–staff partnership activity first proposed by Healey et al. in 2014 and their particular discussion of 'partnership learning communities' – which are at the centre of the model – and the *values* which underpin it. Their work resonates with our project for many reasons (not least because in a 2016 paper re-visiting their original work the authors invite a student response, in much the same way as we worked with our student editorial team to respond to the chapters in Section 2). For Healey et al. partnerships are 'fundamentally a way of relating to the other and to oneself which is both deeply challenging and enables challenge, is both risky and enables taking risks' (2014, 20), and so too in this volume do we see the kind of student–staff partnership activity that takes place through the R=T initiative defined as 'radical' (**Introduction**) and 'transformative' (**2.0**), but also 'troublesome' and 'unsettling' (**1.2**).

Healey et al. (2014) conceptual model for student–staff partnerships is underpinned by a strong set of values which have been drawn from both scholarship and practice. The values are authenticity, inclusivity, reciprocity, empowerment, trust, challenge, community and responsibility (2014, 14–15). Likewise, for Cook-Sather et al. (2014) partnership activity between students and staff is founded on principles of respect, reciprocity and responsibility, while for Marie and McGowan (2017, 12) lessons for sustainable outcomes in partnership work include that 'honesty helps to develop trust' and that 'uncertainty about roles can be paralysing'. Terms such as these all evoke the spirit of community, and it should perhaps come as little surprise therefore that so too do the authors in this volume make reference to such a culture of community: Matthews, Cook-Sather and Healey (**1.1**) argue that the R=T aim, to connect teaching and research through student–staff partnership, is an opportunity to build an 'egalitarian learning community', in which students and staff are *genuinely* co-inquirers in teaching, learning and research. In my own chapter (**1.3**) I make recourse to Lave and Wenger's (1991) communities of practice to posit that postgraduate teaching assistants can make a positive contribution to a research-based education model that is based in a sense of shared responsibility for the continuation of a discipline's norms and practices. Elsewhere in the volume, Sabrina Peters' chapter (**2.2**) recognises that students and staff are part of the same community, with the university providing a platform for both to learn, while Geraniou, Mavrikis and Margeti (**3.5**) discuss their project: to build a 'community of interest' to host a close collaboration between researchers, lecturers and students of mathematics.

Jenny Marie (**1.2**) argues persuasively for the compatibility of the R=T initiative with the concept of participatory democracy and the resulting shift of power from the elite to the population. Her hypothesis is in line with Healey et al. (2014) partnership learning communities: 'partnership places students and staff in different roles and challenges the traditional hierarchical structure of learning and working relationships' (2014, 28). Mina Sotiriou's chapter (**1.4**) discusses the findings of her interviews with some of the students who participated in the R=T initiative to elucidate their impressions of partnership working.

Sotiriou underlines that the aims of the initiative were developed and agreed in collaboration with the students and as such all participants felt a sense of ownership over the project. Again, such a model for partnership resonates with that of Healey et al. who suggest that 'in these new [partnership learning] communities all parties actively participate in the development and direction of partnership learning and working and are fully valued for the contributions they make' (2014, 28). They suggest that the terms of partnership should be agreed 'in time' for partners to get to know one another, and to challenge and unpick assumptions about identity and role (2014, 35).

What emerges from both the literature and chapters **1.1–1.4** is not only that partnership is more likely to be sustained when there is a strong sense of community (Healey et al. 2014, 26), but that partnership work which acknowledges the dual role of students and staff as scholars and colleagues provides an opportunity for all those involved to reflect critically upon (and potentially transform) existing relationships, identities, processes and structures (Healey et al. 2014, 35).

Chapters **1.5–1.9** illustrate what can be achieved when partnership activity founded on the values above is put into practice (similarly, all the chapters in Section 2 are the direct products of our student–staff partnership work: written, peer reviewed and responded to by students in partnership with the three volume editors). The five short pieces are authored by students and discuss their findings from the focus groups that they led with academics and students. In partnership with us, they set the questions and direction of their focus groups and wrote up the resulting discussion with support both from their fellow students and from us as editors. The focus groups all followed one of the Masterclasses which were organised with leading academics and educators and, as such, there are some quite provocative and compelling arguments put forward in the short chapters: in **1.5**, Ran Sing Saw takes connecting students with staff research activities and real-world outputs as her starting point (see also **2.9**), moving on to offer advice on how to scaffold research-based education through the curriculum; Neema Kotonya (**1.6**) discusses transcending disciplinary boundaries in student research activities (see also **2.3** and **2.4**); chapter **1.7** by Masuma Pervin Mishu explores ways of connecting students with the work place (see also **2.10** and **2.11**); the theme of Mariya Badeva's contribution (**1.8**) is the ways in which postgraduate teaching assistants and demonstrators can be more actively involved in large group teaching (see also **2.8**); and lastly, in **1.9** Tika Malla looks at peer-assisted learning and assessment design, specifically exploring a tiered approach to assessment and grading (see also **2.7**).

The chapters in Section 1 were grouped to set the contexts around student–staff partnership activity, specifically in relation to research-based education. The themes that emerge echo much scholarly debate and, as a result, situate our work in the R=T initiative against the larger contemporary landscape of twenty-first-century higher education. As noted, the project has always been a flexible, collaborative and responsive model, whose aims and priorities have shifted as our work has progressed. An example of this is the eventual development of our R=T Framework (see **Introduction**) which grew organically from the students' work to become a unifying feature throughout the volume, giving the book coherence, but also serving as a helpful lens through which our readers can look at their own approaches to student–staff partnership. Healey et al.'s (2014) discussion of partnership communities of practice concludes with a challenging proposition:

> This prompts reflection on the usefulness of current labels like 'staff' or 'students' and the importance of not making assumptions based on perceived 'status'. There may be times in the learning and teaching relationship where staff and students usefully play these traditional roles, but partnership opens up opportunities *for all* to be scholars, researchers, learners, teachers, leaders and so on. (Healey et al. 2014, 35, emphasis added)

By taking a values-led approach to partnership work which places community at its centre, the chapters in Section 1 – and indeed throughout the volume – demonstrate how effective, exciting and rewarding it can be for all members of the higher education community to work together to connect teaching and research and, in so doing, shape their higher education experiences.

References

Bovill, C. and Bulley, C. J. 2011. A model of active student participation in curriculum design: exploring desirability and possibility. In Rust, C. (ed.) *Improving Student Learning (ISL) 18: Global Theories and Local Practices: Institutional, Disciplinary and Cultural Variations. Series: Improving Student Learning (18)*, pp. 176–88. Oxford: Oxford Brookes University: Oxford Centre for Staff and Learning Development. Available from: http://eprints.gla.ac.uk/57709/1/57709.pdf [Accessed July 2017].

Cook-Sather, A., Bovill, C. and Felten, P. 2014. *Engaging Students as Partners in Learning and Teaching: A Guide for Faculty*. San Francisco, CA: Jossey-Bass.

Fung, D. 2017. *A Connected Curriculum for Higher Education*. London: UCL Press.

HEA 2015. *Framework for Partnership in Learning and Teaching. Higher Education Academy.* Available from: www.heacademy.ac.uk/students-as-partners [Accessed July 2017].

Healey, M., Bovill, C. and Jenkins, A. 2015. Students as partners in learning. In Lea, J. (Ed). *Enhancing Learning and Teaching in Higher Education: Engaging with the Dimensions of Practice*, pp. 141–63. Maidenhead: McGraw Hill/Open University Press.

Healey, M., Flint, A. and Harrington, K. 2014. *Students as Partners in Learning and Teaching in Higher Education.* York: Higher Education Academy.

Healey, M., Flint, A. and Harrington, K. 2016. Students as Partners: Reflections on a Conceptual Model. *Teaching and Learning Inquiry* 4(2). Available from: http://tlijournal.com/tli/index.php/TLI/article/view/105/97 [Accessed July 2017].

Lave, Jean and Wenger, Etienne. 1991. *Situated Learning: Legitimate Peripheral Participation.* Cambridge: Cambridge University Press.

Marie, J. and McGowan, S. 2017. Moving towards sustainable outcomes in student partnerships: Partnership values in the pilot year. *International Journal for Students as Partners* 1(2), 1–15.

National Union of Students (NUS) 2012. *A Manifesto for Partnership.* London: National Union of Students. Available from: www.nusconnect.org.uk/campaigns/highereducation/partnership/a-manifesto-for-partnerships/ [Accessed July 2017].

Quality Assurance Agency for Higher Education (QAA) 2012. *Chapter B5: Student Engagement. UK Quality Code for Higher Education.* Gloucester: QAA. Available from: http://www.qaa.ac.uk/publications/information-and-guidance/uk-quality-code-for-higher-education-chapter-b5-student-engagement#.WXXSo1KZMdU [Accessed July 2017].

1.1

Connecting learning, teaching, and research through student–staff partnerships

Toward universities as egalitarian learning communities

Kelly E. Matthews

*Institute for Teaching and Learning Innovation,
The University of Queensland*

Alison Cook-Sather

Teaching and Learning Institute, Bryn Mawr College

Mick Healey

Healey HE Consultants and University of Gloucestershire

1. Introduction

Students and staff engaging together, as partners, in the learning, teaching and research endeavour is gaining prominence internationally. Recent special issues of established journals (e.g. *International Journal for Academic Development*, 21, 1; *Mentoring & Tutoring: Partnership in Learning*, 23, 5) and featured pieces in newer journals (e.g. *Student Engagement in Higher Education Journal*, 1, 1; *Teaching, Learning and Inquiry*, 4, 2) present both principles and practices of student–staff partnership as individually and institutionally transforming. While definitions of student–staff partnership continue to evolve as we develop language to name this new form of engagement, there are basic principles that underpin partnerships. They are manifesting themselves in multiple ways across the globe, and have particular implications for research-based education that embraces student–staff partnerships.

2. Defining student–staff partnerships in higher education

We begin with some working definitions drawing on our experiences, research and practices. Cook-Sather et al. (2014, 6–7) have defined partnership as 'a collaborative, reciprocal process through which all participants have the opportunity to contribute equally, although not necessarily in the same ways, to curricular or pedagogical conceptualization, decision-making, implementation, investigation, or analysis'. Healey et al. (2014, 12) have defined partnership as 'a relationship in which all involved – students, academics, professional services staff, senior managers, students' unions, and so on – are actively engaged in and stand to gain from the process of learning and working together'. Thus, 'the linchpin of partnership', as Matthews (2016, 2–3) has argued, 'is a relational process between students and academics/staff underpinned by a mindset' – what Cook-Sather and Felten (2017) have called 'an ethic of reciprocity'. Such an ethic embraces the principles of respect and shared responsibility, as well as reciprocity, in teaching and learning (Cook-Sather et al. 2014).

As an idea, partnership speaks to an institutional culture that values students as participants in knowledge construction, as producers of knowledge, within the university learning community. This translates into students being active participants in their own learning in the classroom and engaged in all aspects of university efforts to enhance education. For many universities, this is a radical cultural shift from *staff making decisions to benefit students* toward a mindset where *students and staff are working together* – as colleagues, as partners, as trusted collaborators – with shared goals.

There are a number of classifications in the literature of the different ways in which students may act as partners in learning and teaching in higher education (e.g. Healey et al. 2016). One distinguishes between students as teachers, students as scholars and students as change agents:

Students may take on the role of teachers through peer-learning and assessment or through taking on responsibility for co-teaching with staff and other students; they may act as scholars through being involved in subject-based research and inquiry; and they may engage as change agents through undertaking scholarship of teaching and learning (SoTL) projects, co-designing the curriculum and acting as pedagogic mentors and consultants to staff. (Healey et al. 2015, 142)

The advantage of this classification is that it sees 'students as partners' as an umbrella term incorporating, rather than separating, their multiple roles as teachers, scholars and change agents. While engaging students and staff together, in partnership, is pushing the boundaries of how universities typically involve students in the teaching and learning enterprise, how participants in partnership conceptualise their roles and share responsibility for teaching, learning and research plays out differently in different contexts.

3. Examples of student–staff partnerships in higher education

Drawing on the classification model offered by Healey et al. (2015) above, we offer some examples of student–staff partnerships in which students take on the role of teachers through peer-learning, engage as change agents and co-design the curriculum, and act as pedagogic consultants to staff.

Peer-assisted learning models actively involve students in an effort to enhance student disciplinary learning. For example, Peer-Assisted Study Sessions (PASS), or peer mentoring, involve upper-level undergraduates facilitating study sessions in first-year subjects, where student facilitators design and implement learning activities in a safe, low-stakes (no assessment) environment (Brown et al. 2014; Meinking and Sweeney 2016). While student facilitators work with staff to design learning activities for the introductory subjects, they also work with students in the sessions offering alternative explanations for course materials while supporting study habits in the crucial first-year transition to higher education. These approaches value the role of students in the teaching enterprise – students as teachers.

New thinking about the roles of 'students as partners' in the university community is creating space for students and staff to engage in teaching enhancement efforts together. For example, there are programmes where students and staff partner on designated teaching and learning projects (Marquis et al. 2016). In addition, student-proposed and student-led projects (Dunne and Zandastra 2011) as well as university centres (Hald 2011) are also emerging, along with institutional partnerships between student unions and institutional leadership (King et al. 2016). These examples of student–staff partnership position students as scholars and change agents.

Successful examples of students and staff collaborating to co-create curricula highlight the contributions both groups make to designing and implementing courses (Bovill et al. 2011). Students and staff working together to develop and refine curricular materials and new subjects value the role students can play in curriculum development (Duah and Croft 2014; Woolmer et al. 2016). Structured approaches that position students as consultants enable open dialogue between students and staff about teaching as it unfolds in real time (Cook-Sather 2014, 2016).

These exciting practices value the contribution of students, alongside those of staff, in defining and enacting solutions to enhance teaching quality in ways that extend beyond drawing on students as a source of institutional data. Engaging students as co-teachers, co-researchers and co-creators, they embody 'students as partners' practices and demonstrate how students and staff can work together in non-traditional 'student' and 'lecturer' roles to enhance the core functions of higher education: learning and research.

4. Linking student–staff partnership to research-based education

Whereas seeing students as change agents is relatively new, students have engaged in disciplinary research-based learning for much longer (Fung 2016; Healey and Jenkins 2009). Students and staff collaborating in research, particularly at the undergraduate level, is well established and recognised as a powerful learning model where both students and staff benefit as they work together toward knowledge creation. Research-based education originated as part of educational innovations at Massachusetts Institute of Technology in the United States and was expanded with support from the National Science Foundation. These efforts focused on recruiting talented and engaged students to join or lead research activities (Kyvik et al. 2015). A parallel movement has since developed to make undergraduate research available to all students (Healey and Jenkins 2009). However, the language of 'student as producer' and 'student as partner' has been applied to these practices only recently (Neary 2014; Healey et al. 2014).

In the same way that disciplinary traditions and norms inform the ways that teaching and research are linked (Healey 2005), assumptions about realms of responsibility and the roles of students and staff are informed by long-standing traditions. Student–staff partnerships challenge these traditions. They link realms that have traditionally been the purview of one or another constituency and blur the boundaries of roles that have traditionally been clearly delineated and defined.

Such linking and blurring is manifest in one of the most powerful components of both research-based education and student–staff partnership: an insistence on valuing and acting on multiple perspectives. Research-based education that embraces partnership principles of respect, reciprocity and shared responsibility not only positions students alongside staff as legitimate producers of knowledge, it contributes to a culture shift that moves institutions toward a more collaborative mode of operation. Research-based education that embraces partnership principles takes another step toward transforming universities into egalitarian learning communities.

5. Transformative change for egalitarian learning communities

What are the roles of students in shaping the university learning experience? This is a big question, and engaging students and staff as partners in learning, inquiry and curricular and pedagogical co-creation enacts a vision for higher education that positions the perspectives and contributions of both learners and teachers as essential. In our hyper-competitive, increasingly managerial-orientated university settings where everyone is frantically busy, creating genuine learning environments in which students and staff are able to collaborate authentically, will be difficult. Yet, for universities that believe in the values of engaging students and staff as partners in learning, these challenges are being addressed with long-term planning grounded in cultural change. UCL is an example of such a university.

The broad idea of 'students as partners' offers both a new construct and a new language to encompass existing practices and to present new approaches that value students and staff working together on the shared project of teaching and learning in higher education (Matthews 2017). The terms we use to name our practices are tied to communities and their culture – habit of minds, values and reward systems, policies and practices, ways of working and thinking. Student–staff partnership is more than a set of practices with new names; it is an opportunity to transform institutional cultures by harnessing the strength of the relationship between learners and teachers working together.

Because they require and are beginning to constitute a new mode of engagement in higher education, the ideas and practices of student–staff partnerships and the terms we develop for them must be unpacked, debated and challenged through multiple forms of research and reflection. Risks will have to be identified and guiding principles and values framed and reframed as these new approaches and the language to name them evolve. Such evolution necessitates spaces for students and staff, together and separately, to contribute to our shifting understanding. A new journal, *International Journal for Students as Partners*, is such a space, dedicated to advancing the research and practice of student–staff partnerships. It is a journal about partnership, developed and conducted in partnership with a student–staff editorial board from Australia, Canada, the UK and the USA.

International interest in student–staff partnerships is growing and universities will continue to have to grapple with how these partnerships work at the local level. The extent to which we value students and staff working collaboratively informs the transformative potential of partnership. This potential applies not only to individual experiences but also to the shift university cultures can make toward egalitarian learning communities. In such communities, students and staff are genuinely co-inquirers in teaching, learning and research. To realise this potential, all members of the university community will have to embrace new ways of thinking about the relationship between learners and teachers in the process of knowledge creation.

References

Bovill, C., Cook-Sather, A. and Felten, P. 2011. Students as co-creators of teaching approaches, course design, and curricula: implications for academic developers. *International Journal for Academic Development* 16(2), 135–45.

Brown, K., Nairn, K. van der Meer, J. and Scott, C. 2014. 'We were told we're not teachers. It gets difficult to draw the line': negotiating roles in peer-assisted study sessions (PASS). *Mentoring & Tutoring: Partnership in Learning* 22(2), 146–61.

Cook-Sather, A. 2014. Student–faculty partnership in explorations of pedagogical practice: a threshold concept in academic development. *International Journal for Academic Development* 19(3), 186–98.

Cook-Sather, A. 2016. Undergraduate students as partners in new faculty orientation and academic development. *International Journal of Academic Development* 21(2), 151–62.

Cook-Sather, A. and Felten, P. 2017. Ethics of academic leadership: guiding learning and teaching. In Wu, F. and Wood, M. (Eds). *Cosmopolitan Perspectives on Becoming an Academic Leader in Higher Education*, pp. 175–91. London: Bloomsbury.

Cook-Sather, A., Bovill, C. and Felten, P. 2014. *Engaging Students as Partners in Learning and Teaching: A Guide for Faculty*. San Francisco, CA: Jossey-Bass.

Duah, F. and Croft, T. 2014. Can peer assisted learning be effective in undergraduate mathematics? *International Journal of Mathematical Education in Science and Technology* 45, 552–65.

Dunne, E. and Zandstra, R. 2011. *Students as Change Agents – New Ways of Engaging with Learning and Teaching in Higher Education*. Bristol: A joint University of Exeter/ESCalate/Higher Education Academy Publication. http://escalate.ac.uk/8064

Fung, D. 2016. Engaging students with research through a Connected Curriculum: an innovative institutional approach, *CUR Quarterly*, 37(2), 30–5.

Hald, M. (Ed.) 2011. *Transcending Boundaries – how CEMUS is Changing how we Teach, Meet and Learn*. CEMUS, Uppsala University and Swedish University for Agricultural Sciences: Uppsala. www.web.cemus.se/wp-content/uploads/2015/05/TranscendingBoundaries.pdf

Healey, M. 2005. Linking research and teaching: exploring disciplinary spaces and the role of inquiry-based learning. In Barnett, R. (Ed), *Reshaping the University: New Relationships between Research, Scholarship and Teaching*, pp. 67–78. Maidenhead: McGraw-Hill/Open University Press.

Healey, M. and Jenkins, A. 2009. *Developing Undergraduate Research and Inquiry*. York: Higher Education Academy. https://www.heacademy.ac.uk/node/3146

Healey, M., Bovill, C. and Jenkins, A. 2015. Students as partners in learning. In Lea, J. (Ed), *Enhancing Learning and Teaching in Higher Education: Engaging with the Dimensions of Practice*, pp. 141–63. Maidenhead: McGraw Hill/Open University Press.

Healey, M., Flint, A. and Harrington, K. 2014. *Students as Partners in Learning and Teaching in Higher Education*. York: Higher Education Academy. https://www.heacademy.ac.uk/engagement-through-partnership-students-partners-learning-and-teaching-higher-education

Healey, M., Flint, A. and Harrington, K. 2016. Students as Partners: reflections on a Conceptual Model. *Teaching and Learning Inquiry* 4 (2). http://tlijournal.com/tli/index.php/TLI/article/view/105/97

International Journal for Academic Development 21(1).

International Journal for Students as Partners. https://mulpress.mcmaster.ca/ijsap

King, S., Sims, S., Lowe, T. and El Hakim, Y. 2016. Evaluating partnership and impact in the first year of the Student Fellows Scheme. *Journal of Educational Innovation, Partnership and Change* 2(1). https://journals.gre.ac.uk/index.php/studentchangeagents

Kyvik, S., Vågan, A., Prøitz, T. S. and Aamodt, P.O. 2015. Research-based education in undergraduate professional programmes. In Smeby, J.S. and Sutphen, M. (Eds), *From Vocational to Professional Education: Educating for Social Welfare*, pp. 105–23. London: Routledge.

Marquis, E., Puri, V., Wan, S., Ahmad, A., Goff, L., Knorr, K., Vassileva, I. and Woo, J. 2016. Navigating the threshold of student–staff partnerships: A case study from an Ontario teaching and learning institute. *The International Journal for Academic Development* 21(1), 4–15.

Matthews, K.E. 2016. Students as partners as the future of student engagement. *Student Engagement in Higher Education Journal* 1(1).

Matthews, K.E. 2017. Five propositions for genuine students as partners practice. *International Journal for Students as Partners* 1(2), 1–9.

Meinking, K. and Sweeney, M. 2016) The peer mentor: A pivotal teaching and learning partner in elementary Latin. *Teaching and Learning Together in Higher Education*, 19 http://repository.brynmawr.edu/tlthe/vol1/iss19/2

Mentoring & Tutoring: Partnership in Learning 23(5).

Neary, M. 2014. Student as producer: Research-engaged teaching frames university-wide curriculum development. *CUR Quarterly* 35(2), 28-34. http://www.cur.org/DOWNLOAD.ASPX?ID=3070

Student Engagement in Higher Education Journal 1(1). https://journals.gre.ac.uk/index.php/raise

Teaching, Learning and Inquiry 4(2). http://tlijournal.com/

Woolmer, C., Sneddon, P., Curry, G., Hill, B., Fehertavi, S., Longbone, C. and Wallace, K. 2016. Student staff partnership to create an interdisciplinary science skills course in a research intensive university. *International Journal for Academic Development* 21(1), 16–27.

1.2
The relationship between research-based education and student–staff partnerships

Jenny Marie
UCL Arena Centre for Research-based Education

Research-based education and student–staff partnerships are both in vogue at the moment. Evidence suggests that both can enhance student learning experiences but how do the two relate? Is it possible or desirable to use them in conjunction with each other? In this chapter, I show that their pedagogy and politics are compatible. They have common benefits and challenges. At times they overlap but neither fully embraces the other. In short, the links between the two are tangled. In this chapter, I show how they can work together to strengthen each other and how the R=T initiative adds a new dimension to efforts to take the two agendas forward together.

1. What do we mean by research-based education and students as partners?

Students can engage with research and inquiry in four different ways (Healey and Jenkins 2009): they can learn about current research (research-led); they can develop research skills and techniques (research-orientated); they can learn through research and inquiry (research-based); and they can engage in research discussions (research-tutored). Healey and Jenkins (2009) characterise research-based learning as focusing on the research process with students as active participants. Although they did not prioritise any particular form of engagement with research, they noted that students generally do not spend enough time as participants in relation to research (i.e. undertaking research-tutored and research-based activities).

Student–staff partnership is acknowledged to be extremely difficult to pinpoint. As Liz Dunne (2016) points out there are many definitions available. Healey et al. define it 'as *a process of student engagement*, understood as staff and students learning and working together to foster engaged student learning and engaging learning and teaching enhancement' (Healey et al. 2014, 7, emphasis in original). An alternative definition is that of Cook-Sather et al., who describe it as: 'A collaborative, reciprocal process through which all participants have the opportunity to contribute equally, although not necessarily in the same ways' (Cook-Sather et al. 2014, 6–7).

Student–staff partnerships are therefore processes whereby students and staff work together to achieve common goals. There need not be equal responsibility or liability between the partners (QAA 2012, 5) because students are not pedagogical or disciplinary experts (Wenstone 2012, 3; Cook-Sather et al. 2014). However, power does need to be distributed towards students so that they can make an equal contribution through their expertise in the student experience (Cook-Sather et al. 2014).

Staff–student partnership can look very different in practice because of the variety of outcomes that the partners are aiming to achieve. Healey et al. (2014, 23) created a framework for understanding student–staff partnerships in the domain of learning and teaching, where they could occur in learning, teaching and assessment; curriculum design and pedagogic consultancy; subject-based research and inquiry; and/or the scholarship of teaching and learning.

It should be noted that students and staff simply working together in these areas does not necessarily constitute student–staff partnership working. As Allin (2014, 98) points out students tend to be treated as novice researchers, that require facilitation and so the normal power relationships remain. Similarly, Cook-Sather et al. (2014, 138) argue that where students are involved in the research of staff, the staff member's agenda tends to dominate. They thus characterise this as collaboration rather than partnership. Power has not been appropriately distributed to enable equal contribution in these cases.

Bovill and Bulley's (2011) adaptation of Arnstein's ladder of participation to one of student participation in curriculum design is useful for showing that active participation exists on a continuum and that it is possible to go beyond partnership to areas where students dominate. One such case is that of Exeter's 'Students as Change Agents' scheme.

This scheme provided the opportunity for students to define and carry out their own research project into their own learning experiences in order to bring about positive change. Dunne and Zandstra (2011) purposely positioned the scheme beyond partnership, arguing that partnership work tended to be university-driven, rather than student-driven. In this case, students participating in the scholarship of teaching and learning is not partnership because the power has shifted over to the students.

2. What is the relationship between research-based education and student–staff partnership?

2.1 Moving forward together

Research-based education and student–staff partnerships are both processes, and the two can occur at the same time: students and staff can work in partnership on research-based education. However, as noted above, the one does not imply the other. A good example of the two occurring together is the research that Hasok Chang and his undergraduates undertook to collectively investigate the history of chlorine. Chang wrote that 'students take ownership of their research projects, but they are strongly directed by the teacher and by their predecessors' (Chang 2005, 388). While he guided their work, he was not an expert in the area and often had to tell them he did not know the answers to their questions. Their predecessors influenced the work, as their research was passed down between years. Thus the collaboration was not just between the member of staff and individual students but also between each other.

The example above is of partnership in subject-based research, but research-based education can also occur in the scholarship of learning and teaching. Cook-Sather et al. (2014) record how students in partnerships develop their meta-cognitive awareness by enquiring with staff into teaching and learning practices. As such, research-based activity is occurring in partnership into teaching practice. The SALT initiative at Bryn Mawr College provides a good example of this taking place in practice. Students learn about how they and others learn through their inquiry with staff into the best ways of teaching their courses.

Another common relationship between the two is for research-based education to be the goal of the student–staff partnership work. This is the case for UCL ChangeMakers projects, which are intended to forward research-based education (Marie et al. 2016). One example can be found in a project that developed both 3D models of a range of organs and a guide to creating 3D models, so that students could use these to explore the anatomy of different organs (http://www.3d-med.co.uk/about.html).

2.2 Compatible pedagogies

Partnership work and research-based education are both forms of active learning (Bonwell and Eison 1991). Prince says 'active learning requires students to do meaningful learning activities and think about what they are doing' (Prince 2004, 223). This can be clearly seen in partnership work, where students are actively involved in the process of learning and working together (Healey et al. 2014). Research-based education is also a form of active learning, whereby students are strongly involved in their learning and learn to reflect on the research process.

Both research-based education and student–staff partnerships also have strong links to andragogic assumptions. Knowles (1984) outlines five assumptions about adult learning. The second of these is that adults bring their own experiences to the educational arena. Student–staff partnership is premised on the principle that students are experts in the student experience (Cook-Sather et al. 2014). Their experiences are thus the foundation for partnership work, and its utility can be threatened by over-training them, as they risk losing their student perspective. Knowles gives the examples of laboratory experiences, field experiences and problem-solving projects (all forms of research-based exercises) as examples of techniques that draw on the learner's existing experiences.

These existing experiences also cause problems for learning – as Knowles (1984) points out, adults sometimes have to unlearn habitual ways of thinking. Research-based education should encourage this through the development of critical thinking (see Section 2.4, Common benefits). Both research-based education and partnership work can challenge existing preconceptions about the roles of teachers and students, as discussed in Section 2.5, Challenges, and so can help both students and staff to unlearn fixed and unhelpful conceptions of these roles.

Knowles's first assumption is that the learner is self-directing. The research process is self-directing; although the problem to be solved may be set, inquiry is contingent by its nature and students are likely to take the research in different directions, according to their interests. It is highly likely that partnerships will be self-directing for the same reasons. However, it is a particularly strong feature of partnerships that negotiate the curriculum, such as at Queen Margaret University in Edinburgh, where the students and academic staff negotiated the content of modules on an Environmental Justice degree, to ensure that the students developed the skills that they required for their environmental campaigns (Bovill et al., 2011). This particular example is noteworthy, for it also highlights Knowles's assumption regarding orientation to learning, whereby students enter education settings to learn 'in order to be able to perform a task, solve a problem, or live in a more satisfying way' (Knowles 1984, 12).

Research-based education additionally taps into Knowles's assumption that adult learners tend to be more motivated by intrinsic rewards as research draws on students' curiosity. Many of the rewards of partnership work are also intrinsic, with students gaining a feeling of enrichment and fulfilment from undertaking work to benefit others. Students participating in UCL ChangeMakers projects have said: 'Overall, it has been an incredibly enriching experience for me' and that they derived 'the satisfaction of contributing towards enriching the experiences of UCL's student community'.

2.3 Compatible politics

Research-based education and student–staff partnership are both compatible with the concept of participatory democracy, whereby opportunities are created to allow citizens to make meaningful contributions to decision making. Participatory democracy shifts the power from the elite to the population. The relationship between democracy and student–staff partnership is perhaps more obvious: such a partnership is about opening up opportunities for students to contribute to decision making with regards to their learning and teaching (or in another area). Research-based education also shifts the power from an elite (the researchers) to the student population and involves students in making more decisions about their learning. Furthermore, modern participatory democracies require citizens to be able to make decisions in a super-complex world, where the frameworks we have for making sense are themselves disputed. Research-based education provides the critical thinking and skills required to cope and make decisions in such a world (Brew 2006).

At the same time that Higher Education is undergoing a process of massification, it is also becoming strongly influenced by neo-liberal economics, whereby universities are positioned within a marketplace to attract student-consumers. Although there are benefits to this economic model, such as a focus on improving the quality of teaching, it stands in opposition to the idea that learning takes place through the active participation of students with their learning, as described above. Rachel

Wenstone wrote in the National Union of Students' *A manifesto for partnership* in 2012:

> Conceiving of students as consumers is a thoroughly impoverished way of describing the relationship between students and their institutions . . . A narrative of 'competition' and 'choice' within a consumer model offers students a false and inflated perception of their power and encourage [sic] the mind-set of 'the customer is always right' . . . [it] reduces complex interactions to mere transactions and de-values the role and expertise of educators. The consumer model could create a dangerous imbalance . . . student satisfaction is substituted for learning. (Wenstone 2012, 5)

Instead, Wenstone argued for student partnership, where students had the power to co-create knowledge, learning *and*, importantly, the higher education institution. Carey's (2013) analysis of students as participants in curriculum design is interesting in showing that partnership work is affected by the consumerism model and that students sometimes act as consumers because that is the role expected of them. However, he also shows that students do not only act as consumers; the students who participated in the design exercise did so out of altruistic motives. My own work with students has shown that treating students as partners can change their attitudes towards themselves:

> UCL ChangeMakers allowed me to step forward, from an educational consumer to an active participant in UCL.

> Whereas before I think I was content to be a consumer . . . of education here at UCL, the UCL ChangeMakers projects has allowed me to conceive myself in a producing role.

As research-based education is also a form of active learning, it stands in an awkward position with regard to students as consumers and the politics of research-based education can be configured against neo-liberal economics. Neary and Winn write:

> The point of this re-arrangement would be to reconstruct the student as producer: undergraduate students working in collaboration with academics to create work of social importance that is full of academic content and value, while at the same time reinvigorating the university beyond the logic of market economics. (Neary and Winn 2009, 193)

Here students work in partnership with staff to undertake research-based activity in order to create a university that thereby gains a purpose beyond monetary value and the employability of its students. Fung (2016, 31) has also argued that the philosophy behind her model of research-based education is *Bildung*, the idea that education is about developing oneself as a human being with a concern for the common good.

However, it is important to note that research-based education does not need to be based on a politics that opposes neo-liberal economics in higher education. The former Chief Executive of the Higher Education Academy, Paul Ramsden, wrote:

> [Curricula should all:] Incorporate research-based study for undergraduates (to cultivate awareness of research careers, to train students in research skills for employment, and to sustain the advantages of a research–teaching connection in a mass or universal system). (Ramsden 2008, 11)

Here, the emphasis is on research-based education for employability. Students are thus gaining monetary worth through being educated via research-based methods, and as such this is a neo-liberal economic argument. Although this was written as a contribution to the UK Government's Department of Innovation, Universities and Skills' Debate on the Future of Higher Education, it shows that the politics of research-based education are not fixed and that this pedagogy can be used to further different political ends.

I believe that student–staff partnership can also be deployed in support of neo-liberal economic politics. At UCL we invited students and staff to work in partnership specifically in departments with National Student Survey (NSS) results that are lower than the average across the university. The following year, overall NSS satisfaction scores rose on average by 5.0 per cent in those departments. Thus, partnership can be a process towards increasing student satisfaction, and it would be surprising to me if it did not have a positive impact. Nevertheless, the NSS is commonly portrayed as a tool of student consumerism, prioritising satisfaction over learning, and providing information to enable students to choose between universities in the marketplace (Crawford 2012).

Carey (2013) argues that the market ideology within higher education provides one of the challenges for student–staff partnership work, as students act in the ways expected of them and use the opportunity to complain rather than to undertake the type of design thinking Dunne (2016) describes as effective partnership working. Nevertheless, if we are to accept that 'managerisalist principles . . . define contemporary higher education' (Carey 2013, 258), I believe we should be pragmatic in our approach. If we can deliver better student satisfaction at the same time as enhancing learning and delivering the benefits discussed in the following section, that cannot be a bad thing.

2.4 Common benefits

Both research-based education and student–staff partnership increase student motivation, confidence and attainment among those who take part (Healey and Jenkins, 2009; Cook-Sather et al., 2014). UCL ChangeMakers students describe the experience of partnership as transformative: 'ChangeMakers was indeed a changing experience for me. It made the academic year much richer, improved my understanding and provided key insights I otherwise would not have gained.' The work of Brooman et al. (2015) also suggests that partnership working should enhance the educational outcomes for others. They show that student attainment improved as a result of listening to and responding to the student voice in curriculum design. The focus groups run during the project challenged a number of staff assumptions and thus one would expect student partnership to offer the same benefits.

Both research-based education and student–staff partnerships are good for community building. Research-based education helps to create inclusive knowledge building communities because students are welcomed into the world of research where staff normally reside, rather than being excluded from it (Brew 2006). This induction into the research community also improves professional socialisation (Healey and Jenkins 2009). The students who participate in partnership work through UCL ChangeMakers have reported a stronger sense of community with their department and engagement with their studies: 'I genuinely feel more involved with the department and my academic studies.' 'It gives me opportunities to explore my department deeper [sic] which enhances my sense of belonging to my course.'

Brew (2006) argues that to cope in an increasingly uncertain world people require a strong sense of identity. Cook-Sather et al. (2014) describe how student–staff partnerships can develop this for both students and staff. From the student perspective, this can be about developing a sense of themselves as responsible for their own learning, whereas for staff it may be about being confronted with who they are and how they differ from some of their students. Learning through inquiry will encourage students to query who they are and will strengthen their sense of self, particularly as they engage with the community of researchers in their discipline (Brew 2006). Part of this process of self-discovery arises from the more equitable power relationships in both student–staff partnerships and research-based education, which removes the imposition of identity onto students by staff.

2.5 Challenges

One of the major challenges to both research-based education and student–staff partnerships is devolving power sufficiently to students. The appropriate distribution of power for partnership is one of the values that Healey et al. (2014) highlight for partnership work. However, as Cook-Sather et al. (2014) discuss, this is easier said than done. The balance of power should not shift to the students, nor should there be equivalency: partners should be equally valued but their different areas of expertise recognised. When this happens, it should be possible to agree whose opinion should have more weight in any decision and who should contribute more to a specific area of the joint undertaking. A further challenge comes from the fact that staff usually initiate partnerships, so there can be a danger of the process feeling to students as if it is being imposed upon them. The opening up of research to the student population also involves a shift in power from staff to students. As discussed above, when students are excluded from it, research helps to define the staff as elite. By being more inclusive, staff have to devolve more power to students. The shift in power for both research-based education and student–staff partnerships comes about through a recognition that 'different participants have different things to contribute as well as to learn' (Brew 2006, 163).

Both student–staff partnerships and research-based education change the role of staff. In research-based education the staff become facilitators of learning. Cook-Sather (2014) has argued that student–staff partnerships transform concepts of student and staff roles. As one of the UCL ChangeMakers staff partners wrote:

> from a staff perspective, having to think beyond the traditional divide and working with students as truly equal partners can bring vital insights for individuals that may well lead to lasting culture change across the institution.

This can be troublesome and threatening for staff (Cook-Sather 2014) and challenging for students. Carey (2013) discusses how students act out conceptions of them as consumers and Fung (2016) points out that students can find research-based education unsettling.

As discussed in Section 2.3, Compatible politics, both research-based education and student–staff partnership fall more naturally into opposition with neo-liberal economics and this poses a challenge for them both. Separate funding and evaluation of research and teaching strengthens the divide between the two (Brew 2006). Partnerships are inhibited by managerialist principles, which hold staff to account and prevent the flexibility to respond rapidly to student needs (Crawford 2012; Carey 2013). Student input can become meaningless if it is sought through evaluative surveys as these are too late to impact on the students' own experiences and therefore encourage a culture of complaint.

3. Conclusion

Research-based education and student–staff partnership share many aims, benefits and challenges. The two are overlapping, with some research-based education being a form of partnership (but not all) and some partnerships being in the area of research-based education.

As they advance the same educational aims and contribute to the same cultural shifts in higher education, I think it makes sense for the two to try to move forward together. At UCL this is done through both partnership in research-based education and partnership towards it. Partnership on project work, aimed at making the curriculum more research-based is not unusual. The R=T initiative is a slightly different form of partnership, in that students contributed to staff development workshops that were targeted at inspiring staff to relate teaching and research more closely in their practice; the students then researched how the ideas could be applied in practice.

The real lesson of the R=T initiative to me is not that of a new model to follow, but that there are likely to be other areas where we could productively develop student–staff partnerships in aid of research-based education. Mick Healey once said to me that if we want to take student partnership seriously then we need to keep asking the question 'Where are the students?' The R=T initiative demonstrates the power that that question can have.

References

Allin, Linda. 2014. Collaboration between staff and students in the scholarship of teaching and learning: The potential and the problems. *Teaching & Learning Inquiry* 2 (1), 95–102.

Bonwell, Charles and Eison, James. 1991. *Active Learning: Creating Excitement in the Classroom* (ASHE-ERIC Higher Education Reports). Available at: http://files.eric.ed.gov/fulltext/ED336049.pdf [Accessed 26 October 2016].

Bovill, C., and Bulley, C.J. 2011. A model of active student participation in curriculum design: Exploring desirability and possibility. In: Rust, C. (ed.) *Improving Student Learning (ISL) 18: Global Theories and Local Practices: Institutional, Disciplinary and Cultural Variations. Series: Improving Student Learning (18)*, pp. 176–88. Oxford Brookes University: Oxford Centre for Staff and Learning Development, Oxford.

Bovill, Catherine, Cook-Sather, Alison and Felten, Peter. 2011. Students as co-creators of teaching approaches, course design, and curricula: implications for academic developers. *International Journal for Academic Development* 16(2), 133–45.

Brew, Angela. 2006. *Research and Teaching: Beyond the Divide*. Basingstoke: Palgrave.

Brooman, S., Darwent, S. and Pimor, A. 2015. The student voice in higher education curriculum design: Is there value in listening? *Innovations in Education and Teaching International* 52(6), 663–74.

Carey, Philip. 2013. Student as co-producer in a marketised higher education system: a case study of students' experience of participation in curriculum design. *Innovations in Education and Teaching International* 50(3), 250–60.

Chang, Hasok. 2005. Turning an undergraduate class into a professional research community. *Teaching in Higher Education* 10(3), 387–94.

Cook-Sather, Alison. 2014. Student–faculty partnership in explorations of pedagogical practice: A threshold concept in academic development. *International Journal for Academic Development* 19(3), 186–98.

Cook-Sather, Alison, Bovill, Catherine and Felten, Peter. 2014. *Engaging Students as Partners in Learning and Teaching: A Guide for Faculty*. Oxford: John Wiley & Sons.

Crawford, Karin. 2012. Rethinking the student–teacher nexus: Students as consultants on teaching in higher education. In: Neary, Mike Stevenson, Howard and Bell, Les, *Towards Teaching in Public: Reshaping the Modern University*. London: Bloomsbury.

Dunne, Liz. 2016. Design thinking: A framework for student engagement? A personal view. *Journal of Educational Innovation, Partnership and Change* 2(1).

Dunne, Elisabeth and Zandstra, Roos. 2011. *Students as Change Agents: New Ways of Engaging with Learning and Teaching in Higher Education*. Bristol: HEA.

Fung, Dilly. 2016. Engaging students with research through a connected curriculum: An innovative institutional approach. *Council on Undergraduate Research* 18(2), 30–5.

Healey, M. and Jenkins, A. 2009. *Developing Undergraduate Research and Enquiry*. York: HEA.

Healey, M., Flint, A. and Harrington, K. 2014. *Developing Students as Partners in Learning and Teaching in Higher Education*. York: HEA.

Knowles, Malcolm. 1984. *Andragogy in Action: Applying Modern Principles of Adult Learning*. San Francisco: Jossey-Bass.

Marie, Jenny, Arif, Mahmoud and Joshi, Tejas. 2016. UCL ChangeMakers projects: Supporting staff/student partnership on educational enhancement projects. *Student Engagement in Higher Education Journal* 1(1).

Neary, M. and Winn, J. 2009. The student as producer: Reinventing the student experience in higher education. In Bell, L., Stevenson, H. and Neary, M. (eds), *The Future of Higher Education: Policy, Pedagogy and the Student Experience*, pp. 192–210. London: Continuum).

Prince, Michael. 2004. Does active learning work? A review of the research. *Journal of Engineering Education* 93(3), 223–31.

Quality Assurance Agency for Higher Education (QAA). 2012. Chapter B5: Student Engagement. In *UK Quality Code for Higher Education*. Gloucester: QAA.

Ramsden, P. 2008. *Teaching and the Student Experience*. Report presented to Department of Innovation, Universities and Skills' Debate on the Future of Higher Education. Available from: https://www.heacademy.ac.uk/resource/future-higher-education-teaching-and-student-experience [Accessed 1 November 2016].

Wenstone, R. 2012. *A Manifesto for Partnership*. London: NUS. http://www.3d-med.co.uk/about.html [Accessed 7 November 2016].

1.3
Where teaching meets research

Engaging postgraduate teaching assistants with research-based education

Alex Standen

UCL Arena Centre for Research-based Education

1. Introduction

Employing doctoral students to teach, especially on large undergraduate courses, has long been a feature of higher education in the USA. While it is not in itself new in UK institutions, what might be considered a more recent trend is the growing scale on which it is happening, and the increasing dependence of many degree programmes on this – and other – part-time staffing (Park and Ramos 2002; Muzaka 2009). UCL is no exception: the institution has around 6,000 students engaged in doctoral research, and while it is not possible to quantify the number contributing to departmental teaching activities, annual attendance at the university's mandatory training workshop for all PhD students with teaching or assessing responsibilities is around 600, from across departments. This demonstrates the high level of reliance on this cohort for the delivery of a range of activities.

Winter et al. (2015) point to the simultaneous growth in the UK of the professionalisation of the practice of university teaching, citing the development of training courses for graduate teaching assistants (GTAs)[1] as part of this agenda. Again, UCL's recent development of training provision through its Arena programme (discussed in detail in Section 3) mirrors research by Lee et al. (2010), which found that over 50 per cent of UK training courses for GTAs were compulsory, 57 per cent were assessed, and that content was increasingly aligned with the UK Professional Standards Framework (UKPSF).[2]

In 2002, Chris Park and Marife Ramos published the first UK study to explore the experiences of the country's growing body of GTAs – a contribution the authors felt to be already overdue. The study called for further research and discussion around the role, funding and frameworks to support this group, who, the authors concluded, often perceive themselves as the 'donkeys in the department'. Subsequent research has sought to further unpick this 'niche' role (Muzaka 2009), while other research has focused, for example, on the specificities of the international GTA experience (Winter et al. 2015) and how disciplinary differences can shape GTAs' expectations of their training and development (Chadha 2013).

This chapter adds to this small, but growing, literature on UK GTAs by focusing, in line with the overarching aims of the volume, on the role of GTAs in the development and implementation of a research-based education model. As an educational developer running a training scheme for GTAs, and as a contributor to the R=T initiative, I have observed first-hand their role at the meeting point of research and education. Many of our group of R=T student authors, brought together here in Section 2 of the book, form part of the large body of UCL GTAs, while others have current and previous teaching responsibilities that they combine with research and professional roles. I would argue that all of the group, as early-career researchers and teachers, can be said to occupy a unique space which bridges the taught student experience and the research environment.

With an enthusiastic and open-minded approach to their teaching, GTAs are not only receptive to new ideas but, moreover, are often skilled at bringing creativity and originality to the classroom. By first identifying how some of the specificities of GTAs' experience and role can positively impact a research-based education model, and then presenting a case study of a training programme which supports them in creating innovative student learning experiences, I advocate for an approach to research-based education that engages closely with GTAs. In both pragmatic and conceptual ways, their experience and insight can inform and strengthen curricula. At the heart of a research-based education agenda is the breaking down of traditional academic hierarchies, and this approach can offer a vital first step in doing so.

2. GTAs and the research-based education model

Graduate teaching assistants can be considered to hold a unique position at the intersection of research and education. Often only recently emerging themselves from the taught student experience, they can be expected very quickly to start working with undergraduate (and, in some cases, Masters) students in a range of teaching, assessing and mentoring situations. Simultaneously they are on the threshold of their own disciplinary research environment and of the wider academic community. This close proximity to what have sometimes traditionally been two quite delineated communities creates an exciting environment for innovation, which has all too often been ignored due to what are perceived, understandably, as the challenges of giving comparatively inexperienced members of staff substantive teaching responsibilities. Yet, all too aware of the challenges that will face them as they enter a competitive marketplace, GTAs can often be highly motivated to develop themselves professionally, and are receptive to exploring new approaches and methods.

While there is little doubt that GTAs need to be properly trained and supported to undertake teaching and assessment, and that their main priority must always be their doctoral studies, there is great potential to be explored in creating opportunities for their close engagement in the experience of taught students. Having recently completed a programme of study, for example, might provide a GTA with insight into both the positive aspects and drawbacks of an established course, which existing staff members may be unable to identify. A survey of undergraduates, GTAs and staff in a social sciences department at the University of Sheffield sought to explore the beneficial and problematic aspects of GTA-run seminars. One of its findings of perceived benefits for students suggested that GTAs 'recent university experience gives them additional awareness and knowledge of what might work best for students in this setting, thus helping to keep "seminars useful and interesting"' (Muzaka 2009, 4). Students also commented that GTAs were better at stimulating discussion and were not afraid of trying new methods. Staff, meanwhile, suggested that GTAs tend to be more open to innovative teaching methods, more enthusiastic about learning to teach and more capable of providing an informal learning environment (ibid.). For programme and module leaders, GTAs can offer valuable support in suggesting and implementing change.

Yet, in spite of these compelling arguments (and there are likewise pragmatic ones: in a culture of growing student numbers, GTAs and other part-time staff allow for scalability of provision), there remains an assumption that GTAs will only undertake teaching in bounded situations with little space for autonomy or responsibility (Park and Ramos 2002; Muzaka 2009). This does, of course, reduce the risk of them being over-burdened and, for departments, could be perceived as a necessity for matters of quality assurance, but this lack of ownership over course content and delivery negatively impacts both the GTAs and their students:

> This has an important bearing on the GTA's sense of identity and academic value, particularly for those who see themselves as apprentice academics. It severely restricts the GTA's ability to exercise academic leadership and responsibility, and compromises the way their students see them. (Park and Ramos 2002, 51)

Mazuka's (2009) survey indicated much the same. However, it also suggested that while GTAs rarely saw themselves as having ownership of, or authority in, their teaching responsibilities, many staff, by contrast, did indeed perceive them as 'academic apprentices' (Mazuka 2009, 10). This might suggest, in turn, a willingness to allow them some freedom and creativity in their teaching practices.

It seems salient at this point – as we begin to touch on ideas of innovation – to turn to our central question of engaging GTAs in a research-based education model, and the specific advantages associated with this. Scholarship advocating a closer integration of teaching and research suggests a number of arguments which – when considered in our context – provide compelling reasons to further this agenda. Jenkins et al. (2003, 41–8) suggest that enhanced motivation for both staff and students is a likely outcome of a curriculum which emphasises the linkages between teaching and research. They argue, for example, that staff discussing research with students is an opportunity to develop trust and intimacy, and share interests (and discover the interests of the student). Such conversations can be used to discover learner goals, explain why knowledge is useful and make learning interesting and relevant. The authenticity with which many GTAs would no doubt discuss their research may provide a motivating factor for students to engage more deeply with the discipline.

Similarly, research-based education encourages staff to share their learning experiences and frame themselves as fellow learners rather than experts (Jenkins et al. 2003, 41–8). GTAs can act as role models, presenting a possible pathway for less experienced learners and an archetype of the experience of seeking knowledge for intrinsic good, rather – as may be the case for some learners, particularly at the outset of their studies – as learning for short-term benefits and strategic goals. Sharing the challenges of research is of equal importance, and by doing so, GTAs (as all staff members) can help students develop strategies to ease anxiety. Once again, it is the distinctiveness of their particular position that increases the potential gains here: GTAs will be no strangers to setbacks in the research process, and, coupled with their concurrent experiences of robust processes of feedback, peer review and criticism, they can introduce to learners (over-achieving ones in particular) the realities of dealing with uncertainty and the threat of failure. Turning again to the findings of the University of Sheffield survey, Mazuka argues that, 'being a GTA, and not necessarily an "expert", could be beneficial in that a GTA's own inquiry into the subject area may help to convey students the message that knowledge is not transmitted but actively constructed' (Mazuka 2009, 9). What some students might, understandably, perceive as a lack of knowledge or experience in their teaching staff could be usefully reconceptualised to emphasise the role of higher education not as knowledge transfer from 'expert' to student, but to create an environment designed to foster independence, critical thinking and the ability to handle change and uncertainty.

At our R=T Launch Event, Professor Elizabeth Shephard, UCL Biosciences, described what she viewed as one of the fundamentals of research-based education in the scientific disciplines – which in itself can be suggested as a means of reducing anxiety and learner stress. In this undergraduate model, integration into both the discipline and the research environment is a stepped process: the first year is about developing the relevant skills set, learning the technology, building confidence and becoming numerate, coupled with a first-year tutorial system that includes a lab visit in which all students meet research staff. In this way students begin to appreciate the people behind the research. The second year involves group work and guided projects. By the final year, students are ready to challenge themselves and carry out an independent research project. The aim, for Liz, is to 'inspire students to be enchanted by science' (R=T Launch Event).

It is a traditional model for curriculum design, which has been well-used in the sciences – and to varying extents in the arts and humanities – but it can also be re-conceptualised as something more innovative than that. In a study of first year undergraduates' experiences of research, Levy and Petrulis (2012) found that, by the middle of the first year, many students were not able to explain what research by advanced scholars might entail. They therefore emphasised 'the need to help first years to situate and connect their own experiences of inquiry and research more clearly with those of more experienced researchers in the discipline . . . to move students towards more advanced conceptions of inquiry and of themselves as student-researchers' (Levy and Petrulis 2012, 98). It is this connection that is happening in the Biosciences tutorial system and is a conclusion that aligns with Lave and Wenger's (1991) communities of practice, in which learning occurs socially and 'novice' members of the community learn to think like members of the discipline by participation in its work.[3] Angela Brew (2012) suggests that for the maintenance and continuation of this community, its experienced members have a responsibility to induct its new members into it. Her argument reinforces the legitimate sense of community proposed by Lave and Wenger, in which there is a shared responsibility for the maintenance of the community, for carrying on its traditions and for moving it forward to the future. Returning to many of the scientific disciplines, there can already be the convention that at each stage of a career, one has the responsibility to induct those at the stage below: the postdocs induct the postgraduates, for example, and the principal investigators the postdocs. It should not be too great a step to see the GTAs inducting the taught students.

Indeed, implementing a through-line of research to a degree (as proposed by Fung's Connected Curriculum [2017], and which is, to a certain extent, the Biosciences model) might mean an 'apprenticeship' model where mistakes need to be made early on and steps need to be repeated and practised – something which GTAs are ideally placed to support. That said, this model used in the sciences is not without its faults: it implies a one-way transmission of information and expertise, while in Lave and Wenger's framework teachers' and students' activities are not seen as separate, and learning is reciprocal. Similarly, in other disciplines (such as the humanities) in which research work can be less collaborative – where colleagues' research interests are sometimes only tangentially linked, and the progression from student to PhD to postdoc to Principal Investigator is not so clearly defined – it might be challenging to see how the model could be put in place, but it is not impossible. Encouraging all members of the community to participate in its work and learn collaboratively within it will foster both a collegial environment and an identification with a department, discipline or culture, and is ultimately of benefit to all. As Brew argues:

> The development of academic communities of practice where both students and academics engage as legitimate peripheral participants cannot take place without the relationships between students and their teachers changing. What I have suggested means breaking down the distinctions between teaching and learning as both teachers and students explore the issues which confront them. (Brew 2012, 111)

For me, a vital step in this process is the greater involvement of GTAs and other early-career researcher–teachers in taught provision. Above,

I noted how engaging with research-based education can be beneficial for staff as well as students, and also how GTAs are often intrinsically motivated to develop themselves professionally (and our collection of chapters in Section Two of this volume certainly provides evidence of both). Centring their discussion on GTAs' engagement with teacher development programmes, Winter et al. suggest that:

> Engagement with [a] GTA course can potentially enhance [...] GTAs' understanding of the expectations upon them in their wider PhD role. In order to develop academically, the PhD candidate as a student-researcher must become reflectively aware of their meta-cognitive strategies within the appropriate cultural context as well as developing their research potential; these are interlinked practices which are increasingly recognised by the institutions governing research careers [Vitae, 2011]. (Winter et al. 2014, 40)

Resources such as Vitae's Researcher Development Framework (2011) recognise the value and importance of teaching (and teacher development) to the early-career academic. Moreover, it is instructive to acknowledge that in a research-intensive environment such as UCL, staff can be the beneficiaries of a reconceptualised relationship between research and education (Brew 2012). However, where studies have predominantly discussed how research can inform teaching, Winter at al.'s findings thus suggest possibilities for advocating the benefits of 'teaching *for* research' (2014, 40, emphasis mine). The training and development of research students is a key strategic priority for many UK higher education institutions.[4] I would argue that not only should doctoral candidates and early-career researchers be encouraged to teach, but that they should be closely and actively involved in the development and implementation of a research-based education model. UCL's development programme for GTAs, Arena One, seeks to prepare research students for their teaching responsibilities in a research-intensive environment; in Section 3 of this chapter I offer it as a case study for how an institutional programme can help to support GTAs as they cross some of the boundaries from student to teacher.

3. Case study: A training ground for research-based teaching practitioners

UCL's Arena One is a training pathway composed of three steps: an initial, mandatory 'Gateway' workshop for all PhD students who teach, assess or support students' learning; an optional five-session course based around peer dialogue and self-reflection; and finally the opportunity to submit an application for Associate Fellowship of the Higher Education Academy (AFHEA). The case study focuses on the full process from first workshop to successful completion of the application, in order to foreground the GTAs' burgeoning self-confidence and their increased understanding, and implementation, of research-based learning activities.

The Gateway workshop is most PhD students' first introduction to teaching, and many are understandably anxious. Participants are encouraged to engage with an online learning environment in advance of the first session and contribute to an activity designed to demonstrate that these anxieties are common and reasonable. An anonymous 'hot question' function invites them to submit a query or concern and then vote for one of the others. The top concerns are addressed directly in the session, and it is hoped that indirectly many of the others will also be considered. Alongside the validation that comes with recognising that they are not alone in their worries, the exercise models a helpful teaching technique that the GTAs can go on to try with their own classes. The 'hot questions' posed across all workshops are remarkably similar: how to respond to a question to which you do not know the answer; how to engage students to participate actively in class; how to manage quiet or disruptive students; what are the boundaries for giving support and feedback; how to ensure marking is at the appropriate level; and how to work with students from diverse backgrounds. In response, the workshop introduces participants to the principles of active learning and introduces them to classroom techniques that promote student participation, rather than being tutor-led. Its central aim is to welcome and induct GTAs into the community of UCL teaching staff and to provide an opportunity to meet fellow GTAs: there is a strong institutional focus to the session and plenty of occasions for GTAs to network with peers from across the disciplines.

GTAs who wish to progress from the Gateway workshop to the full Teaching Associate Programme are required to have some prior teaching experience or to be teaching at the same time as following the course. This allows them to put into practice what they are learning and means they are able to write about their experiences in their future applications for AFHEA. As this is an optional programme, it tends to attract the most highly motivated research students who are willing to engage actively with both their continuing professional development and their educational roles. That said, the majority do not have responsibilities for course design and most of their teaching remains small group or lab-based, rather than more traditional lecture style (as was noted above to be common across the sector). They are nonetheless encouraged to try out new techniques in the environments available to them and are given support in designing sessions and activities.

The programme is centred around peer dialogue and group activities, with the tutors' role being predominantly to facilitate interaction and discussion. Both formal and informal feedback garnered from the GTAs suggests that what they most value from the course are these opportunities to learn from and interact with their peers, alongside the modelling activities that they can take forward to their own classes. The second session builds on the basics of active learning discussed in the Gateway workshop and expands on this to introduce the GTAs to research-based teaching, both as a concept and as it is being put into practice institutionally. The GTAs work in groups to design a research-based learning activity, and their resulting ideas are often inventive and sophisticated; they are also, perhaps most importantly, generally realistic and achievable. Here are three examples of the activities proposed:

My group decided that we would create a walking route and communicate this to students ahead of time. Students would be placed in small groups and required to select a building located on this walking route to present to the class. Roughly, students would be looking at the who/what/when/where/why/how related to the building's construction, its current status, and could potentially remark on the building's future. The class would thus consist of a tour created by the students themselves. The outcome of this exercise is to get students applying processes/terminology discussed in previous classes into a real-world context. Teamwork will be required in order to create a thorough and cohesive group presentation. We are interested in the following: what can we know about the building by experiencing it? And conversely: how does our knowledge affect the experience? (Doctoral student in the UCL Slade School of Fine Art)

My group decided that we would present the class with an object/ text/plan (we all come from different disciplines – but all wanted to approach an object in a practical way) and discuss possible approaches or solutions to it. For example, if it is a text to be translated, how we would consider certain words or phrases. In the case of an art object, we would consider its material, its techniques, etc. We would then split the class into smaller groups and present each group with a different object, expecting them to go through the same process again, but without being led by the teacher. The students would come up with their own approaches to the object at hand, and then later feed this back to the other groups. This way the teacher plays a limited role, and it is the students who really guide the learning of the whole group through their interactions with one another, and their engagement with a specific problem (as problem-based learning). (Doctoral student in the UCL School of European Languages, Culture and Society)

This activity was aimed at science students learning about microbiology. The activity involved students taking swabs from their home environment (kitchen, computer, bathroom, living room, etc) and cultivating them, identifying the organisms and then doing standard antibiotic resistance testing. Learning outcomes for this activity would include practical tasks of micro culture, resistance testing, microscopy, sample collection. The results could be collected and collated and the activity repeated over several years to build up a temporal picture of microbiological species in the environment and resistance patterns that would be built on by future classes. (Doctoral student in the UCL Division of Surgery and Interventional Science)

Interestingly, many of the activities were similarly based around this 'legacy' concept, whereby the outputs produced by students could be modified and built upon by subsequent cohorts. As many of the GTAs had recently completed a taught programme of study, they were perhaps all too aware of the frustration of their own, 'valuable essays simply [sitting] in piles collecting dust for three years, then [getting] thrown out' (Chang 2005, 387). Unwittingly, the GTAs had designed activities similar to the innovative work of a previous UCL colleague, Hasok Chang, who designed just such a project, ultimately resulting in a collaborative monograph. Chang has described the resulting volume as, 'the product of a unique educational experiment, a pilot project aimed at a full integration of teaching and research at the undergraduate level' (Chang and Jackson 2007, 383). Likewise, as one student from the UCL School of Slavonic and East European Studies reported:

The aim of our activity [gradually developing with subsequent student groups a peer-reviewed volume in Political Science or an online archive in History] would be to familiarise students with the research process and to create learning conditions in which they encounter the frontier of research in a certain field as opposed to relying on text books. If the students are producing a publication, they would have the satisfaction of seeing their work in print. Likewise, if the students gradually produce an archive, they would not only become very familiar with the content of the source materials they were cataloguing, but they would also become adept at locating and working with primary sources. (Doctoral student in the UCL School of Slavonic and Eastern European Studies)

The final stage of the GTA training programme is the option to submit an application for AFHEA. For many, this is a major incentive for participating in the course: the opportunity to gain professional recognition is understandably appealing to students on the verge of entering the competitive job market. It is highly gratifying to read these applications and to observe how, with even a limited teaching load, but by participating in a peer-led, supportive training environment, GTAs can quickly come to be inspired by one another to create innovative student learning experiences. Reflecting back to the initial Gateway workshop and how so many of the concerns raised centre on, 'But, what if I don't know the answer?', the GTAs gain an understanding that they too are experts, and that by integrating their own research into their teaching they can establish their expertise and authority. Moreover, they develop an appreciation of how exciting this can be to students and how they can play a role in making student learning relevant, challenging and inspirational.

4. Conclusions: GTAs and the R=T initiative

The unifying thread – and unique element – of the chapters written by the GTAs in the R=T initiative is that they are authored by academics at the meeting point between the taught student experience and the research environment. Working with this group on the R=T initiative has reinforced my belief in the fundamental importance of an approach to research-based education that engages coherently and robustly with GTAs and other early-career academics. The benefits to students, staff and the individuals themselves are unmistakeable. In a higher education environment which is seeking actively to encourage individuals and teams to think deeply about the nature and practices of their own research, to invite students at all levels to learn through engaging in some of those distinctive practices, to take students to the edge of knowledge, and to change the nature of the dialogue between staff and students (Fung 2017), there is a key role to be played by those at the confluence of research and education.

Notes

1. At UCL, doctoral students who teach are known as PGTAs (postgraduate teaching assistants), and go by a variety of other names at different institutions. It is common in the literature to use the term GTA, which has thus been adopted for the purposes of this chapter.
2. Based on a survey with 68 respondents, of which 82% offered developmental opportunities to GTAs.
3. See Dwyer (2001) for an analysis of the core tutorial programme in UCL Geography, which centres on geography as research practice. One of the first activities involves students 'meeting the researcher': interviewing an experienced member of staff about his or her research, the challenges, processes and 'messiness' of the research process (2001, 359).
4. See, for example, the 2016 UCL Doctoral Education Strategy: http://www.ucl.ac.uk/gs/doctoral-education-strategy/Doctoral-Education-Strategy.pdf [Accessed October 2017]

References

Brew, Angela. 2012. Teaching and research: New relationships and their implications for inquiry-based teaching and learning in higher education. *Higher Education Research and Development* 31, 101–14.

Chadha, Deesha. 2013. Postgraduates as teachers: Exploring expectations and highlighting disciplinary differences. *Practice and Evidence of Scholarship of Teaching and Learning in Higher Education* 8, 2, SEDA/PESTLHE Special Issue September 2013, 93–103.

Chang, Hasok. 2005. Turning an undergraduate class into a professional research community. *Teaching in Higher Education* 10, 387–94.

Chang, Hasok and Jackson, Catherine (eds) 2007. *An Element of Controversy. The Life of Chlorine in Science, Medicine, Technology and War*. British Society for the History of Science, UK. Available online: http://www.bshs.org.uk/wp-content/uploads/file/bshs_monographs/library_monographs/bshsm_013_chang-and-jackson.pdf. [Accessed October 2017].

Dwyer, Claire. 2001. Linking research and teaching: A staff–student interview project. *Journal of Geography in Higher Education* 25, 357–66.

Fung, Dilly. 2017. *A Connected Curriculum for Higher Education*. London: UCL Press.

Jenkins, Alan, Breen, Rosanna and Lindsay, Roger. 2003. *Reshaping Teaching in Higher Education: Linking Teaching with Research*. London: Kogan Page.

Lave, Jean and Wenger, Etienne. 1991. *Situated Learning: Legitimate Peripheral Participation*. Cambridge: Cambridge University Press.

Lee, Ann, Pettigrove, Malcolm and Fuller, Michael (eds) 2010. *Preparing to Teach in Higher Education*. Lichfield: UK Council for Graduate Education.

Levy, Philippa and Petrulis, Robert. 2012. How do first-year university students experience inquiry and research, and what are the implications for the practice of inquiry-based learning? *Studies in Higher Education* 37, 85–101.

Muzaka, Valbona. 2009. The niche of Graduate Teaching Assistants (GTAs): Perceptions and reflections. *Teaching in Higher Education* 14, 1–12.

Park, Chris and Ramos, Marife. 2002. The donkey in the department? Insights into the Graduate Teaching Assistant (GTA) experience in the UK. *Journal of Graduate Education* 3, 47–53.

Vitae. 2011. Vitae Researcher Development Framework (RDF). Available from: https://www.vitae.ac.uk/vitae-publications/rdf-related/researcher-development-framework-rdf-vitae.pdf/view [Accessed October 2017].

Winter, Jennie, Turner, Rebecca, Gedye, Sharon, Nash Patricia and Grant, Vivien. 2015. Graduate teaching assistants: Responding to the challenges of internationalisation. *International Journal for Academic Development* 20, 33–45.

1.4

Investigating student perceptions of student–staff partnership

Mina Sotiriou

UCL Arena Centre for Research-based Education

1. Introduction

As one of the academic leads of the R=T initiative, I worked closely with the students on the planning of the Masterclass series and focus groups. My close working relationship with some of them gave both me and them the opportunity to discover each other's roles and develop a relationship based on trust. My first-hand, positive experience of working in close partnership with students prompted me to delve further into the principles and theoretical perspectives involved in student–staff partnerships and investigate students' experiences of being involved in these. Specifically, I was interested in finding out what the students thought of the R=T initiative, which I consider unique as a structure.

This chapter will discuss the findings of interviews I held with five students who took part in the R=T initiative, and their perceptions of partnerships.

2. Background: from engagement to partnership and beyond

In 2011 Axelson and Flick wrote that 'few terms in the lexicon of higher education today are invoked more frequently, and in more varied ways, than *engagement*' (2011, 38–43). Five years later (2016) and the term 'engagement' is no less used. Furthermore, in addition to researchers, policy makers have also adopted it extensively, and it has become common parlance within the learning and teaching literature.

The term refers to how involved or interested students appear to be in their learning and how connected they are to their classes, their institutions and each other. Ashwin and McVitty (2015) provide a very informative account of the problem of defining student engagement. They argue that when we talk about student engagement it is important to focus on the object of engagement or what it is to be 'formed' through that engagement. With this approach in mind, Ashwin and McVitty define three broad objects of engagement:

- engagement to form individual understanding – how student engagement can help students to improve their learning outcomes;
- engagement to form curricula – how students can help to form the courses that they study in higher education;
- engagement to form communities – how students can be involved in helping to shape the institutions and societies of which they are part.

For the Quality Assurance Agency (QAA), the independent body which monitors and advises on standards and quality in UK higher education, student engagement is about students getting involved, raising their views, feeling empowered and shaping their education. The QAA

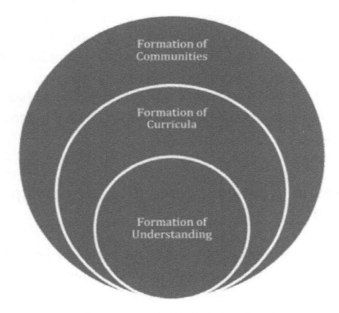

Formation of Communities

Formation of Curricula

Formation of Understanding

Figure 1.4.1 Nested hierarchy of the object of student engagement in Ashwin and McVitty (2015)

sees its role as bringing students and university staff together to influence decision makers, share good practice and ensure students are at the centre of the process (QAA 2012).

But is student engagement synonymous with partnership? As Healey et al. (2014, 7) argue, 'all partnership is student engagement, but not all student engagement is partnership'.

The distinction, according to NUS (2012, 8), is that, 'the sum total of student engagement activity at an institution does not equate to partnership; this is because partnership is an ethos rather than an activity'.

The same philosophy has been adopted by the UK Higher Education Academy (HEA). In the foreword to Healey et al. (2014), HEA's Deputy Chief Executive Philippa Levy argues that '"student engagement" has become a core aim for the [HE] sector' (Healey et al. 2014, 4).

Where the QAA sees partnership as an outcome, Healey et al. (2014, 12) see partnership as a *process* of engagement. It is a way of doing things, rather than an end goal, in which all those involved – students, academics, professional services staff, senior managers, students' unions, and so on – are actively engaged in and stand to gain from the process of learning and working together.

The common denominator in all three initiatives is students. Students, therefore, were the focus of the R=T initiative. We invited current UCL students to express an interest in participating in the initiative, and the resulting testimonies demonstrate that students were interested in forming partnerships that will not only change their perceptions and help them gain knowledge, but also transform their education:

> Encouraging students to engage more with current research, as well as attempt their own, leads to more natural and long-lasting learning. Research-based education also gives students the opportunity to teach their fellow students about their findings, therefore encouraging and reinforcing new ideas between peers. This sense of ownership over their degrees and learning outcomes leads not only to better scholarship, but a more confident interaction with the cultures in question. (Mary)

> By going through the research-based approach, learners are able to realise their full potential by understanding how knowledge is created. Initiatives such as R=T initiative give learners and researchers the chance to see behind the scenes, to learn crucial skills early and be prepared to undertake research at any level, because innovation is possible at any stage. (Mariya)

3. Context

Although student–staff partnership is a well-researched topic nowadays, research on students' perceptions of such partnerships is quite rare.

I was particularly interested in gaining an understanding of students' perceptions of:

- student–staff partnerships in the context of the R=T initiative;
- criteria for successful partnerships;
- benefits of student–staff partnerships;
- teachers' roles and purpose of higher education.

As a result, I conducted face-to-face interviews with five students who took part in the R=T initiative, and who also contributed to this publication. All five students – four female and one male – were postgraduate teaching assistants. They were from:

- Eastman Institute,
- Institute of Sustainable Heritage,
- Translation Studies,
- Institute of Education,
- Chemical Engineering.

4. Research findings

4.1 Perceptions of partnership

Partnerships can be seen as one-to-one, one-to-many or many-to-many. The R=T initiative is a many-to-many partnership which involves:

- students and academics (including academics leading the R=T Masterclasses);
- students and students;
- students and the academic leads in the R=T initiative.

In my discussions with the students, I was particularly interested in exploring their perceptions of 'partnership', and how they saw their partnership within the R=T initiative.

The majority of the interviewees described partnership as a network of people or one-to-one relationships, where participants are working together towards the development of an idea or project with all the parties involved. Partnership was seen primarily as engagement in learning and teaching. In the words of one interviewee, 'the object of the partnership is for students to understand teaching and staff to develop that teaching' (Dallas).

A similar view was also expressed by another interviewee who defined partnership as 'students talking to teachers about what they want to learn or need to learn . . . [Partnership is when] the student and the teacher are collaborating in the actual course content' (Ellen).

Partnerships, though, require a structure that is formed by the exchange of ideas and agreed by all participants. As one interviewee (Preeti) described it, 'a partnership is an open window for dialogue'. For the dialogue to be effective, a sustainable long-term plan is necessary. As such, the students identified continuity as an essential criteria for forming a partnership. Another interviewee (Eirini) argued that 'the aim of the partnership is not to be on–off, but to be . . . long term; it is something that can be repeated in the future and involve more people'.

In every partnership, it is also necessary to have a context for implementation. Preeti also commented, 'there are three settings [in] which students and staff interact: the classroom, research and assessments. Student–staff partnerships should negotiate the rules of engagement on all these areas and students and staff should articulate the scope together'.

Evidently, the interviewees see partnerships as an opportunity to actively contribute to the development of their teaching, learning and research experience, and be co-developers of their curriculum.

4.2 Criteria for successful partnerships

A variety of authors have identified a number of essential criteria for successful partnerships. Healey et al. (2014, 14–15) summarise these as:

- authenticity – all parties have a meaningful rationale for investing in partnership, and are honest about what they can contribute and the parameters of partnership;
- inclusivity – partnership embraces the different talents, perspectives and experiences that all parties bring, and there are no barriers (structural or cultural) that prevent potential partners getting involved;
- reciprocity – all parties have an interest in, and stand to benefit from, working and/or learning in partnership;

- empowerment – power is distributed appropriately and all parties are encouraged to constructively challenge ways of working and learning that may reinforce existing inequalities;
- trust – all parties take time to get to know each other, engage in open and honest dialogue and are confident they will be treated with respect and fairness;
- challenge – all parties are encouraged to constructively critique and challenge practices, structures and approaches that undermine partnership, and are enabled to take risks to develop new ways of working and learning;
- community – all parties feel a sense of belonging and are valued fully for the unique contribution they make;
- responsibility – all parties share collective responsibility for the aims of the partnership, and individual responsibility for the contribution they make.

Many of these same criteria were also identified as critical in my interviews with the students.

In terms of the structure of the R=T initiative, however, two criteria were highlighted as particularly important: 'community' and 'reciprocity'. It is important to note that the aims of the R=T initiative were developed and agreed in collaboration with the students and as such all participants felt a sense of ownership or, in the words of one interviewee (Preeti), 'it is [as] much your baby as it [is] mine'.

It should be said, though, that a consistent and a regular dialogue was also identified as a critical element for building and sustaining partnerships. Interviewees felt that limitations of time and a lack of continuous engagement can affect a partnership and its outcomes. For this reason, all interviewees valued the regular contact with the academic leads of the R=T initiative, which helped to build up trust and commitment.

4.3 Benefits of student–staff partnerships

In their report, 'Developing successful student–staff partnerships', Killen and Chatterton (2015) discuss the numerous benefits that such partnerships can offer to students, staff and institutions:

- gaining knowledge and experience of leadership and influencing change;
- gaining experience of using research to shape change;

- recognition of achievements through accredited leadership and extra-curricular awards;
- increased confidence and skills (e.g. communication, team-working, management, research skills);
- enhanced networking with the wider professional community;
- improved employability and job prospects;
- driving the development of the digital environment for students at their institution.

Similarly, the HEA is promoting student–staff partnerships as an effective way of developing student engagement and enhancing learning and teaching (HEA 2016).

My interviewees also discussed the perceived benefits of participating in the R=T initiative. They described gaining knowledge, improving skills and enhancing networking, as identified by Killen and Chatterton above.

While networking with the wider community was of particular interest to all interviewees, partnership was seen as a way of finding out what is happening in the institution. In the words of one interviewee (Eirini):

> I have been a postgraduate student in smaller universities where every student activity was easier to disperse and easier to be heard of. While in UCL (because it is very big) there are too many information and you need to prioritise. It is very difficult to find the group of people you want to talk to and this partnership looked like a way to come closer to people who have similar interests. It was also a way to understand what is the goal of the institution. [sic] (Eirini)

Interviewees also claimed that the partnerships in the R=T initiative offered the opportunity for bilateral negotiations and ideas: it was seen as an iterative process where ideas were continuously created. As the result of this process, any perceived hierarchies were dissolved and diluted, and all partners effectively had equal rights: 'in a partnership all parties have responsibilities, otherwise it is a leadership' (Ellen).

It is worth noting, however, that although the interviewees confirmed the benefits cited by both Jisc (an organisation for digital services and solutions in the UK; see Killen and Chatterton 2015) and HEA, they also indicated a distinction in the focus of the partnership. Specifically, in contrast to the Jisc and HEA results, where attention appears to be on the outputs, our results from the interviews demonstrate instead a focus on the process of the partnership, as discussed by Healey et al. (2014), in order to form communities (Ashwin and McVitty 2015). According to interviewee Eirini, the partnership offered her the opportunity to discuss with other members 'how the educational system can be changed or transformed'.

Another benefit for the students of the R=T initiative, and acknowledged by the interviewees, was interdisciplinary knowledge awareness. Specifically, the students valued the knowledge gained by the interdisciplinary character of both student–staff and student–student partnerships:

> I particularly liked that many people [were] involved in the partnership and their voices were represented. I attended Masterclass sessions by people from different disciplines than mine and I gained by watching them. I saw how their methods applied in my area. You can get an overview of what is going on in academia especially if you want to teach afterwards. (Eirini)

Such an approach is closely aligned with the views of Brew (2006), where partnerships lead to the development of an inclusive scholarly community.

4.4 Teachers' roles and purpose of higher education

Flint, in his Jisc report (2015, 3), argues that

> partnership is a particularly useful lens when looking into change agency, as it focuses on the role of staff and students. As a relationship and a dialogic process, partnership presents opportunities to start new conversations and to open up new spaces for learning, change and innovation. It offers transformative potential because it prompts us to question the assumptions we make about one another and the learning process, in a way we don't often make explicit.

The current roles of teachers and students were topics that came up in the interviews, and the interviewees argued that a redefinition of roles is required if student–staff partnerships are to be successful. In the words of one of the interviewees (Preeti), redefining the role of teachers should begin by asking 'what are we doing in the class, [and] why are we doing it?'

Similar concerns were echoed in the R=T Masterclasses by the invited professors. I was particularly taken by the views of Professor Jeremy Levesley, who argued that 'my work is not to give answers; my work is to ask questions. My work is to stimulate confusion. Because learning is all about learning and resolution, in my mind. You have to destroy your old to create your new' (2016).

It was clear that the students felt that their involvement in the R=T initiative gave them the opportunity to voice their views and question the educational status quo. In her chapter 2.4, Agathe Ribéreau-Gayon argues that 'traditional educational models are no longer suitable for today's students' needs'. She 'explores the suitability of research-based teaching as a new education model'.

It remains to be seen if the research-based education model is a suitable educational model for all higher education institutions. However, the need to redefine the purpose of higher education is a necessity argued by all interviewees.

> Students got the mentality that education is education for jobs. This is what needs to be questioned. We prioritise the wrong things. (Saya)

Saya's views are also reflected in the students' chapters here, and it is worth taking a moment to question the current system and in particular the purpose of assessment. It appears to be a consensus among the students that assessment, as it is currently practised, 'is of learning rather than assessment for learning'. The fact that students' success is defined as 'the correct answer' is an issue that needs to be addressed.

5. Conclusion

My interaction with the students in the R=T initiative, and the in-depth interviews conducted with a number of them, offered me the opportunity to question my own views and practices. While generally the emphasis on student–staff partnerships is on the students and what they will benefit from partnership, I would argue that in this particular initiative I gained more than I put in.

The interviews with the students allowed both me and them to question what we thought we knew and to learn from each other. Although the students who took part in the R=T initiative focused initially on the object of engagement to form individual understanding, during the process it became apparent that they were interested in shaking up the status quo: 'students want their voices to be heard so they can change the institution they are in; and through this you also change people's experiences and what they take after leaving the institution' (Eirini).

Students' involvement in the R=T initiative created a precedent for future UCL partnerships. Students were instrumental not only in the planning and execution of the tasks assigned by all parties, but also in the development of ideas for the research-based education approach that UCL champions. Engagement was not restricted to forming understanding or curricula or communities, but to forming all three dimensions.

The aim of the R=T initiative was not only to create a student–staff project which would enhance students' learning and provide pedagogical examples for staff development, but – crucially – to create an ethos of partnership in the whole institution and initiate a dialogue between students and staff.

The success of such an institution-wide initiative can only be possible if all partners share the same values. The students who took part in the R=T initiative were the co-creators of the research-based education approach, and their views in this book, as Preeti says, is an 'open window for a dialogue' for all of us in higher education.

Students' perceptions as discussed in this chapter can help institutions plan their educational strategy with students in mind. Although the R=T initiative is based on research-based education, what it is important to stress is that whichever approach an institution applies, student–staff partnerships are a crucial element for success in higher education. Students want their voices to be heard.

References

Ashwin, P. and McVitty, D. 2015. The meanings of student engagement: Implications for policies and practices. In A. Curaj et al. (eds) *The European Higher Education Area*, pp. 343–59. Springer International Publishing.

Axelson, R. D. and Flick, A. 2011. Defining student engagement. *Change: The Magazine of Higher Learning* 43, 38–43.

Brew, A. 2006. *Research and Teaching: Beyond the Divide*. London: Palgrave.

Flint, A. 2015. Students and staff as partners in innovation and change. *The Journal of Educational Innovation, Partnership and Change* 1, preface.

Flint, A. in Killen, C. and P. Chatterton. 2015. Developing successful student–staff partnerships. JISC, Available online at: https://www.jisc.ac.uk/guides/developing-successful-student-staff-partnerships [Accessed 30 July 2016].

Healey, M., Flint, A. and Harrington, K. 2014. Engagement through partnership: students as partners in learning and teaching in higher education. York: Higher Education Academy. Available online at: https://www.heacademy.ac.uk/engagement-through-partnership-students-partners-learning-and-teaching-higher-education [Accessed 26 July 2016].

Higher Education Academy (HEA). 2016. Students as partners. Available online at: https://www. heacademy.ac.uk/enhancement/themes/students-partner [Accessed 1 August 2016].

Killen, C. and Chatterton, P. 2015. Developing successful student–staff partnerships. JISC. Available online at: https://www.jisc.ac.uk/guides/developing-successful-student-staff-partnerships [Accessed 30 July 2016].

Levesley, J. 2016. 'UCL R=T Masterclass'. UCL Arena.

NUS. 2012. A manifesto for partnership [Internet]. London: National Union of Students. Available online at: www.nusconnect.org.uk/campaigns/highereducation/partnership/a-manifesto-for-partnerships/ [Accessed 30 July 2016].

Quality Assurance Agency for Higher Education (QAA). 2012. Chapter B5: Student Engagement. UK Quality Code for Higher Education [Internet]. Gloucester: QAA. Available online at: www. qaa.ac.uk/publications/informationandguidance/pages/quality-code-B5.aspx [Accessed 29 July 2016].

1.5

Connecting students with staff research activities and real-world outputs

Ran Sing Saw
School of Pharmacy, UCL

1. Challenges

Several issues were raised in my focus group, the most prominent one concerning the availability of resources to involve students in research. Ideally, students are paired with staff and their research projects to best engage and to provide optimum support to the students. However, this only works if there are reasonable staff–student ratios in all departments. While there are differences between disciplines, one of the main challenges is low staff availability, which makes the inclusive involvement of students in staff research projects difficult. The inadequacy of spaces and facilities is also an issue when trying to accommodate large student cohorts, for example into scientific laboratories – even just for a tour. Specialist equipment, such as laboratory instruments, may be sophisticated and very expensive and therefore require appropriate training, which, again, needs staff and resources.

Another challenge to incorporating research into teaching is that some research requires deep understanding of certain topics. Staff reportedly found it difficult to introduce the latest research into curricula, especially into those of first-year undergraduates. The focus group also noted a lack of interest among students towards some of the existing programmes and initiatives. One academic staff member who has been teaching for many years shared his experience of conducting a workshop series that encourages students to find information and think critically to solve the problems given. He found that some students prefer being given straightforward answers instead of doing the searches and researches themselves.

In addition to improving technical knowledge, there are also a number of activities or projects that aim to develop 'soft' skills such as team-working, time management, and oral and written presentations. Although these skills are transferable, and essential to doing research in the future, the link may not seem obvious to students in the early stages of their study. Consequently, as described by another participant of the focus group, there appears to be resistance among some students towards completing coursework before they have realised its importance in building their soft skills.

Some of these issues could stem from a lack of connection to the 'real world'. Take the dissemination of research work and findings, for example. If these fail to be communicated to an audience wider than the few people involved in the marking process, they will be less powerful as a tool to link students to the world outside the classroom. This is possibly one of the factors that leads to low motivation among students in carrying out particular research tasks. Hence some consideration has to be made to translate their efforts into outcomes that have deeper and wider impacts.

2. Recommendations

2.1 Overcoming the resistance

It was generally agreed among participants in the R=T Masterclass and focus groups that the development of transferable skills through coursework and projects can be the first step towards involving all students in research. However, students themselves have to be able to see the importance of this progression to avoid the lack of interest that potentially leads to students' resistance in doing the work as identified in the focus group. To help students to see into the future and appreciate the essential skills they will need, whether for research or their career, alumni who are distinctive in their own fields can be invited to give talks to students sharing their experience of using skills acquired at undergraduate level which helped them in their research. It can be helpful for students to see the work alumni have produced and hear how they got to where they are now. As most students are able to relate themselves more readily to alumni – who might have had a similar experience to them in previous years – these former students can become role models and a source of inspiration.

Traditionally, only final-year students carry out a dissertation or final-year project. However, not all look forward to it, and there are many who see it merely as something they have to do to graduate. If students are able to find out where their passions lie during their early years at university, it can serve to build up the enthusiasm, knowledge, skills and excitement that are often lacking when carrying out that important final piece of work. Hence, opportunities for students to explore various subjects of their choosing should be promoted. Short exploratory classes featuring staff research activities can serve as a platform which, at least briefly, involves students in the research carried out in the university. Such classes can also help to introduce a wide variety of topics without students having to commit to an entire module; this can encourage them to look beyond their degree courses towards multi- or interdisciplinary studies. As students begin to get an idea of what they are most interested in, they will become proactive in finding out more about the topic and progressively accumulating related knowledge. Introducing real research at this stage is the best way to encourage students to continue developing their knowledge and skills in areas that interest them. Hopefully, they will be able to further develop these interests in their dissertation or final-year project – and work on it with passion.

2.2 Enhancing connections to the real world

Professor McCrindle encouraged universities to grasp every opportunity to partner with enterprises and industries, as well as form links with charities, museums, collections, societies and, in some cases, professional bodies. Building on these relationships, collaborations with partner organisations can be expanded through guest lectures, competitions, awards, real-life projects and even summer placements. These opportunities enable students to transfer and improve the skills learnt throughout their course into real-world systems while gaining different perspectives on the world outside the classroom. This is undoubtedly valuable for students' personal and professional development as well as for future employment prospects. The chance of getting their work 'out there' and making an impact will encourage students to put in more effort, leading to higher-quality products and invoking a sense of pride that could hardly be obtained through standard assessments alone.

2.3 Developing abilities

Although it is inevitable that some research requires deep knowledge that may be beyond the understanding of undergraduates, students can nonetheless be encouraged to read secondary sources to get a good overview in the early stages. However, it is just as important to expose undergraduate students to primary literature, not only to be better informed of the field, but also to advance their critical-thinking and analytical skills so that they can later develop their own research. Selecting journal articles that are easier to understand, breaking them down to allow students to learn section by section, forming clear and defined learning outcomes, and providing guidance on how to go about writing a section of an article are some of the ways to help students get more familiar with primary literature.

Setting up a research unit providing training and support to promote entrepreneurship and business acumen should also be considered. This could provide relevant support through facilitating the delivery of short training courses, summer classes and internships, as well as linking students with external organisations for research projects. Developing the knowledge and skills of students is essential to prepare them for carrying out their own research.

2.4 Linking students with research activities

As discussed previously, the main obstacle to involving most, if not all, students in research is the lack of available staff. One of the focus group participants recommended using more postgraduates, especially PhD students, to ease the burden. Postgraduates are often looking to engage with undergraduate students, and having them assist, supervise and teach research will create immense opportunities for both sides. Giving postgraduates greater responsibility will also reflect positively on their personal experience and further develop their skills.

One way to facilitate this idea is through a mentorship programme, whereby PhD students and postdoctoral researchers act as mentors to small groups of undergraduates. Students should be able to sign up online, stating their research interest, and then be matched to a mentor with a suitable background. To begin with, mentors would be responsible for linking students to research by explaining the projects that they are working on, and potentially explaining the wider context of the materials taught in lectures to reinforce understanding. Undergraduates could also be used to provide extra help with projects, a great way to gently introduce them to the work, techniques and skills essential to a researcher. Further down the line, mentors would provide guidance and support to students in developing ideas for their own research.

While these initiatives may encourage inclusiveness in research-based teaching, it is worth recognising that only a fraction of students are interested in pursuing research as a career. There needs to be an element of selectivity in how research opportunities are offered, so that more support and guidance is available to develop the skills and abilities of those students who want to carry on their research journey after their undergraduate degree.

3. Conclusion

While connecting students with staff and their research activities is lauded as the way forward in higher education nowadays, the implications of the change for both staff and students need to be acknowledged and addressed. Staff workloads will most probably increase, while some students may find it difficult to adapt to a different learning experience particularly in the initial stages. Hence, good communication between the staff and the students, as well as from the university itself, is crucial. Otherwise the approach could be a source of frustration for all, as expectations are not met. Students should have more opportunities to act as departmental and faculty representatives, with a voice in developing research-based education in their respective areas of study. Training and incentives should be given to both staff and postgraduate students.

In addition to institutional initiatives, motivated students can also help to develop research skills and opportunities through student clubs and societies. Activities such as workshops, competitions, talks and seminars can be organised by students and supported by the university and staff to enhance learning outside the classroom. The wider participation and deeper involvement of students in the implementation of this initiative is, in its own right, a real-world output, which will have lasting and positive impacts on students' education and experience.

Ultimately, connecting students with staff research activities and real-world outputs requires the collaboration of many sides, and thus its successful implementation depends heavily on the collective effort of everyone involved.

References

Healey, M. and Jenkins, A. 2009. *Developing Undergraduate Research and Inquiry*. York: Higher Education Academy.

Rauschert, E., Dauer, J., Momsen, J. L. and Sutton-Grier, A. 2011. Primary literature across the undergraduate curriculum: Teaching science process skills and content. *Ecological Society of America* 92, 396–405.

Walkington, Helen. 2016. Pedagogic approaches to developing students as researchers, within the curriculum and beyond. York: Higher Education Academy. https://www.heacademy.ac.uk/system/files/resources/walkington-pedagogic-approaches.pdf [Accessed 1 April 2016].

1.6
Transcending disciplinary boundaries in student research activities

Neema Kotonya

Department of Computer Science, UCL

1. Key themes from the R=T Masterclass

I have identified two broad issues and challenges, which audience members stated hinder the fostering of relationships between departments. Rapport-building is an essential starting point for honest and nuanced conversations that could lead to joint research efforts.

The first challenge is overcoming the problem that arises when students specialise too early. The issue here is that students might not have the depth of knowledge required to engage in conversations with people from difficult fields. Also, if someone is from an insular field, they might not be particularly open to accepting new perspectives or helping a student from outside their field understand the complexities and intricacies of their own research area.

The second challenge is that if universities take a top-down or central approach to this task, they risk undermining any work that has been done building contacts and relationships. Conflicts arise when administrators attempt to bring departments or research teams together for projects, while ignoring the bonds that have already been painstakingly formed between teams in different departments. Universities should therefore approach this task both cautiously and transparently.

In the Masterclass there were also questions about what specifically constitutes a student research activity. Bob Eaglestone stated that in his two disciplines (English and History), a simple discussion of a book in a seminar environment is a research activity. In engineering and sciences, however, research activities are longer, more involved processes that usually involve the development of mathematic models and require the execution of several experiments. It might therefore be more difficult to initiate interdisciplinary projects in these disciplines.

2. Focus group findings

I identified broader, more general issues and challenges during the Masterclass conversation. However, I still needed to gather information on subject-specific issues regarding cross-disciplinary student research to gain a better understanding of how to remedy the problem. I opened the conversation by asking the students if they had any experience undertaking interdisciplinary projects during their time at university. Only one student had experience of collaborating with people from a different subject area, and this was a fairly recent experience, which he had acquired since arriving at UCL. Some participants expressed concerns that they were often not aware of activities in other departments, or even of the existence of other departments, which makes it harder for them to bridge the divide between their discipline and others.

3. Connecting the challenges to the theme of the R=T Masterclass

The issue of transparency is linked to democratising research and teaching, something Bob Eaglestone touched upon when he introduced the audience at the Masterclass to the work of Paulo Freire (1970). Freire was a proponent of democratising the education process through rethinking the dynamics of the teacher–student relationship and viewing education as an exchange. A substantial number of the problems highlighted in both the Masterclass and the focus group are also linked to a lack of communication. Poor communication can be a hindrance.

4. Focus group recommendations

The focus group participants provided recommendations for the direction in which universities should steer in order to encourage students from different academic backgrounds to pursue research projects together. The focus group's suggestions can be summarised as follows:

1. organise small projects and events;
2. create student-led initiatives;
3. find a case study from within the university.

It is important to approach the task of interdisciplinary student research activities in bite-sized chunks, rather than bigger projects. One way of doing this is perhaps by expanding the UCL's series of Lunch Hour Lectures, and encouraging student researchers to give some of the lectures. Hour-long lectures are much more accessible than longer lectures.

Educators should focus on a bottom-up rather than a top-down approach to ensure that ownership of the research/ideas stays with the originators and that the projects remain people-focused. This will encourage researchers to get involved and may improve the chances of the projects running to completion (retention). Also, taking a decentralised approach means that the burden of expectation for researchers is lifted. There is less pressure on them to 'tick boxes', and they are less likely to be reluctant to join a project for fear of the venture not being successful.

It is crucial to examine cases where interdisciplinary collaboration at the university has already garnered astonishing results and is flourishing. The example brought up in the focus group was the UCL Institute of Biomedical Engineering (IBME), where researchers from Mechanical Engineering, Computer Science, Medical Sciences, Electrical Engineering, Chemistry, Biochemical Engineering, among other departments, are working together to develop medical technologies to improve the quality of healthcare provided by clinicians.

5. Personal recommendations

I have two recommendations for how universities should go about encouraging interdisciplinary student research. These are:

1. early-years research projects;
2. expanding the possibilities for final-year bachelors and taught Masters projects.

Universities must encourage first- and second-year undergraduate students – not just final-year undergraduates and taught Masters students – to take an interest in the research that is being undertaken in their departments. There should be a particular focus on interdisciplinary research activity. One method for achieving this is through the home department hosting research presentations by educators from other departments in the university. In my opinion, only introducing students to postgraduate research opportunities in their penultimate or final year is far too late; by this time a significant proportion of the class have already begun to make decisions. This leads to the brightest and most capable students being lost along the academic pipeline from undergraduate to postgraduate studies.

Furthermore, departments should provide a broader range of final-year project options, including cross-disciplinary suggestions from external departments. Currently, students from my home department (Computer Science) must seek out interdisciplinary dissertation options themselves, as only departmental supervisors' suggestions are listed on their website.

6. Conclusion

After reviewing the challenges and issues presented to me by staff and students at the university, I firmly believe that the most pertinent issue for universities to tackle is sensitivity when broaching the topic of inter-departmental collaboration. It seems that a 'bottom-up' approach could be more beneficial than a 'top-down' one. The most pressing subject-specific issue is definitely ensuring that connections and relationships are formed between different departments, faculties and schools, especially those schools that are newer to the university.

Of the recommendations that were suggested to me, I would advise that the university pursue three of them as part of a trial:

1. an extension of the Lunch Hour Lecture series;
2. support for early-years student researchers;
3. offering a wider range of final-year projects (not restricted to students' home departments).

As the infrastructure already exists to support the Lunch Hour Lecture series, it would not be as costly, in terms of expenditure or the institution's reputation, to extend it. With regards to my second and third recommendations, as they would both be department-led I think they would be more impactful, as departments would have full control in specifying exactly how they wished to carry out these projects. Regarding final-year project selection, I think that a UCL online communication platform, where students could discuss ideas with potential supervisors from other departments, would be a great solution.

Taken as a whole, the question of transcending disciplinary boundaries in student research activities is an important one. Bridging this gap doesn't just offer academic success for the institution and its constituent departments; it will also bring academic rewards and a sense of personal success to students.

References

Freire, Paulo. 1970. *Pedagogy of the Oppressed.* New York: Herder and Herder.

1.7
Connecting students with the workplace

Masuma Pervin Mishu

Department of Epidemiology and Public Health, UCL

1. Challenges and issues

As research-based education is a comparatively new area, establishing it requires the involvement of different groups of people, both within and outside the university. But, currently, not all members of the university are aware of research-based education or are ready to adopt it. The process of implementing it will also differ from department to department. One issue to emerge from the focus group discussion was that although there are some scattered examples of student involvement in research, it is not very organised, planned or widely practised in all departments. One participant said: 'Most of the graduate or students on Masters of Science (MSc) courses don't know what the scope of research is in their department'. This is true for many departments.

Another barrier to engaging students in workplace research is scarcity of resources. 'There are not even adequate places to sit in the office', said one of the academics in the focus group discussion, 'so how can we invite at least some of the students to get involved in our research work?' For students, there is a vast field of work outside academia. Professor Fleming said that after completing their studies, only 15 per cent of students remain in academia, with the rest working in non-academic jobs. Therefore, enabling students to increase their employability for jobs in industry is a very important issue. There are several basic skills – creativity, logical and critical-thinking, research communication, teamwork, leadership, being able to work under pressure and so on – that students could acquire from research-based higher education. But many students are not aware of these transferable skills that are so useful when they enter the job market.

There are opportunities for work or industrial placements in some departments, but these are still very limited. Creating opportunities on a wider scale is a real challenge, as it involves multidisciplinary groups working together, both within and outside the university.

2. Recommendations

The practical implementation of research-based education across the university is a complex process. The first step should be to spread awareness of this teaching approach to every academic and research staff member, particularly senior colleagues. There should be a central recommendation from the university to every department to put this new approach into practice, backed up with a strategic implementation plan, as well as financial resources and other material support from the central authority.

Each department should be willing to engage students in its various research projects. Some changes or redesigning of the old curriculum may be necessary to fit with this research-based education system. Tutors may also need some new training. To involve students in research, tutors have a very important role. Tutors could integrate research into their teaching by involving students in their own research projects, for example by giving them some specific duty, responsibility or fieldwork experience. Tutors could also design assignments that are focused on real-life research activities, such as the practice of writing a grant application, giving a presentation or peer reviewing.

To prepare students for connection to the workplace, tutors should help make students aware of the transferrable 'soft' skills that they are acquiring through research. These skills should be flagged to students to give them more confidence about approaching the world of work, for example being able to refer to them in a job interview or apply them in their real working life.

Incorporating more multidisciplinary research into higher education could help to widen students' horizons of future work opportunities. The university should collaborate with industry and local government to allow students to connect with the workplace through work placements, internships, volunteering opportunities or collaborative projects. This would really help students to make the smooth transition from theoretical knowledge to practical work, and also benefit industries by increasing the supply of innovative workers.

Professionals from industry or business could be invited to the university to give short lectures or career consultations on practical ways to apply the knowledge gained at university into working life. They could also speak to students about work patterns and the workplace environment, which would help students make more informed choices about their future jobs.

Academics usually have a wide network of both academics and non-academics. They should use their existing networks to help their students. Two academics at the focus group suggested that professors are sometimes reluctant to let students use their network, as they are worried about the impact it might have on their own reputation. They said there should be a central industrial placement system within the university.

The implementation of research-based education by connecting students with the workplace is most certainly a noble concept. If universities want to make it happen, staff and students will need to work in partnership. Academics should also get official recognition for being involved in research-based education. It should be seen as rewarding for their careers, otherwise they are unlikely to really engage with it and do the extra work required.

1.8
Involving tutors, demonstrators and teaching assistants more actively in large-group teaching

Mariya Badeva

The UCL Bartlett Faculty of the Built Environment

1. What are the general challenges?

One key challenge that arose in my focus group about large-group teaching was how to eliminate the passiveness of students in this context. It was acknowledged that many students do not feel comfortable or lack the opportunity to share their thoughts in front of a large group. Many of the issues identified during the focus group were found to be dependent on the professors, teaching assistants and demonstrators who lead large-group sessions. These leaders are perceived as an important factor to integrating and involving students in large groups, dictated mainly by the strategies they use and how well prepared they are for a particular class. Inevitably, different teaching contexts require different approaches. By attempting to tackle the various challenges, we can achieve a much better involvement of both tutors and students in the context of large-group teaching.

2. Recommendations

One way to improve large-group teaching might be to accept and perceive it as a system. Knowledge can be seen as information that flows through this system. Ostensibly, professors and students might sometimes have largely differing views and perceptions about the system, and therefore it is important that teachers and teaching assistants are aware of students' perceptions and vice versa. This will increase the understanding of both sides and improve communication between the two groups. It is critical that teaching assistants and tutors can situate themselves on the other side of the system. In this way, they will know how students feel and thus make improvements in certain areas to increase students' involvement in large groups.

Another suggestion is to offer additional tutorials, especially for first-year students, to ensure they are well prepared and have a good understanding of the material delivered in class. This will facilitate greater interaction and involvement of teaching assistants in large-group teaching.

A further recommendation would be to provide adequate means for redesigning courses to help students think and be engaged in large-group contexts. The *sustainment of curiosity* was identified as a crucial aspect of student engagement in large groups. It is suggested that through more practical exercises and/or experiments there would be much better involvement of both tutors and students in large groups. This is especially valid within disciplines such as Biomedical Studies, Physics, Chemistry and Computer Science. The involvement of PhD students in courses that they have previously undertaken – sharing their experience by being integrated in the main lectures – could also positively contribute to the learning process.

Lecture theatres play a significant role in how teachers and teaching assistants interact with students. The space can be perceived as an important stage where the roles of actors (tutors) and spectators (students) constantly interchange within an arena of mutual involvement and conversation. It is suggested that by going around the lecture theatre and asking questions at various points within the space, might dramatically improve the interaction between participants, helping students in all parts of the room to feel more engaged.

It is also recommended that tutors should look on each new group of students not as a single group but as individuals, and take the time to provide more individual feedback. Some tutors tend to give very general feedback that is applicable for 75 per cent of a group, but this is seen as a negative practice. Instead, teachers and/or teaching assistants should provide specific feedback, as each student is unique and makes individual mistakes. Focused, specifically prepared feedback will inevitably have a better effect on students' performance as compared with general feedback that focuses on the result rather than on the learning process and what aspects of it can be improved in the future.

Last but not least, writing is seen as one of the most crucial skills in life, one that needs to be acknowledged by students. Writing means the ability to communicate, and therefore students must learn how to do this properly. It is suggested that assessment through writing might turn into a positive practice, as writing is one of the most valuable skills learnt in university. Therefore, tutors and teaching assistants should facilitate moments of writing during large-group classes. This will aid the mental engagement of both teachers and students in the large-group setting and, if practised regularly, might lead to many positive results both inside and outside the university.

3. Concluding remarks

Tutors, demonstrators and teaching assistants face a number of challenges when approaching large-group teaching. The focus group I conducted identified areas that could be improved, including assessment and feedback, the integration and delivery of tutorials as well as teachers' preparation for large-group sessions. It is recommended that if tutors and teaching assistants have a more personal approach towards the delivery of their lessons, it will have a positive effect on their involvement within the specific large group or class. In addition, employing simple tasks and actions such as innovative writing or questioning techniques will increase both tutors' and students' engagement. All in all, it is felt that the student–staff partnership in research-based education is of key importance for the successful implementation of large-group teaching and learning.

Peer-assisted learning and assessment design

Tika Malla
Department of Biochemistry, UCL

1. Background

Often in universities, there are different modes of assessment designed to determine the understanding and abilities of students. Some of the most conventional methods are coursework, tests and the 'unforgettable' exams! To help learners prepare for these assessments, they have access to online learning materials, university-facilitated subscriptions to journals and publications. In some cases, to further facilitate the students' learning, even a recorded version of their lectures is available online as a podcast. Moreover, learners are encouraged to request new books and resources in the library if they are not already available. All these sources of information are at their disposal so that they are equipped with the proper resources and skills to excel in their degree. However, it is far from universally agreed that the conventional mode of assessment – based on average upon a two-hour written examination – is the best way to determine learners' academic capabilities and understandings.

The other significant point to consider is that, nowadays, these vast sources of knowledge are not the preserve of higher education institutions: in our digital world, they are readily available to learners, literally at the tips of their fingers. The idea of institutional education stemmed from the fact that in ancient times the sources of information were scarce. There were few books and even fewer people to disseminate and decipher the subject matter correctly. However, it is evident that this is no longer the case. This plausibly creates a demand for the tutor–pupil relationship to evolve.

2. R=T Masterclass and focus group outcome

In the focus group, there was a discussion as to whether exams might impose an invisible barrier to the inquisitive nature of students. And although coursework may present a brief window of flexibility for exploring outside the set core modules, it still does not fully promote self-learning. One of the alternative forms of assessment suggested by Professor Levesley in the R=T Masterclass consists of a tiered grading method. Rather than marks being based on exams and tests, students would need to demonstrate a basic understanding of the fundamental concepts to achieve a first-year pass. In progressive years they would have to present a higher understanding and analytical skills to be awarded a lower-second honours degree classification, and demonstrate in-depth knowledge and application for an upper-second honours degree classification or above. The cohort in the focus group generally approved the idea. Personally, I find this system very appealing. Once the learners have acquired the fundamental concepts, there would essentially be the freedom to pick the topics to be further, independently explored. Students would not necessarily have to abide by the compulsory syllabus and core modules, but could choose to spend time on what truly interested them.

The other highlight of the focus group discussion was the idea of peer-assisted learning. Professor Levesley had suggested this as the principle method that suits the current era where students have immediate access to immense sources of knowledge. It involves students meeting periodically to discuss whatever they are independently learning with tutors. Among the focus group it was unanimously agreed that it is a good tool for learning. However, some interesting concerns were raised. As students may pick and explore different subjects, realistically there may not be sufficient staff to accommodate this, as current student–staff ratios are very high. To allow students to explore a wide range of subjects and effectively manage this, the student–staff ratio would need to fall, as it would not always be possible to break down the interests of students into a broad category and run a massive lecture. This system would require a more tutorial-like environment.

Another prominent idea that was integrated into the focus group discussion was peer-assisted assessment. However, it was suggested that as peers would be considered to have the same level of abilities and skills, it might give rise to disputes and unjust feelings among learners. As a student I can relate very well to this. There are times when I suspect that my coursework has not been marked fairly, but I console myself with the fact that the marks and feedback are from experienced experts in that field. Were it to be marked by my peers, these suspicions would only have room to grow and I am certain this would apply to all the other students as well. The feedback would not be taken seriously. Comparing peer-assisted assessment with the standard method now, I see the potential. However, it would require the reorganisation and perhaps complete overturn of the current management structure and logistics in universities.

The idea of the UCL Connected Curriculum was also suggested as a way of changing university-level education from research-led to research-based. For instance, here at UCL, research-led education is already embraced. The lecturers integrate their research into their teaching, meaning learners are readily informed of recent advancements in their field of study. However, the idea of research-based education is to engage students in research activity, so that students work alongside teaching staff as co-creators of knowledge. The idea is very novel and full of new opportunities for students, breaking the traditional tutor–student barrier. However, the focus group participants questioned the validity of the knowledge that would be co-produced by learners. While it might be a good idea to involve students in research, to co-produce knowledge might be challenging for tutors, as it may require students to have expertise and skills that they don't yet possess. But there certainly remains scope for students, as they extend their skills, to play a role in generating information. It would depend upon the complexity of the information being generated. However, increasing the opportunity for learners to co-produce their education would enhance their educational experience and would be a major step towards research-based education.

3. Conclusion

Research-based education is an alternative perspective, or rather just one of the reforms, that the contemporary education system needs. For learning to be integrative, inspiring and innovative in nature, there is a dire need for different learning and assessment methods to be sampled, as times have definitely changed.

Section 2
Connecting Research and Teaching Through Learning

2.0
Research-based education
Engaging staff and students in praxis

Lauren Clark
UCL Institute of Education

As an American doctoral student studying British higher education, I am uniquely placed as both an insider and an outsider. Not only am I a student reflecting on the process of higher education while studying it, I am also an international student coming from outside the British context. Throughout my educational career, I have had many different experiences that have not only shaped my interest and passion in higher education; they have also shaped me as a person. I have had the opportunity to engage in student–staff partnership in several contexts, inspiring a love for education and research. One such opportunity occurred while getting my bachelor degree in California, where I had a research internship with a professor. This experience taught me a multitude of research skills, while also inspiring me to go on to further study. When starting my masters in the UK, I was surprised by the lack of student–staff partnership in a research-oriented psychology of education programme. Despite this I went on to pursue a PhD at UCL, where I once again had the opportunity to get involved in a student–staff partnership through UCL ChangeMakers.

Reflecting on my experience with student–staff partnership as an undergraduate, I can now see how important it was in shaping my future. I learned so much about the process of doing research, and gained an appreciation of how knowledge is socially constructed and that truth is sometimes hard to pin down. Now I see that the process that I was engaged in was a cycle of theory, action and reflection, or *praxis*. Praxis is a process wherein people can apply a theory to their actions, and then reflect upon those actions; this is then fed into new theories for future actions. This is a process that staff and students engage in when participating in research-based education. As staff conduct research with students they apply a theory to their practice, and then reflect upon that approach. Students can help with this process as well, by giving feedback to staff and exploring pedagogy together (Cook-Sather 2014). Students engage in praxis in research-based education as they apply the knowledge learned in class to their research project and then reflect on the process, or how it has changed their thinking about their subject. Being involved in the production of knowledge through research-based education can encourage students to develop a critical awareness of how knowledge is created and socially situated, with a view to encouraging critical reflection on how they have been moulded by their own experiences (Kincheloe and Steinberg, 1998a).

A significant amount of the literature on research-based education focuses on the instrumental reasons for engaging students in research– increased student engagement, increased retention of knowledge, development of research skills and preparation for the workforce. Although I do not wish to detract from the importance of those outcomes, I want to focus on the transformative aspects of research-based education and student– staff partnership – how using these approaches in higher education can lead to a change in thinking for students and staff, and can inspire students to become change agents (Kincheloe and Steinberg, 1998b; Cousin 2010). Cook-Sather (2014) suggests research partnerships are threshold concepts, in that they provide opportunities for change in action and mindset, asking staff and students to engage in situations that might seem contrary to 'common knowledge' or common ways of doing things, like letting students teach. Engaging with threshold concepts can be 'productively disruptive', threatening and transformative (Cousin 2010; Cook-Sather 2014). Transformation takes place when staff and students display 'an ontological as well as a conceptual shift' (Cousin 2010, 2). This can occur through critical reflection or dialogue with others.

1. Research-based education: Encouraging student–staff partnership

Collaborating on research can encourage students (and staff) to question the traditional power dynamic in education. This is a trend throughout this book, mentioned in all of the 11 student chapters. In Jawiria Naseem's chapter (**2.10**) on connecting graduates with the real world, she points out that as research-based education is more student-focused than traditional transmission methods of teaching, it makes a step toward creating a more equal dynamic between staff and students. Similarly, in reference to Bryn Mawr's SaLT programme, Cook-Sather (2014) reflects on the changing dynamic between staff and students when students are employed as curriculum and pedagogical consultants. Researching around this threshold concept of having students consult on teaching led both students and staff to engage in critical reflection about the roles of teachers and students. Although not all staff were able to transform their perception of students as partners, many of the staff members identified partnership with students as 'productively disruptive' (Cook-Sather 2014, 190). Some teachers found giving up their power too difficult, especially when students have so little experience with teaching or knowledge about education, aside from their experience as students. Cook-Sather (2014) suggests that 'if faculty can recognize students as differently situated knowers with insights to share as partners in exploration but not ultimate authorities', they can experience a fundamental shift in how they perceive the contributions of students (2014, 191). You will see this echoed in this book, where student editors identified the need for both staff and students engaged in partnership to realise and appreciate the value of each other's input for the partnership to be successful.

Learning through research-based education can encourage student–staff partnership, but even in situations where students and staff do not collaborate on research projects, engaging in the research process can help put staff and students on a more equal footing. When students have the experience of producing knowledge themselves, instead of passively receiving it, they may learn to appreciate that no one knows it all, and in some situations, students may even know more than staff. For example, in **2.6**, Eirini Gallou talks about the use of technology in research-based education, and how this interaction can help challenge the traditional hierarchical relationship between staff and students. Using technology in the classroom sometimes puts students in the role of teacher if the staff member is not technologically fluent, or can create environments where students can take on a more equal role in the class, such as sharing resources or engaging in a discussion with peers on Moodle, or developing videos to teach others about physics research at UCL (**3.7**).

If students are included as legitimate co-producers of knowledge, this interaction can create a space where genuine dialogue can take place, further enforcing a change in the hierarchical dynamic between staff and students. In **2.3**, Ellen Pilsworth suggests that dialogue in research-based education can lead to a more equal partnership between staff and students, where students and staff both benefit from learning together and receiving feedback from their research partners. However, just involving students in research is not enough – to be a true partnership, students need to be involved from the beginning. Several authors have come up with different models to conceptualise levels of student participation (Arnstein 1969; Healey and Jenkins 2006). These models help distinguish between involving students in a tokenistic way as opposed to being true partners (Arnstein 1969), although Healey and Jenkins' (2006) model looks more at how research is used in the curriculum, differentiating between students as participants or as an audience. I think these models can help both staff and students realise that there is more to research-based education and student–staff partnership than just working on projects together – other dynamics come into play, specifically regarding power and choice. For example, Ira Shor (1996) points out that power-sharing empowers students and instils a critical awareness of the benefits of challenging the boundaries between knowledge producers and knowledge consumers, as well as other dynamics that may be taken for granted. This will empower students to take ownership of their education and give them the power to shape it, rather than just accept it as it is (Shor 1996, 200). This view is echoed in **2.8**, where Preeti Vivek Mishra touches on the importance of involving students in a deconstruction of subject knowledge in order to inspire them to rethink dominant knowledge. Mishra also questions the purpose of higher education, stating that it should lead to empowerment, emancipation and critical reflection.

2. Research-based education: Research as a critical exercise

Students who are involved in research-based education learn a lot about the process of doing research and are more likely to see it as just that – a process. As Sabrina Peters argues in **2.2**, where she writes about a student research blog, engaging with research promotes the idea of research as a process rather than just an end result. Viewing research in this way not only shows students that mistakes are a part of the research process and offer important learning opportunities, but it also moves away from the instrumentalist way of thinking about learning. Engaging in research-based education also involves students as co-producers of knowledge, transforming them from consumers of knowledge to creators. This process can be emancipatory and transformative, as students begin to realise what it is like to be a knowledge-producer, possibly leading them to question and become aware of how other knowledge is created. For example, in **2.1** Ahmet Alptekin Topcu talks about how engaging in research-based education can show students that there is usually more than one way to answer a question, and definitely more than one way to arrive at an answer. Teaching through research shows students that failure is not the end, or necessarily a bad thing – many revolutionary and innovative ideas have come from 'mistakes'. It also shows students that knowledge is not created in a vacuum. Approaches to problems, or even the questions that researchers are trying to answer, are all influenced by social and political factors that play a role in the production of knowledge. Further, 'Research becomes a way of life, a way of approaching the world. In line with higher orders of cognition, those who embrace critical research view answers as tentative – findings are always in process' (Kincheloe and Steinberg, 1998b, 241). This speaks to the realisation that knowledge is always changing and being built upon, and may be context specific. Students engaged in research are more aware of this because they see, as mentioned in **2.1**, that there is often more than one answer, or that researchers are constantly building upon and sometimes disproving previous research.

Teachers engaging in research with students may also view knowledge in a different way. Agathe Ribéreau-Gayon, in **2.4**, claims that teachers doing research are more likely to see knowledge as evolving, whereas teachers who are not engaged in research may be more likely to see and portray to students that knowledge is fixed and should be 'consumed' without question. She goes on to say 'I believe developing this integrated, active, research-based teaching approach is crucial for students to understand the limitations of knowledge and education, and for them to appreciate the research process'. Mishra (**2.8**) agrees, stating that establishing a dialectical relationship between research and teaching through research-based education inducts students into a culture of critiquing disciplinary knowledge. This also relates to what Light and Calkins (2014, 347) referred to as 'teaching by modeling critical enquiry'.

3. Research-based education: Engaging staff and students in praxis

Taking part in a research partnership can be beneficial for both students and staff. The majority of the student–staff partnership and research-based education literature seems to focus on the benefits for the students, in an aim to improve the student experience and student engagement. This focus may be a factor in deterring staff from getting involved in student–staff partnerships, because all they see is more work and giving up their authority in the classroom with no obvious benefit for them. Others may find it hard to see the value in student perceptions on curriculum and pedagogy due to lack of experience or knowledge, missing out on a uniquely situated perspective of the classroom. Cook-Sather (2014) uses the reflections of staff to demonstrate that although student–staff partnership can be a troublesome threshold concept, staff as well as students benefit from this work. Not only did staff gain a critical awareness of their pedagogy through interaction with student consultants, they also gained insight into the student perspective, and how students experience their classrooms. This can lead to an improvement of teaching practice, as well as a desire to partner more with students on projects outside the classroom. One staff member said that participating in the partnership 'made her a better scholar, as well as teacher, as it allowed her to integrate the various dimensions of her identity – indeed, to co-construct them with students' (Cook-Sather 2014, 192).

This process of praxis – theory, action, reflection – occurs in both students and staff when they engage in student–staff partnership. Wasley (2007) discusses a project at Bringham Young University (USA) where students act as pedagogical consultants, offering staff the opportunity to see their course through the eyes of the student consultant, and giving students the chance to approach learning in a different way. Students involved in the process said that after being involved in the programme they had more empathy for their professors, and also realised that they were experiencing their own classes in a different way. One benefit of this kind of interaction is that students learn more about how they are learning, or they think about thinking, also known as meta-cognition. Students who develop meta-cognition through student–staff partnership and research-based education are more likely to have the opportunity to reflect on what they want from education, and what they need to do in order to make those changes. Students as researchers could ask of the curriculum, or of education more broadly, 'What is worth knowing here? How do we come to know it? . . . What benefits do we derive from knowing it? What can we see or do as a result of gaining a specific understanding that we were unable to see and do before?' (Kincheloe and Steinberg, 1998b, 238). Students engaged in research-based education may also transfer these critical thoughts from their academic lives into their everyday lives, as discussed in Sharp et al. (2009). As student authors reflected on their transformative experience of research-based education, they said 'we no longer viewed thinking as an activity best conducted for the enhancement of grades; thinking could also provide a foundation for the interrogation of everyday activities making us critically aware of our surroundings' (2009, 375).

For staff and students, engaging in research-based education and student–staff partnership requires a change in the way they think about teaching and learning, as well as their assumptions about how higher education should work. As Fielding (2004) puts it: 'Transformation requires a rupture of the ordinary and this demands as much of teachers as it does students. Indeed, it requires a transformation of what it means to be a student; what it means to be a teacher' (2004, 296). Engaging with this 'threshold concept' (Cook-Sather 2014) means that staff and students will have to interrogate and possibly change the way they have previously viewed higher education and the staff–student dynamic to make way for a new kind of pedagogy. Aside from the transformative (and often troublesome) aspects of this endeavour, staff and students still have to simultaneously manage institutional constraints, societal expectations, and a lack of resources in the university. This can make a drastic change in pedagogy very challenging on a practical level, and would be difficult without the support of the institution in which the changes are being made. This was a sentiment expressed by many of the authors in this book, as well as the student editorial team.

4. Students in student–staff partnership: agents for change

Praxis is a cycle, which means it doesn't just end with reflection. As students engage in student–staff partnership and research-based education, they enter a cycle of 'interpretation and action' (Cook-Sather 2014) which encourages them to reflect on knowledge (or theory) in action. The development of student voice is a trend in student–staff partnership research, looking at how student–staff partnership can empower students to realise that they have valid and valuable opinions and knowledge, and how they can use these to affect change. However, student–staff partnership that is not authentic and does not involve students in a more equitable relationship where they have a voice and power becomes tokenistic and can be more harmful than helpful. Projects that take advantage of students and manipulate them while ignoring their valuable input fall to the bottom rung of Arnstein's (1969) ladder of participation. Arnstein's framework is a helpful tool when thinking about student participation, as it encourages both students and staff involved in projects to reflect on whether their project involves true partnership. This is important because 'transformation is more likely to reside in arrangements which require the active engagement of students and teachers working in partnership than those which . . . treat student voice as an instrument of teacher . . . purposes' (Fielding 2004, 306). Sharp et al. (2011) found that students engaged in authentic student–staff partnership were empowered to take on leadership positions and challenge the status quo. This was perhaps because once students realised they had a voice, and what it felt like to make a difference, they were more likely to want to get involved in student government, student representation and student committees. The students involved said 'Our voices were developed academically, empowering our intrinsic abilities to formulate our ideas into action' (Sharp et al. 2011). Students engaged in student–staff partnership are perhaps more likely to question the status quo of higher education, and realise that students as well as staff can make productive changes to the way things are. Mishra supports this view in **2.8**, where she asserts that deconstructing where knowledge comes from and who created it may give students the opportunity to engage in projects to rethink dominant knowledge and 'muster the courage to change it'. In **2.1**, Topcu highlights how students who were encouraged to take ownership of their education through the more active learning strategies involved in research-based education were more likely to feel motivated to get involved in making changes through programmes such as UCL ChangeMakers.

5. Conclusion: Research-based education as transformative

To conclude this chapter, I would like to look at how engaging in research-based education and student–staff partnership can be transformative for both staff and students, and the impact this could have on higher education. However, I also want to look at the challenges involved in performing and planning research-based education and student–staff partnership. Finally, I will reflect on my own experience of beginning to challenge the status quo and how this has led to my involvement in student–staff partnership projects and student-led initiatives.

Based on the amount of research done on research-based education and student–staff partnership, it is clear that staff as well as students are interested in making higher education a place for more equitable collaboration, transformation and empowerment. Much of the research mentioned here focuses on the use of research-based education and student–staff partnership in a more holistic way, rather than the more instrumentalist approach, which focuses on the development of skills for the workforce or improving student satisfaction for the sake of university league tables. As British higher education becomes increasingly marketised, these programmes may become more and more instrumentalised, stripping away their transformative and empowering intentions. For this reason, I argue that it may be more effective to empower students to fight for these changes. In this marketised system, the 'student-consumer' has a lot of power – student satisfaction is an important metric when it comes to the ranking of universities. Therefore, if students demand more staff–student research collaboration, more space for conducting research, more funding for student initiatives, they may actually be heard. Students can use this system to their advantage to make the changes they think are important.

The aim of involving students in research-based education and student–staff partnership, and therefore praxis, is not to produce a student who knows everything or knows more than other students. Instead, the aim is to encourage students to listen to those who have been marginalised and learn from them, and realise that the dominant view is not the only way to approach the world.

Kincheloe and Steinberg (1998a) assert that 'a good education should prepare students as researchers who can "read the world" in such a way so they can not only understand it but so they can change it' (1998a, 2). They continue, by summarising the empowering effect research-based education and student–staff partnership can have on students as the potential to 'gain a power literacy – that is, the ability to recognise the ways power operates to create oppressive conditions for some groups and privilege for others. Thus, students as researchers gain new ways of knowing and producing knowledge that challenge the common sense views of reality with which most individuals have grown so comfortable' (Kincheloe and Steinberg, 1998a, 2). I think that developing this kind of critical student researcher is particularly important in our knowledge society, where people have instant access to infinite information on the Internet and social media and the authority of the university as a knowledge producer is in decline (Høstaker and Vabø 2005). Although the Internet has undoubtedly opened access to many people who may not have previously been exposed to this knowledge, many do not have the capacity to differentiate between fact and fiction, or critically evaluate what they are reading.

My research is on the use of critical pedagogy in higher education, which, in a way, looks at how staff can engage in praxis to make their classrooms more critical, and encourage students to model these practices. As such, a lot of the reading I do for my research is based on the deconstruction of knowledge and examining how social and political contexts shape our world and the status quo in which we operate. It is through this reading and thinking that I have been empowered to get involved in my university through student-led initiatives like UCL ChangeMakers and this student editor project. Although I understand the challenges associated with student–staff partnership, and the difficulty that both staff and students encounter because of our socially constructed perceptions and expectations of education, I feel that getting involved in these projects can not only make a difference in its own right, but in the case of R=T, I hope the projects will inspire other students to fight for changes in their own universities.

References

Arnstein, S. R. 1969. A ladder of citizen participation. *Journal of the American Institute of Planners* 35(4), 216–24.

Cook-Sather, A. 2014. Student–faculty partnership in explorations of pedagogical practice: A threshold concept in academic development. *International Journal for Academic Development* 19(3), 186–98.

Cousin, G. 2010. Neither teacher-centred nor student-centred: threshold concepts and research partnerships. *Journal of Learning Development in Higher Education* 2, 1–9.

Fielding, M. 2004. Transformative approaches to student voice: theoretical underpinnings, recalcitrant realities. *British Educational Research Journal.* 30(2).

Healey, M. and Jenkins, A. 2006. Developing students as researchers. *Education*, 3.

Høstaker, R. and Vabø, A. 2005. Higher education and the transformation to a cognitive capitalism. In Bleiklie, I. and Henkel, M. (eds) *Governing Knowledge*, pp. 227–43). Springer Netherlands.

Kincheloe, J. and Steinberg, S. 1998a. Critical visions, emancipatory insights. In Steinberg, S. and Kincheloe, J. (eds) *Students as Researchers, Creating Classrooms that Matter*, pp. 2–19. London: The Falmer Press Teachers' Library.

Kincheloe, J. and Steinberg, S. 1998b. Making Meaning and Analyzing Experience – Student Researchers as Transformative Agents. In Steinberg, S. and Kincheloe, J. (eds) *Students as Researchers, Creating Classrooms that Matter*, pp. 228–43). London: The Falmer Press Teachers' Library.

Light, G. and Calkins, S. 2014. The experience of academic learning: Uneven conceptions of learning across research and teaching. *Higher Education* 69, 345–59.

Sharp, H., Stanley, L. and Hayward, M. 2009. Critiquing undergraduate student participation in academic research using Kincheloe and Steinberg's eight cognitive benefits. *The Student Experience, Proceedings of the 32nd HERDSA Annual Conference*, Darwin, 6–9 July 2009, pp. 369–78.

Sharp H.L., Stanley, L. and Hayward, M. 2011. Breaking research boundaries: Academics and undergraduates engaged in collaborative research. *Staff-Student Partnerships in Higher Education*, pp. 201–14. London: Continuum.

Shor, I. 1996. *When Students have Power: Negotiating Authority in a Critical Pedagogy.* Chicago: University of Chicago Press.

Wasley, P. 2007. How am I doing? *Chronicle of Higher Education* 54(9), A10.

2.1
The unifying role of learning across higher education

Ahmet Alptekin Topcu
Department of Mechanical Engineering, UCL

with Professor Peter Abrahams
Warwick Medical School, University of Warwick

As a fellow scientist, from a different discipline, it is heart-warming to see a young mind thinking both laterally and globally and questioning all our previous experiences both in learning and teaching as well as in the field of assessment. Ahmet has reached a stage in his own intellectual development that is 'seeing the light' of the links between interdisciplinary research. It is connection through team learning that he passionately feels should move our institutions of higher learning towards a more integrated future. Personally, coming from the field of clinical medical science and the modern recent wave of 'evidence-based medicine', it is so very rewarding to be able to endorse a young engineer who wants to challenge and empower the youthful student experience, democratise education and challenge conventions. It gives me great pleasure to see that the R=T initiative at UCL is causing a small revolution in many younger research workers. Hopefully they will be the vanguard and continue to challenge the learning process and the status quo. Higher education is not about data and the gathering of isolated facts to be regurgitated in exams but about putting them into a knowledge base provided by the teacher. The teacher's task is then to show the wisdom of this knowledge and thus enthuse, stimulate and encourage the student to want to find new knowledge and wisdoms across their discipline for use in our modern society. I will follow Ahmet's academic career with interest, and as my mother – a dedicated and very practical teacher – always taught me: 'Pupils *may* learn. Teachers *must*'.

Professor Peter Abrahams

1. The antique roots

In the era of Classical antiquity, the majority of humankind had a relatively limited collection of knowledge about the universe while most phenomena were explained through myths and stories. In that particular time, the Library of Alexandria (Figure 2.1.1) was opened as a pearl of wisdom as the very first research institute ever known in the history of the world. It truly was a citadel of human consciousness, the centre of education and science in the Hellenistic world, where laws of the nature were enthusiastically sought for and taught to subsequent generations. Among the greatest minds educated were Eratosthenes (Roller 2010), a great polymath and father of geography who claimed planet Earth was spherical and calculated its circumference to a surprising degree of accuracy (1% error) about 1,700 years before any scientist, even after Magellan's circumnavigation. Aristarchus (Heath 1913) hypothesised a heliocentric solar system almost 2000 years before Copernicus (1566). The examples go on with Euclid, Archimedes, etc., indicating that for great discoveries,

Figure 2.1.1   The Royal Library of Alexandria (third century BCE) was part of the Temple of the Muses. (Image used under Creative Commons CC0)

perhaps one does not need that much equipment beyond basic tools and paper combined with a great deal of curiosity and imagination.

The Alexandrian Library is of particular importance in exploring the systematic collection and sharing of information, as the first institution to have lectures, reading rooms, meeting offices, public halls and an extensive library. It was an early model of a university, where knowledge is learned, shared, enriched and taught so to be passed on. It was perhaps one of the earliest centres ever to integrate research and teaching. It was through the formation of influential contemporary teams, in which learning, inspiration from and imitation of great minds apparently had taken place, that a cultural evolution was able to progress. In other words, it has been possible through preliminary *memes*: ideas, behaviours and cultures spreading between individuals in a society.

The library was progressively forgotten over the following six centuries, with most of its contents either lost or burnt. It would take many more centuries until the Enlightenment to surpass level of comprehension attained there. Yet successors have adapted and flourished even more. The collection of information keeps on expanding in the twenty-first century. It is more extensive, fluid, abundant and easy to find than ever before. Yet with time becoming ever more limited, all this information is also hard to process. Accordingly, we can and will eventually find a way again of adapting to the renewed necessities of this age to prosper even further. We should not forget what brought our species to the current distinct position: the systematic accumulation of knowledge about the cosmos and its successful transfer to subsequent generations. Hence, this chapter relates specifically to the production and sharing of knowledge and even more distinctly on the human components of knowledge-generation and sharing: teacher and student. Specifically: research and teaching.

2. The overlapping of research and teaching

In research, unknowns are sought, while in teaching the known is taught. Importantly both share the act of learning. Therefore, any process that enhances the quality of learning should theoretically develop teaching too. Hence this section considers whether there is tangible evidence that indicates a mutually beneficial correlation between research and teaching (Breen et al. 2003).

Research and teaching are two core academic traits of modern universities and policies determine the time allocated to both. Time invested in either one is reallocated from the other – for example, teaching-focused universities do not prioritise research (Marsh 1979). Yet there are complementary insights in their mutual interaction. In many ways, learning and teaching reinforce each other. Imagine teaching a colleague. Suddenly, you realise gaps in the knowledge that was assumed extensive. It is apparent that a thorough understanding of teaching and learning are interactively beneficial to each other. A teaching person is assumed to have learnt better than a pure learner. The potential cause of this positive interaction is often explained through comparison of different teaching methods and information retention rates among students after a learning session.

Substantial changes, however, are observed in the case of participatory or active learning (Mosaica and The Corporation for National Service 1996) as retention rates increase to 50 per cent in discussion groups, to 70 per cent in practice groups and finally to about 90 per cent for individuals who teach others. This comparison displays the substantial improvement in information retention associated with active learning methods (Chi et al. 1989) which is about three- to ten-fold better than other methods. As a form of problem-based learning, research has proved that more active methods create situational interest among students, which then increases the amount of time engaged with the subject, while also motivating exploratory behaviour and better knowledge acquisition (Rotgans and Schmidt 2011). Universities and research institutes are therefore not being optimally efficient in their teaching methods if they continue with passive methods (Wingfield and Gregory 2005). Current higher education should therefore prioritise active learning as standard procedure across the curriculum. Although there is a trend towards problem-based learning, the pace of progress is quite slow.

Focus group studies point to increased efficiency in the research environment when research is related to teaching. When staff are actively taking part in recent research, this can shape and update their research interests. From the student perspective, the inclusion of recent research into the curriculum is known to affect student perceptions, conveying the impression that staff are enthusiastic about the course (Jenkins 1998). This allows them to better appreciate how research is incorporated into the lives of lecturers. Moreover, involving students in research fosters an inclusive culture, where students become part of a larger team. Personally, looking back to my undergraduate years, I quite vividly remember becoming part of a research group in sciences. I felt a strong need to imitate my advisor and took pride in belonging to a group of researchers. From that point onwards, my goals were much clearer: excel at research related courses and quickly learn as much as possible.

The studies on the relationship between research and teaching usually aim to find a premise for the following: they are either positively or negatively correlated, or not related. Instead of that simplistic model, Marsh (1979) postulated a connected model of their interaction and how the abilities to be effective in research and teaching might be positively correlated as a function of ability and time (Figure 2.1.2). In the UK, there is a strong correlation between the external national rating of departments for teaching, research and teaching quality assurance (Cooke 1998). The connection is not evident in other countries, such as the USA and Australia (Ramsden 2003), indicating that a high research output does not necessarily relate to effective undergraduate teaching. Moreover, drawing on a meta-analysis of 58 studies, some researchers even state that this relation might be a myth or carry a lower correlation than assumed (Hattie and Marsh 1996). The simple assumption that more research automatically equals better learning is under suspicion (Ramsden 2003), emphasising the need for deliberate and carefully built links between them.

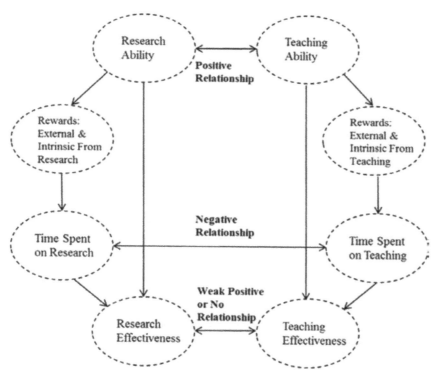

Figure 2.1.2 Differential variables method suggested by Marsh for research and teaching relationship. Adapted from Marsh (1979)

Since research and teaching have many confounding factors – such as different students, staff, departments, universities and nations in the broader context – direct comparisons of their quantitative analyses are a hard task indeed. What I intend to do with R=T is not entirely new but it is a novel approach looking further into this question. Instead of continuing the decades-old debate, the aim is to concentrate on how they overlap across higher education and focus on a unifying force between them.

3. The adhesive force: learning

Humboldt was an influential Prussian philosopher in the eighteenth–nineteenth centuries who suggested an educational concept that holistically combines research and education (Verburgh et al. 2007). Often accepted as one of the best education ministers in modern history, he had a vision of a holistic education, *Humboldtian Bildungsideal*. It would not only provide vocational training for the needs of the labour market but also cultural knowledge and the freedom for individuals to shape their character according to the best knowledge of themselves: *Ausbildungsfreiheit*. The academic freedom and economic autonomy in educational institutions were innovational for the Enlightenment and seen as a template for many other national education systems. Humboldt's inspirations live on to this age and, in the same way, research and teaching could be examined as similar practices with a single core goal: to promote learning and access to knowledge across all stages of university life.

Research and teaching share one common factor: the act of learning (Brew and Boud 1995). In fact, learning can be thought of as the glue between research and teaching (hence R=L=T). The elements of any learning process conventionally involve at least two individuals: a teacher and a learner. Innately, there is an information gap often resulting in a hierarchy. This creates a problem, as the lecturer already knows before a lecture that there isn't much to learn. This passive learning model leads to very low knowledge-retention and constitutes an inefficiency. The solution might be symmetrical learning in a lecture to engage both the lecturer and students, where everyone is active and interacting continuously. In fact, a recent study conducted on undergraduate STEM (science, technology, engineering and mathematics) students has shown that transforming passive listeners into active participants through hand-held 'clickers', short group discussions or randomly calling on individuals/groups to speak in class not only boosted grades by about one half standard deviation/half letter grade (i.e. B to B+, equivalent to about 6 per cent) but also reduced failure rates in the class (Freeman et al. 2014).

Imagine a learning environment where everyone is equal and there are no limits on the roles for teacher and students in the classroom. This could be achieved by creating an environment where no one knows the answers or the problems, revolutionising established hierarchies. One way to accomplish this is through course design. Research and teaching could be achieved in one unified package throughout a course. In fact, five distinct means to this end were identified through reports of academic staff regarding their experience of the research–teaching relationship. Two of them are particularly relevant to enhancing the quality of student learning: (1) teaching by modelling critical inquiry; (2) research and teaching sharing a learning community (Light and Calkins 2014). Learning could be a binding force between R=T, expanding the title further to R=L=T as all three are interconnected.

Accordingly, Professor Levesley, hosting one of the R=T Masterclasses, shared the following quote while inspecting the role of lecturer in the lecture: 'I am god and the stage is mine' (Levesley 2016). Apparently, there are alternative views of knowing adopted by different lecturers. In the above-quoted form of absolute knowing, knowledge is viewed as certain. It has to be acquired from an authority (Baxter Magolda 2004), it could be described as the lecturer pouring information into the students' brains. On the other hand, in transitional knowing or independent knowing most knowledge is uncertain; everyone has to think for themselves. In a classroom utilising independent knowing, a lecturer is just someone with more experience in the journey of learning, guiding the student on the path of learning if and whenever necessary.

In fact, a study of undergraduates participating in higher research programmes to bring them together with postgraduates/researchers has shown that this is likely to develop students as better learners. Epistemological reflection was measured and recorded by students, which was then compared to control groups, indicating that they became more self-confident learners and independent problem-solvers (Baxter Magolda 2004). This suggests that mentor-assisted approaches are promising. Even subject mastery classes like biology, chemistry and mathematics could be designed in ways that develop students as learners. This can be done through directing students into thinking like scientists, asking the necessary questions and designing experiments to hypothesise from eventual results.

Research-oriented, student-assisted content creation is an important tool that seldom finds support. In an ideal research, learning and teaching (R=L=T) scenario, student-centred investigation processes could serve two purposes: (1) involve students in staff research to accelerate the learning process; (2) supply research projects with fresh minds that could easily provide novelty and vitality. There is an element of reciprocity: while students are learning further, lecturers might have unexpected sparks of insight through observation. Hence everyone can benefit from a R=L=T scenario. The result is an enthusiastic environment where both parties progress and learn. This can enhance intellectual development and have long-lasting effects on the inquiring society (Clark 1997). Whether students continue in academia or move into industry, the effects would be long-lasting for society. There would be challenges in integrating research into teaching as it means changing curricula at the faculty, university and national level. Moreover, how students and lecturers react to such changes is another question. Change is not always easy, but if the positive outcomes of an integrated R=L=T environment can be proven to larger audiences, there is the potential for a wider acceptance.

4. Challenging conventions: research vs. teaching

The following question often startles me:

> Why is there a disparity between the rules separating research and teaching when they are exercised closely under the same roof?

Perhaps every student in education has criticised exams as unfair at one point or another. Currently, competition is fierce and grades are the major determinants of success. This is not only stressful but also different from how research works. Researchers, scientists and engineers often work collaboratively in teams with a common goal. Everyone in the team wins when a journal article, research grant or project is successfully completed. Think of NASA's Mars Rover project, the International Space Station or the discovery of the Higgs Boson at CERN (Aad et al. 2012). They comprise cooperative international groups of individuals with a common purpose. When someone in the team improves, so does the whole team. Most of today's high-impact research is increasingly national/international in scope, and has many researchers working in collaboration with separate groups.

A typical lecture hall includes a teacher who is responsible for the flow of information towards students, while students are assigned to the activities of listen and learn. In research, you are your own teacher, responsible for figuring out what to learn and where to find it. Research is an open-book exam indeed, where you can use endless resources to solve open-ended problems related to materials, society, nature and the universe at large. In research and life in general, only yourself is the ever present advisor.

Typical assessments often come in multiple-choice format: many similar choices and only one correct answer for each question. In research too there are multiple answers to most of the questions, many of which are correct in their own way. One becomes resistant to the fear of failure. If your publication is rejected then you are, hopefully, given corrections and recommendations. Criticisms and harsh rejections might be embarrassing in the short term, for example at a conference in public. However, they also motivate a scientist to become a better researcher. In fact, failure is an important part of the learning process. Every research project is a series of trial-and-error experiments with the hope that some will prove lucky. Research is often full of false starts and wasted time. Yet the road to success depends on learning lessons from these experiences and moving on to the next with greater knowledge.

For many postgraduates, research has been and still is, different from teaching/learning. In research, there are no right answers that lead to clear rewards and you do not need to be right in the first trial. There are many opportunities to experiment and gather skills and passions in surprisingly novel ways. If one happens to discover something groundbreaking, the status quo might be hardly disturbed. Dan Shechtman observed a five-fold rotational symmetry (Figure 2.1.3) in aluminium–manganese alloys in 1982 (Shechtman et al. 1984). The discovery challenged the concepts of translational symmetry, on which modern crystallography was based. Shechtman was looked upon by other scientists as proposing something against the laws of nature and was eventually forced to resign his lecturer post at a university. However, he persisted with his discovery and published further findings, eventually receiving the Nobel Prize in Chemistry in 2011.

These examples provide comparisons and the urge to question the current rigid education structure to prepare students in higher education for their future lives. Should we continue using double standards for research and teaching? Among all people, researchers especially should not be afraid to leave their comfort zones, have acceptable disregard for the impossible and turn conventional ideas upside down.

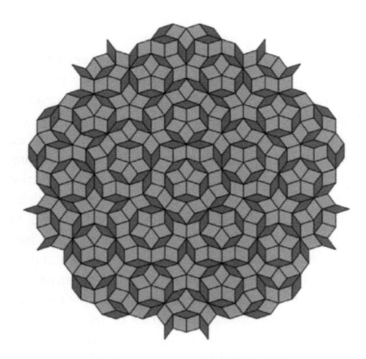

Figure 2.1.3 A quasi-crystal pattern with five-fold symmetry forced the International Union of Crystallography to officially change the definition of 'crystals'. (Image used under Creative Commons CC0)

5. Careful: more tuitions ahead

The first R=T Masterclass was hosted by Professor Lora Fleming (2016) from the University of Exeter. With over 30 years of academic expertise spanning both UK and US educational establishments, Fleming compared the differences between the two countries. The outlook for research funds is perhaps better in the USA – but what about obtaining them? The USA might be a very competitive place indeed. It is common to master grant applications during postgraduate studies. In fact, the start of Fleming's personal academic career was unexpectedly quite straightforward: she was told to apply for funding, obtain a grant, start teaching and subsequently she would be employed as a researcher. That was it. She found herself teaching and doing research soon after.

Professor Fleming sees UK higher education as being in a transition stage, as there has been a substantial increase in tuition fees from almost zero to about £9000 a year within the space of less than ten years. Moreover, the price cap will be removed starting from 2016/17, so expect tuition fee increases in line with inflation (or more during

Brexit) in a few years' time. This is something that has been accepted in American society for some decades already. Correspondingly, student expectations of education in the UK have also increased. Perhaps that is why there are more questions being asked and more answers sought today. Current fee-related changes are likely to push research, teaching and universities towards a more student-oriented higher education to address what students really want to adapt to their changing needs. More satisfaction surveys and reports within UK academia are likely. Academia is slow to adapt to the changing needs of work, industry and society in general. Finally, Professor Fleming's advice to university students was to develop communication and transferable skills through practising clear, tight, pitch-like presentations and participating in volunteer projects.

The opportunities we look for do not necessarily need to be in our discipline, as there is now more unity in research through interdisciplinary work. Professor Robert Eaglestone (2016) of the Department of English at Royal Holloway, University of London hosted an R=T Masterclass and expanded his take on transcending disciplinary boundaries. As a researcher who enjoys and values interdisciplinary work, he believes that scientists may perhaps strive to talk across different disciplines even more. What is a discipline and why do we allow our brains to be bound by rigid structures anyway? It does not necessarily mean that disciplines should form limiting barriers, since they are likely to have evolved from solutions found yesterday and perhaps are still useful today. But we cannot expect them to be practical tomorrow. In the information age, particularly, the rate of knowledge growth is exponential, causing revisions to knowledge. Once we leave the comfort zone of our discipline and venture into the unknown, the potential benefits for research and teaching are enormous. That is the reason why collaboration across disciplines may enlighten our path further in the search for the truth, just as geology utilises physics to inspect geology problems. After all, the truth would accept all forms of currencies.

6. Curiosity vs. pragmatism

The human mind has always been curious. It seeks explanations. Today, ever more serious questions are being asked to reach the essence of truth. Research and teaching promote an inquiring society in higher education by letting students take control and ask questions freely. As part of the current reigning culture, however, expediency and pragmatism seem to dominate and rule over any visionary intuition. Courses, assignments and research projects are completed just for their sake. In fact, this is the worst thing that can be done to research, but it is forced by current assessment methods. Open-ended assessments offer a solution. Their suitability will depend on the subject and university and are not particularly common in science and engineering. In the interests of assessment justice, instead of a single person grading the performance and knowledge of each student, assessment should be through peer evaluation (Levesley 2016). Many students comment on the performance, comprehension and knowledge of one another throughout the course, with the final grade based on the average of all these multiple grades.

How exactly did we end up in a society that values pragmatism more than curiosity and reflection (Figure 2.1.4)? This is not easy to answer. It is no surprise that university degrees are commoditised too. Many lectures are almost automatised – not only for teachers but also for students. There is often a silent status quo with everyone forced to focus on the next goal.

One might argue that there is quality control to prevent any of these problems. Commonly used audits, surveys and grades evaluating lecturers/students would provide solutions. Yet they fail to provide meaningful answers. The key solutions in academia for lecturers/researchers are usually reduced to numbers and dichotomies: publish or perish; teach

Figure 2.1.4 'It is a miracle that curiosity survives formal education.' Albert Einstein (Image used under Creative Commons CC0)

or leave; secure funding or leave. For students it changes to: memorise/produce results or fail. These are deliberately oversimplified to emphasise some of the crucial flaws that are, well, quite normal these days.

It is hard to notice whether you have an interest in research in a curriculum that reserves independent projects until the later stages. A solution could be in diversity: higher education should in fact offer an extensive menu, to allow students to 'taste' every flavour. After all, it is hard to know what to like without any prior knowledge. R=L=T provides a method for students to engage with research to see their potential fields of interest. This not only provides increased efficiency in finding potentially suitable researchers. It also gives students ownership of their choices while they are engaged in higher education, and offers them a glimpse into creative, wide-open approaches to research.

There is an appreciation and value attached to research in our world's society. The positive correlation between research and economic productivity is the reason for this (Seltzer and Bentley 1999). The value attributed to research is important, so are the skills for doing research and a desire for further education. The mutual benefits between research and its applications are already accepted as vital. It becomes even more important as the benefits have been increasing exponentially over the last decades. In fact, research and related research skills are perceived as the key to knowledge economies.

Why is there a need to change parts of a higher education system that is already working? Because the successful integration of research into teaching can supply an enhanced intellectual and spiritual vitality to the work done within universities. Laboratory sessions do not have to be time-limited sessions where strict procedures are followed. Instead, they can be an opportunity for student-driven research questions, with answers discussed in a spirit of refreshed curiosity. Even routines can be transformed into valuable parts of advisor-driven research. Thus, students should be infused throughout their time in higher education with a sense of the potential that their work has in a larger context; something empowering for both students and universities. This could be realised through re-engineering the curriculum in light of R=L=T in such a way that develops and motivates students as ever-inquiring learners.

7. Conclusion: change in the making

The accumulation of frustrations with conventions might be the driving force for seeking change. During the R=T Masterclasses, observing genuine criticism from professors in sincere group discussions has been enlightening; seeing that most scientists are aware of the problems and are looking for answers was partially relieving. The joy of working on common goals as part of a large family is hard to explain in words. It has been really motivating, so I had to write about it. What I understand from R=T has been these three mantras: democratise education, challenge conventions and empower everyone involved. Something is genuinely different this time, perhaps because everyone really wants real change.

The intellectual core aims of universities are to help students devise sophisticated conceptions of truth and knowledge. The aim of this chapter was to investigate how to unleash potential by combining the experience and knowledge of researchers with the boundless curiosity of youth. The link between learning and research is open for exploitation through the better design of courses. There is much to learn about learning by inspecting successful researchers' ways of operating. A convergent approach to research and teaching is proposed as they share one thing in common: the learning itself (R=L=T).

Teaching students how to become better, independent learners should be a primary goal for higher education. Accordingly, environments should be designed to enrich the learning process. The aim is to harness the benefits of interaction between Research and Teaching by focusing on learning across the curriculum with the assistance of deliberate course design. Research in higher education indicates that such designs are possible. Active and participatory learning should be extended throughout all possible departments and curricula, due to proven positive outcomes in both grade increments and reduced failure rates (Freeman et al. 2014). In order to improve the cognitive outcomes in class-specific materials, passive learning methods should be replaced with active, experiential learning (Michel et al. 2009). Second, harnessing the benefits of an integrated Research and Teaching approach can be possible through problem-based course designs, where students and teachers stand on an equal footing for a particular course. Perhaps they could choose research questions after group discussions. Group work would be a key standard across the curriculum, with randomly selected individuals to limit biases. This is important due to the necessity of teamwork towards accomplishing learning goals.

Finally, exams or assessment systems might need to be altered. Open-ended assessments should predominate. Lecturers are already using open-ended, peer-review based assessments (Boud et al. 2001). Eventually, learning could become more collaborative, problem-centred and peer-directed. From either a research or teaching perspective, learning is the key ingredient (R=L=T) that has the potential to transform higher education.

As scientists, we sometimes tend to forget the importance, beauty and extent of the work we do. As a UCL ChangeMaker, my aim is to involve both parties and stimulate enthusiasm in everyone. Let us not forget that reform is a process; it is not a single event. And I think that it might have already started in the realm of UCL. Specifically, I know of at least one group of individuals for whom the combination of UCL Arena, Connected Curriculum and ChangeMakers has succeeded in making a meaningful difference by inspiring them to take action.

Initiatives focusing on bringing together research, learning and teaching (R=L=T) might potentially help the higher education system to evolve for the better. Let us not forget that the questions of today are derived from the answers of yesterday and there is a growing accumulation of knowledge snowballing with original and increasingly complex questions. As institutions mostly focused on research and teaching, universities should keep an open mind and be willing and able to ask the bravest, most daring questions that need to be asked for the prosperity of science. We should seek it for our society and future generations. It is our responsibility in higher education not only to question but also to conserve and develop the tradition of our brilliant predecessors who contributed in bringing humankind to the once unimaginable point where we find ourselves at present.

References

Aad, G. et al. 2012. Observation of a new particle in the search for the Standard Model Higgs Boson with the ATLAS detector at the LHC. *Physics Letters B* 716, 1–29.

Baxter Magolda, M. B. 2004. *Making Their Own Way: Narratives for Transforming Higher Education to Promote Self-development*. Sterling, VA: Stylus.

Boud, D., Cohen, R. and Sampson, J. 2001. *Peer Learning in Higher Education: Learning from & with Each Other*. London: Kogan Page.

Breen, R., Brew, A., Jenkins, A. and Lindsay, R. 2003. *Reshaping Teaching in Higher Education: A Guide to Linking Teaching with Research*. London: Kogan Page.

Brew, A. and Boud, D. 1995. Teaching and research: Establishing the vital link with learning. *Higher Education* 29, 261–73.

Chi, M. T. H., Bassok, M., Lewis, M. W., Reimann, P. and Glaser, R. 1989. Self-Explanations: How Students Study and Use Examples in Learning to Solve Problems. *Cognitive Science* 13, 145–82.

Clark, B. R. 1997. The Modern Integration of Research Activities with Teaching and Learning. *The Journal of Higher Education* 68, 241–55.

Cooke, R. 1998. Enhancing Teaching Quality. *Journal of Geography in Higher Education* 22, 283–4.

Copernicus, N. 1566. *De revolutionibus orbium coelestium, libri VI*. Hennepetrina.

Eaglestone, R. H. 2016. Transcending disciplinary boundaries in student research activities. 3 March. UCL Arena R=T Masterclass 4.

Fleming, L. 2016. Connecting students with the workplace through research. 29 February. UCL Arena R=T Masterclass 1.

Freeman, S., Eddy, S. L., McDonough, M., Smith, M. K., Okoroafor, N., Jordt, H. and Wenderoth, M. P. 2014. Active learning increases student performance in science, engineering, and mathematics. *Proceedings of the National Academy of Sciences USA* 111, 8410–15.

Hattie, J. and Marsh, H. W. 1996. The relationship between research and teaching: A meta-analysis. *Review of Educational Research* 66, 507–42.

Heath, T. L. 1913. *Aristarchus of Samos: The Ancient Copernicus.* Oxford: Clarendon Press.

Jenkins, A. 1998. Assessing David Blunkett on teaching and research. *Teaching Forum* 45, 8.

Levesley, J. 2016. Peer-assisted learning and assessment design. 16 March. UCL Arena R=T Masterclass 5.

Light, G. and Calkins, S. 2014. The experience of academic learning: uneven conceptions of learning across research and teaching. *Higher Education* 69, 345–59.

Marsh, H. W. 1979. *Annotated bibliography of research on the relationship between quality of teaching and quality of research in higher education.* Los Angeles: Research and Teaching University of Southern California, Office of Institutional Studies.

Michel, N., Cater, J. J. and Varela, O. 2009. Active versus passive teaching styles: An empirical study of student learning outcomes. *Human Resource Development Quarterly* 20, 397–418.

Mosaica and The Corporation for National Service. 1996. *Starting Strong: A Guide to Pre-service Training.* Washington, DC: Mosaica, The Center for Nonprofit Development and Pluralism.

Ramsden, P. 2003. *Learning to Teach in Higher Education.* London: RoutledgeFalmer.

Roller, Duane W. 2010. *Eratosthenes' Geography. Fragments collected and translated, with commentary and additional material.* Princeton, NJ: Princeton University Press.

Rotgans, J. I. and Schmidt, H. G. 2011. Situational interest and academic achievement in the active-learning classroom. *Learning and Instruction* 21, 58–67.

Seltzer, K. and Bentley, T. 1999. *The Creative Age: Knowledge and Skills for the New Economy.* London: Demos.

Shechtman, D., Blech, I., Gratias, D. and Cahn, J. W. 1984. Metallic phase with long-range orientational order and no translational symmetry. *Physical Review Letters* 53, 1951–3.

Verburgh, A., Elen, J. and Lindblom-Ylänne, S. 2007. Investigating the myth of the relationship between teaching and research in higher education: A review of empirical research. *Studies in Philosophy and Education* 26, 449–65.

Wingfield, S. S. B. and Gregory S. 2005. Active versus Passive Course Designs: The Impact on Student Outcomes. *Journal of Education for Business* 81, 119.

Links to the R=T Framework

Charlotte Collins

Department of Geography, UCL

- Ahmet's key message is that learning by 'doing' is far more effective in terms of knowledge retention than the more conventional dictation of information. While a research/teaching binary still exists, time should be shared more equitably to allow students to engage with practical research as a pedagogic tool. Students seem to prosper and be more enthusiastic about learning when they are playing a productive role and when their work contributes meaningfully to progress within their respective discipline. Learning partnerships would not only be beneficial to the development of students, but may also work to dissolve the traditional staff/student hierarchy and encourage lecturers to deliver topical and dynamic teaching, transforming 'passive listeners into active participants'. Therefore, the main sentiment is to create a learning environment of equality and equal opportunities, to allow both parties to thrive – through working together to find answers and solutions to research problems.

- The real benefit of promoting active forms of learning through research is the encouragement of independent thinking. Students in particular will feel that their work is more meaningful and, in turn, invest more time and effort into their studies. This will not only allow them to be more engaged and focused on their studies, but will also contribute to innovation in research within their department as a result of research-based teaching methods. Similarly, student–staff partnerships in the learning environment will foster greater equality – while academic staff will offer highly developed knowledge and connections, students can contribute 'curiosity, vitality and passion' to deliver more holistic and integrated research.

The main barrier to active learning is the curriculum framework, as a new form of teaching would require an overhaul of current teaching methods and a complete reconfiguration of university space to allow for hands-on learning. Moreover, one of the greatest concerns of traditional research-led teaching was the lack of engagement of students, however there is no guarantee that a new form would significantly alter their willingness to participate, and may potentially benefit some students over others. Additionally, certain standards would still need to be imposed in order to ensure that the level of learning and progression is consistent and sufficient across all departments.

- The main principle that goes beyond a context-specific framework is attitude. A seemingly straightforward realignment of the student–staff relationship would open up a wealth of opportunities. More value should be placed on the empowerment and enfranchisement of students to allow them to understand that they are able to contribute to ongoing research. This sentiment should be made clear when students first enter into higher education as most will expect to be met by the same pupil/teacher dynamic as experienced at college, high school or sixth form. Teaching staff also need to realise the merit in involving students on an equitable basis to bring new and innovative ideas, perspectives and opinions to research. In this way, I believe that students in particular will excel through having the opportunity to be active, not passive learners and benefit from the long-term merits of research involvement.

2.2
Learning through mistakes
An important part of the learning and research process

Sabrina Jean Peters
Department of Civil, Environmental and Geomatic Engineering & The Centre for Urban Sustainability and Resilience, UCL

with Professor Elizabeth Shephard
Department of Structural and Molecular Biology, UCL

Learning from mistakes is key to understanding how things work when students enter the research laboratory. Sabrina describes the value of working in a system where everything does not work perfectly and the unlikely can always happen. She illustrates how we learn from practice. Her chapter is highly recommended to those embarking on a research career. It is a confidence booster. She highlights great discoveries arising from the unexpected result. Sabrina demonstrates how understanding why a mistake happened can be turned into a very positive outcome.

Professor Elizabeth Shephard

1. Introduction

The opportunity to make mistakes aids both learning and mental resilience. Unlike research, the current nature of education – favouring the errorless pursuit of learning – often overlooks the value of the serendipitous. This chapter reflects on how research-based teaching can remove the barriers between education and research by creating space for students to explore the unexpected, to change their perspective as well as gain invaluable knowledge and experience of the research process.

Here in the sciences we are relatively lucky – to my knowledge it is likely that you will have been exposed to laboratory or other experimental work during your journey. This may have varied in its success due to the very nature of experimental work. Experiments are the perfect environment for things to go 'wrong' or, arguably, 'right'. The value of mistakes can be easily downplayed in an academic system that solely celebrates a narrow definition of success and arguably cultivates a 'will this be in the exam?' culture. In my experience, I learnt more about the science and technical aspects of, for example, analytical equipment when trying to solve why it was not working, than I ever did when it went according to plan. The process that follows from the initial mistake opens up a plethora of opportunities for learning via analysis and feedback loops between the student and their teacher(s), peers and even students themselves through self-evaluation and future reflection.

That is not to say that I find making mistakes an enjoyable experience and I imagine it would be difficult to find someone who does. Whether it is the fear of vulnerability, looking ignorant or going against the social norm, largely we do not deal well with these inevitable life events. These feelings can be made worse in a high-risk environment where we may become hyperaware of our surroundings, ourselves and the perception of others. University can indeed feel like a high-risk environment, where the future is at stake and your future colleagues and employers are the audience. To see a mistake, error or diversion from the plan as a new opportunity for learning (or research) takes both practice and resilience. I believe research-based teaching will be instrumental for students' development of these qualities, as the boundaries between textbooks and research are replaced with experience. As a researcher, this exposure to mistakes and the subsequent problem-solving they require is our job, the research itself (or at least an integral part of it). Therefore, a research-based approach to university teaching will expand this environment so that students can make mistakes while learning just how normal they are, but through exposure rather than words.

2. Momentous mistakes

Early on in my exploration of research-based teaching methods I recognised the potential for it to be used as a tool that allows students to make mistakes in a safe environment. This led me to consider how mistakes are integral to both learning and research. The interpretation of mistakes has shaped both the research environment and the discoveries themselves.

Setting out towards an unknown with the belief that you will find one correct solution, on the first attempt, for a single problem can blind an individual to the potential of serendipity. For instance, I would love to have been able to ask Wilson Greatbatch how he viewed one of his greatest mistakes for the people it has saved. When producing a prototype for a device to record heart rhythms, he accidentally fitted the wrong resistor, creating a device that instead produced intermittent electrical pulses – otherwise known as the pacemaker.

Discoveries from mistakes like this in medicine are relatively well known. Arguably, one of the most famous examples is Alexander Fleming's contaminated staphylococcus cultures. His mould-contaminated petri dishes could have been discarded as part of the main experimental goals; instead they led to the discovery of penicillin, which later changed the world. Another drug that has affected the lives of people all around the world was originally known by Pfizer as UK94280, which underwent unsuccessful trails as a treatment for angina, a heart condition where valves are constricted. The drug was initially going to be removed from further trials until volunteer feedback revealed an unusual side effect. After further testing, UK94280 was renamed Viagra and has since become one of the fastest-selling drugs of all time. However, it is not solely medical research that has found success in mistakes. Roy Plunkett was carrying out research for DuPont into a new refrigerant in 1938 when he found that one of his experiments had formed a resin resistant to extreme heat and chemicals. This later become known as Teflon.

As these examples show, just making the mistake is not enough. The researchers also had to see its potential, as well as having the desire to explore and analyse it. Individuals need to be aware of the larger process, opening their mind to mistakes and understanding that deviations from the expected are not automatically uninteresting, worthless or failures. It is within the hands of the researcher that these deviations can either become a mistake or a success. To quote Plato: 'Science is nothing but perception'. But perception is not beholden to science alone. Along with consideration for the serendipitous, it is arguably part of the process of research.

Learning how mistakes are intrinsic to research and knowledge-acquisition, as well as creating a safe environment in which to explore these concepts, can be achieved through research-based teaching methods. At UCL, I met with two professors, Elizabeth Shephard and Anson Mackay, at the R=T Launch Event, during which they shared case studies from their own teaching practice. We talked about innovative research-based methods that allow students the space to fail and make mistakes.

3. Research-based teaching in practice: the practical

Practice is key and the ability to repeat and learn from practice is crucial. In the laboratory, however, time is restricted. We therefore designed a virtual learning platform (VLP) to provide additional support for a hands-on research project in DNA cloning and analysis. The VLP allows students to practise numeracy, reagent preparation and experimental procedure. We wanted a platform that students could use in private, one where mistakes could be made and exercises repeated as many times as required. Practice and repetition has built confidence, aided further learning and enjoyment, and encouraged students to develop more advanced research skills. Repetition in a class laboratory environment is not always possible and there is little time to redo an aspect if a mistake is made. By building an understanding through practising the component parts of an experiment when mistakes are made, we can turn these into a positive learning process.

Professor Elizabeth Shephard

Professor Elizabeth Shephard believes that teaching in the life sciences is entrenched in research and therefore using a research-based approach comes naturally. The hardest aspect of this process is preparing the students for using the laboratory and trying to find new ways to engage them with safety and methods beforehand. As part of their studies, undergraduate students are required to clone a section of DNA. To support this, the department designed a virtual laboratory where students can go through the steps of a real experiment and get familiar with the methods and equipment. Students adapt quickly to the programme, enjoying earning points for making the right choices and being able to repeat the exercise until they either pass the activity or are satisfied with their score. These virtual activities are useful for ensuring students understand health and safety, methods, instrumentation and the general layout of a laboratory before the experiment begins. However, the virtual experience cannot replace reality: perhaps unsurprisingly, in modules that mixed virtual and real laboratories the students exhibited a preference for the latter.

Despite this preparation, mistakes can still be made and some students will find that their experiments fail to clone the DNA. Elizabeth explained how she goes through the work with her students as an important aspect of their understanding of the practical. She encourages students to consider the experiment in a real-world setting, reminding them that outside of a module practical the process would be repeated until they got it right. She believes students need to learn and understand that not everything is perfect. The practical is not one where all factors are manipulated in their favour; it is a reflection of research. Therefore, problems may arise as a natural by-product of the experience. Importantly, Elizabeth has noticed that on contemplation the students comment that they learn better through mistakes.

Even here the environment for making mistakes is shown to be hugely important. It helps students to understand that one failure in the laboratory does not mean they would not succeed with repetition, as by using virtual resources Elizabeth and her department have developed a programme that allows students to practise. For the numerical aspects of the course, this approach has been applied through creating a quiz that asks different questions for both different students and attempts. This was felt to be particularly important, as numeracy often requires practice. This level of repeatability could not be achieved on paper, nor could paper assessment and feedback be provided with such immediacy.

From being able to make mistakes and repeat tests for factual knowledge to learning through practice, the next logical question becomes: Is this factual knowledge enough? It is then the role of the practical to allow students to explore how they can apply this knowledge and gain additional skills in the process. One method of assessment used in my department (Civil, Environmental and Geomatic Engineering, UCL) that illustrates research-based teaching and assessment is the use of scenarios. A group of students are given a brief, just as they would be if they were carrying out a project in the workplace, and it is their responsibility to complete it using the resources available to them. These resources may include a site visit, online resources or a member of industry and will have been backed up by a series of lectures on frameworks and theory, scientific principles, etc. The students need to assign themselves roles and complete tasks both individually and as a team to create different solutions for the brief. It was noted in the discussion with Elizabeth and Anson that peers learn very well from each other and that peer review and engagement can be an effective way of creating an environment for mistakes that aid the learning process.

4. Research-based teaching in practice: writing and feedback

The motivation for creating an advanced-level assessment in the form of a 14-week blog was to engage students, in depth, in an environmental issue. But the unintended consequences have been just as important, and which speak to the topic of this chapter. Students are fearful of making mistakes. We judge and grade them on their mistakes; they judge themselves and they judge one another. Allowing students to write publicly – effectively rehearsing and developing an argument in a series of blog posts – raises their confidence in terms of both writing styles and research skills. Peer-to-peer feedback allows other students (and indeed anyone from around the world) to contribute to this learning process. Readers make criticisms, but these are nearly always constructive. It is how a student takes these on board that allows us to see their learning in progress.

Professor Anson Mackay

Laboratory or practical exercises are not the only environments in which mistakes play a key role in the learning process. What happens when students fail and how these failures can be incorporated into teaching, learning and assessment are important considerations when designing research-based approaches. Professor Anson Mackay described one of his assessments in the Geography department at UCL to try and achieve this.

Third-year undergraduate and Masters of Science (MSc) students are required to write an academic, yet public, blog, publishing regular posts over three months. The subject, design and research direction are under the total control of the individual within an environmental focus in either the sciences or humanities. As the blogs are publicly available online, fellow students and Anson can leave feedback and praise in the comments as well as instigate debate, helping the students to develop a deeper understanding and support learning. The assessment is designed in a way that accepts that mistakes or areas of weakness may exist. Through the course of the task, students should address these weaknesses, improving the quality of the blogs over time. This approach means that the students develop a voice as well as peer-to-peer skills. The task also offers a novel assessment, using technology in a way that benefits learning, while introducing students to a versatile media. It may be interesting to explore the difference between the perfect, polished product that is an essay and the developmental nature of blogs. This scope for self-correction as a result of further research or understanding, peer review and feedback creates an opportunity for students to identify and explore their mistakes.

Understandably, at first many students are nervous. However, Anson noticed that after approximately four weeks there is a marked improvement in both the quality of their work and the students' enthusiasm. I feel this is a result of the students taking ownership of their own work and being given the opportunity to express their perspective in an environment that encourages discussion between peers. Students come to university for many reasons, including education but also personal growth. I believe choices are more often made based on passion and therefore it is understandable that having a platform to explore and present this, as well as being encouraged to discover the cutting edge of their interests alongside their peers, would be met with enthusiasm.

An assessment like this is in stark contrast to the norm. Breaking from the mould in this way is something I think I would have enjoyed and found inspiring during my undergraduate studies. Elizabeth supported this assessment approach arguing that you should not worry about pushing the boundaries of the student's academic comfort zones, because in the end they come back to you and say it was the best experience. This viewpoint was supported by feedback on Anson's module, which shows the assessment is enjoyable and often a highlight of the student's degree experience. However, Anson also noted that while this assessment works brilliantly and receives good feedback, it requires a lot of energy on the part of the assessor.

5. The importance of peer review

In academia, the application of peer review is integral for opening oneself up to outside opinions and, through this, the publishing process. Just because an individual believes their work is fantastic, it does not mean that reviewers or peers will agree. Elizabeth mentioned that when students come to her, asking how to make their work perfect, she explains this uncomfortable truth to them. Like students, academics must submit their work. Sometimes reviewers will respond with praise, at other times they will suggest necessary additions or improvements. Everyone feels uncertainty and pressure, but after you have had more exposure, you have practised taking the knocks required for success. In other words, you need to learn to make mistakes. This also relates to the undergraduate experience, where a student's pursuit of knowledge may only be witnessed by their examiner. Universities should provide a platform of learning for a community that does not end in the lecture theatre or with graduation ceremonies. Research-based teaching provides an opportunity for teaching staff to break down the barriers between researcher and student, encouraging students to become researchers themselves and take an active role in the exchange of knowledge and ideas.

6. Interdisciplinary relevance

Arguably the science sector already uses research-based teaching. A university-wide shift towards this approach is therefore an opportunity for both further improvements and sharing knowledge and experience across disciplines. Critical thinking integrated with active learning (such as through a laboratory practical) is a key part of university education that teaches students how methods and knowledge are applied to research questions in their discipline (Healey 2005, 183–201). However, in the case study from Elizabeth's teaching approach, it can be seen that laboratory experience alone is not enough. It needs to be supported by allowing students to practise basic principles in a safe environment that allows them to fail (an approach that can be applied widely across subject boundaries) while putting tasks into a real-world context. One way to achieve this may be through the use of outward-facing assessments that promote module design directed towards real-world problems, applications and public engagement, as seen in the case studies above. This would allow students the opportunity to learn how to apply their knowledge, skills and experience in a relative context.

To allow cross-disciplinary discussion about how to effectively incorporate mistakes into the teaching method, it may be important first to clearly understand and define how failures are approached and engaged with (perhaps differently) across disciplines; how we define what makes our students successful; and how we encourage students to seek opportunity from the unexpected. My university experience has been largely dominated by the sciences. However, during the progress of this discussion I have often thought back to how different my experiences of mistakes were in my A-level English literature and art classes compared to my pre-university science and other subjects. For instance, our art teacher constantly encouraged us to look for opportunity at every stage of our project development, to question how we defined when our work was completed and not to give up in the face of what we perceived as errors. Incorporating unexpected spillages, wonky interpretations of reality or being unable to physically form the exact vision in your mind was placed in the context of the developmental process, which allowed us to learn cross-disciplinary problem-solving skills and resilience. As students we were taught to search for both the positives and the opportunities: even if we had to start again, how could we apply what we had learnt? How had this changed our perception and ideas? Sometimes starting again is necessary and does not reflect your ability. In this context, what may have been labelled as a failure elsewhere was only truly one if you allowed it to be such: *if you failed to learn*.

7. Conclusion

For me this conversation has highlighted how, as teachers, researchers and students, we do not need to limit peer exchange to what are perhaps arbitrary definitions of a discipline in the face of learning. This is especially true where mistakes are concerned – a common currency of humanity.

One benefit of research-based teaching is that it allows the creation of a safe space to make mistakes and build resilience: accepting that it is okay to fail. It is how the community and the individual deal with mistakes that defines the experience and value gained. Allowing students to develop the confidence to take a chance that may result in failure, teaching them how to respond to mistakes and changing their perspective on the serendipitous can only be good news for research and learning within universities. We need individuals with their minds open to learning, engagement, opportunity and discovery, not crippled by an impossible pursuit of 'perfection'.

Research-based teaching provides us with the opportunity to enhance the university experience at all levels of the learning community. It allows us to grasp valuable benefits by encouraging collaboration and discourse at earlier stages of career development and by supporting research. Overall, it feels appropriate to end this chapter with the conclusion of our discussion where I asked Elizabeth to describe research-based teaching in one word. For both the students and myself: *inspirational*. But in two words: *wanting more*.

References

Healey, M. 2005. Linking research and teaching to benefit student learning. *Journal of Geography in Higher Education* 29, 183–201.

Links to the R=T Framework

Francesca Peruzzo
UCL Institute of Education

- Sabrina argues for the importance of considering mistakes as an integral step in the learning process when approaching research-based education through student–staff partnerships. Engaging with the opportunity of making mistakes opens up reflections over the reasons why errors have been made throughout the research process, in turn building confidence both through practice and analytical learning methods. However, hands-on research approaches not only allow participants to critically assess mistakes by the practical reiteration of procedures, but they also enable them to benefit from peer-to-peer feedback. The research process thus becomes a joint learning experience, with students and staff partaking in the practice of creating knowledge and constructively informing the design of a research-based approach. By valuing and discussing the importance of making mistakes throughout the research process, the partnership between staff and students allows for joint elaboration of scientific knowledge and the critical assessment of each step of the learning experience.

- Students can often feel pushed and overwhelmed by exams and evaluation procedures. A research-based approach creates a safe learning space within which students can turn their fear of making mistakes into self-exploration in a non-judgemental environment. Critical self-correction and the development of an ability to peer-review are facilitated by a hands-on research space, which enables students to push their knowledge boundaries. In fact, approaching mistakes from a constructive viewpoint means not only making sense of the real world by analytical adjustments, but it also opens up a more flexible approach to learning processes. Gradual and practical attempts to make the real world intelligible promote active learning and create opportunities for staff to rethink their pedagogic and didactic approaches.

Mistakes are mostly considered on the part of students, taking staff teaching methods as unquestionable. Despite being facilitated by the opportunity to adjust their didactics to research methods, staff face difficulties in conjugating theoretical and practical knowledge in such a way that provides students with a critical approach to practice. Assessment of mistakes can represent a constructive solution by promoting discussion about the impact of diverse theoretical perspectives on real-world research. However, a lack of resources in terms of time, funding and staff can undermine the benefits.

- The research-based education approach through student–staff partnership requires delimited environments and pre-set settings, within which to create knowledge and assess outcomes of applied methods. Taking into account these specific conditions of a research-based teaching approach, examples of successful case studies can become powerful tools, used both as applied methodologies and as theoretical instances. However, critical aspects of creating knowledge are to be taken into account from both students and staff. The positioning of the researcher is to be constantly questioned throughout the research process. By these means, reflexivity comes to be embedded into a constructive engagement with research choices encompassing the whole investigation. Reflexivity, both in social and scientific research, calls for closer examination of the diverse outcomes that stem from the application of different theoretical perspectives in investigating the real world. Therefore, by critically discussing the influences of taking different stances in the application of case studies to the real world, students and staff can jointly engage with critical and research-based approaches to the learning process.

2.3
Research = Teaching = *Dialogue?*
Dialogue as a model for research-based learning at university

Ellen Pilsworth

Department of German, UCL; now at University of Bristol

with Professor Robert Eaglestone

Department of English, Royal Holloway, University of London

Paulo Friere, one of the twentieth century's most influential theorists of education, didn't want imitators but reinventors. His argument was that education should proceed through active and engaged dialogue, and not simply consist of a teacher 'banking' deposits of information in students' heads. Ellen has used these insights to begin to develop a 'dialogue lens for research-based teaching', aiming to make her own teaching more dialogic and more responsive and to show how these ideas can be developed in a range of disciplines. This empowers the student and helps to connect research and education by bringing to the fore the dialogical elements in all university learning activity.

Professor Bob Eaglestone

1. Introduction

In discussion with Bob Eaglestone, in preparation for an R=T Masterclass, one of the first things he told me was that his approach to teaching throughout his career had been fundamentally shaped by a reading of Paulo Freire's slim but hugely influential volume, *Pedagogy of the Oppressed* (1968). My own reading of this book has had no less of an impression on the way I plan to approach teaching and learning in the future. This chapter is an exploration of some of the ideas that came out of discussions with Bob as part of the R=T initiative exploring research-based education, informed by my reading of Freire as well as other writers who have carried his flag on into the twenty-first century – primarily Jane Vella's programmatic *Learning to Listen, Learning to Teach* (revised edn, 2002). As a student of German literature, and a teacher of translation, my own focus is naturally on the humanities and on the process of language learning. Sections 2–4 of this chapter therefore reflect generally on the model of dialogue as a way of integrating research and teaching, with examples drawn from a variety of disciplines, whereas Section 5 follows my own subject-specific interest in translation. Section 6 is a final, personal reflection on how the ideas gathered in discussion at UCL, together with subsequent readings and ruminations, will shape my own teaching practice going forward. If any of the ideas presented here prompt you to reflect on your own teaching practice, that will be an added bonus to what has already been of great benefit to me in putting all of this together.

2. Pedagogy of the Oppressed

Freire's crucial argument about our traditional forms of education is that they uphold systems of oppression and domination by following a 'banking model'. In this model, teachers hold all the power and knowledge and only they can bestow it on the learners, who remain passive recipients throughout the learning process. To counteract this 'student–teacher contradiction' (Freire 1996, 53), Freire puts forward a new model of 'co-intentional education', in which 'Teachers and students . . . are both Subjects' (1996, 51). Both student and teacher are emancipated from hierarchical structures, and approach the subject to be learned through a *dialogue* in which they take on equal roles. Instead of the teacher dictating the path of the students' learning, the students should determine their own path through dialogue with the teacher: 'Education should not present its own programme but should search for this programme *dialogically* with the people' (1996, 105). Although Freire does not discuss the idea of research-based teaching, his model of dialogue proves very helpful as a way of integrating the two processes in education practices, as will be explained below.

3. What is a dialogue?

Outlining her twelve principles of dialogue education, Vella (2002, 3) explains the meaning of dialogue with reference to its roots in Greek: '*Dia* means "between", *logos* means "word". Hence, *dia* + *logue* = "the word between us"'. This is how dialogue is understood in an everyday sense, as a synonym for 'conversation'. However, dialogue can be used as a model for the learning process not only when it is understood in this literal sense. For example, Bakhtin's theory of dialogism explains human thought processes as working in the form of dialogue. Dialogue can be internal as well as external (Greenall 2006, 69).

Another way in which the process of learning can be seen as a dialogue is through exchange and transmission. Words go between interlocutors in opposing directions: there is a to-ing and fro-ing of ideas between people, and this exchange of ideas itself enacts a to-ing and fro-ing between the known and the unknown. I exchange what I know for what you know – I listen to what you know, you listen to what I know – we share our knowledge and produce more knowledge. This oscillation between subjects, and between the known and the unknown, should surely be the primary goal of all university education. In encouraging students to seek the unknown, they should therefore be taught to engage dialogically with it, both in a literal and more abstract sense. The process of research can itself be modelled in the form of a dialogue with the unknown. Following this logic, we arrive at the equation suggested in the title of this chapter: R=T=*dialogue*. But how can we apply this concept practically across a variety of university disciplines?

4. Disciplines as dialogues

The primary question of my R=T Masterclass with Bob Eaglestone was one of how disciplinary boundaries can be overcome by students in their research. Naturally, we became preoccupied with the task of defining what exactly is meant by the term 'discipline'. Bob suggested that instead of thinking of disciplines as particular topics for study, they should instead be defined by the kinds of research processes in which those who study them engage. He suggested, for example, that what historians have in common, as opposed to students of English, is the set of questions that they would ask of a given text. This set of questions becomes a characteristic research method, by which a discipline then becomes recognisable. (Another point raised by Bob in our discussion is that disciplines are first born when they become self-reflexive: when people within them begin to ask, 'what are we actually doing here?') The discipline of English, he suggested, was defined primarily as the act of reading and discussion itself, rather than as a set of objective texts to be 'covered'. For example, to have read the complete works of Shakespeare does not make you a literary scholar. Rather, it is the way in which you have read and responded to these texts that marks you out as such.

Reading and discussing texts is a model by which most humanities subjects function, although their discussions will look and sound different, depending on the discipline. It follows that humanities disciplines can be defined as *dialogues* in both a literal sense (they are built on discussion) as well as a metaphorical sense (they are about thought processes, an exchange of ideas and an encounter with the unknown). A student of English might ask research questions such as 'how is language working here? What is the effect of this text on me as a reader?' A historian, on the other hand, might ask 'what does this text tell us about the government of Mercia in 650 AD?' Perhaps a philosopher would ask 'what is the argument of this text?' In each of these cases, a metaphorical dialogue takes place between the reader and the text. An actual dialogue between students who asked these questions and exchanged their own ideas would form the second part of the active, dialogic research process. After many years of having such dialogues, literary scholars, historians, and philosophers will have been produced.

The dialogue model applies equally to research-based teaching in the science disciplines. For example, Prigogine and Stengers (1984, 42) describe scientific enquiry as a 'Dialogue with Nature':

> The experimental method is the art of choosing an interesting question and of scanning all the consequences of the theoretical framework thereby implied, all the ways nature could answer in the theoretical language chosen. (Prigogine and Stengers 1984, 42)

A hypothesis is brought forward by the scientist, based on what he or she already knows, and this knowledge is then added to by what the experiment demonstrates. Nature 'speaks' to the scientist, just as the written word speaks to the reader of poetry, philosophy or theology.

This method of experimentation – the set of questions answered – becomes the discipline itself. To illustrate this idea in our masterclass, Bob drew on the example of making a titration, as the kind of experimental process that a student of chemistry must go through, and argued that this active process is itself the act of learning: it is not something to be 'got through' to reach the knowledge 'on the other side', (although it might sometimes feel like it!) Scientists are best taught when the research = the teaching = the experimental dialogue.

To gain more examples of how this dialogue lens for research-based teaching could be applied to various disciplines, I interviewed friends about their teaching and learning experiences at university. The following case studies document real examples of learning tasks at undergraduate level (interviewees' names have been changed).

Chris, Music and Sound Technology

In groups of about eight people, students were asked to create six track-length pieces of music in different genres within a set time frame. Each student had to play an instrument with which they were less familiar on at least one track, and they were encouraged to experiment on the other tracks as well. The exercise was research-based in that students had to first determine their own resources, ('we didn't know what instruments everyone played, so we had to figure that all out first'), before coming up with new music through explorative jamming. The dialogue model can be applied here. Students had to engage in actual dialogue to get the ball rolling, before the process of jamming took over, and the dialogue became metaphorical. It was an exchange of ideas and sounds between people and instruments.

What was learned? Students learned new things about themselves – that they could work with others and with different instruments – as well as new practical techniques from each other through the process of collective jamming.

Julie, Pure Maths

Julie described the weekly problem sheets that were set for students to work through independently. They would be preceded by a lecture in which students would be shown new proofs. However, the problem sheet would require students to create their own proofs to complete the tasks. Students might use similar techniques or ideas to those shown in the lecture, but would be coming up with something entirely new. This often meant that students had to try a variety of approaches, or ask a number of different questions, before arriving at a proof that worked. They engaged dialogically with the problems by trying various proofs until they got a positive response. Negative responses did not imply failure, as these were necessary steps on the road to finding the correct proof. After completing the problem sheet, students would then get feedback from the teacher in small-group tutorials. When I asked Julie if she had enjoyed these weekly problem sheets, she said: 'It was hard. I think if you put in the time it's much more rewarding than just reeling off examples . . . You've got to have actual understanding of the subject matter.'

What was learned? Students learned to think creatively using proofs that had been discussed in the lecture to develop their own, entirely new, proofs. They had to try a variety of approaches to a problem, engaging in the kind of experimental dialogue in which negative responses are also helpful, to find a solution.

Roz, Physics

At the end of first year, students were given a five-week research project to work on in pairs. The task was to create fractal feedback by setting up a webcam facing a computer screen, and then to analyse the fractal dimension using MATLAB, an easy-to-use programming language. The teachers deliberately left the students to figure out the experiment on their own, giving them an opportunity to work independently: 'It was a real introduction into research. We were just told the idea and given the webcam.' Roz described the problems she and her lab partner had at every stage, from the frustration of setting up the equipment to understanding the programming language and explaining the final results. She was glad to have her partner to work with, as their teacher remained deliberately aloof. 'We didn't actually have that much discussion [with the supervisor]. The dialogue was like, "That's ok, keep trying."' While oral dialogue between teacher and learner was not a key part of this learning exercise, there was a constant dialogue between the students, although it took a while for this to produce useful results. (Roz described the process of learning programming using the computer and webcam as 'asking questions and mostly getting the answer "no".') They were thus in a kind of dialogue with their apparatus. Although progress was slow, and the process frustrating, Roz said that this experience 'was really unlike other things we'd done. . . . It's funny because [...] it stood out because it was *so good*.'

What was learned? The students learned how to set up real experiments without artificial boundaries – and gained an understanding of the many possible challenges involved – by working independently and using the process of trial and error: 'I guess you can't teach that. As in, you can't *tell* someone how to do that.'

If we apply the idea of dialogue in the metaphorical sense of an exchange of the known with the unknown, then disciplines themselves become specific types of dialogic methods or practices: they are the *questions* that you ask, the *actions* that you take, and the *methods* by which you to enter into the unknown. These kind of exploratory, dialogic, research-based learning tasks prove more fruitful than monologic learning styles in which the teacher speaks and the learner listens. They also overcome the 'student–teacher contradiction' in that they enable the student to engage in their own research dialogue.

the discipline = the research activity = *dialogue*

What does your own discipline look like through this lens?

How would you describe your discipline – as a method or process?

Which actions do you take? Which questions do you ask?

How could you encourage your students to think of their discipline as a dialogic process, and what would this achieve?

5. Example: translation as a model for R=T=dialogue

As well as being the only subject of which I have any experience as a teacher, translation presents itself as an apt example for thinking about R=T=dialogue. The whole process of learning a foreign language, and studying its literature and culture, boils down to the act of translation. Without it, how can we, as learners, express or even understand what we have learned in the foreign language? Although translation has long been excluded from dominant language learning approaches – especially at school – Cook (2010) makes a compelling case for the myriad benefits that practising translation offers to language learners. Despite frequent criticisms that it is too academic an exercise, it is in fact a fundamentally task-based endeavour: 'Translation is a real-world activity outside the classroom. It is outcome-oriented: a successful translation is one that works' (Cook 2010, 30). It follows naturally that translation should form a compulsory part of any university language course, although this is not always the case.

However, translation can also be seen as a discipline in its own right, as competing theorists have long sought to define the parameters of the activity: how much is actually possible when we try to shift meaning between languages? The process of dialogue is often used metaphorically to explain the translation process. For example, Greenall (2006) uses Bakhtin's theory of heteroglossia to explain what goes on between a source text (ST) and a target text (TT): 'a TT is at once in the voice of the author, the translator and the audience' (Greenall 2006, 71). She explains that there is rarely a one-to-one correspondence between languages, and that solutions have to be arrived at through a process of dialogue between the two languages, as well as between the author and the translator. This, she argues, is why computers cannot translate. They cannot grasp the whole context of a phrase, and cannot consider the abundance of possible word choices, along with their particular connotations:

> The intuitive, intricate, 'no-real-beginning-and-no-real-end' quality of dialogical relations in texts might not be so easily captured by mathematically based systems. In fact, it is not even easily captured in words: any attempt at analysis will tend to belie the complexity of the processes involved . . . (Greenall 2006, 70)

The idea of 'no real beginning and no real end' fits well onto the concepts of both research and teaching, since neither process should be viewed as finite. When theorised in this way, the practice of translation can therefore be seen as a prime example of research-based teaching. Furthermore, it is highly dialogic. Greenall calls for 'a focus on the notion of dialogue itself, in order to capture the multitude of different meaning-creating relations which the translator has no choice but to enter into, in his or her work' (2006, 81).

Although it is bound to be mostly 'hands-on', a translation class as part of a language course could benefit students by also engaging (at least superficially) with the theory of translation as a dialogue. There is no manual for translation. There are no hard-and-fast rules to memorise. Rather than a subject to be passively learned, translation is a discipline that requires the kind of dialogic thinking that makes learners into subjects in their own right. Returning to Freire's idea of overcoming 'the student–teacher contradiction' (1996, 53), students of translation should above all be encouraged to think of themselves as already translators, on a par with the teacher, who becomes just another translator (albeit more experienced). Fully embracing their autonomy as individuals, able to engage in their own personal dialogue with the source text, they might perhaps avoid the pitfall of trying to work like machines, looking for the 'correct' solution, when there is no such thing. Both the student and the teacher would engage with the source text on their own terms, and the teacher's role would be merely to guide the student in reaching their own conclusions, rather than spoon-feeding them the solutions to difficult problems.

6. Embracing dialogue in my future teaching

I feel very strongly that I want to work to overcome the 'student–teacher contradiction' with future cohorts, allowing students to be empowered to act as translators in their own right. This is especially important for translation beginners, because they need to feel able to make their own choices, employing critical thinking and sensitivity, to be able to achieve translation at all. Otherwise, they will make the same random choices that a machine translator would (see Greenall 2006, 79). They should not be allowed to remain in the 'dependent' mindset, but must fully embrace their new status as subjects and decision makers.

The greatest difficulty this poses for me is in the practice of assessing students' work and giving feedback. I have long been troubled by the problem of what to do when a student has simply got it wrong. It is all very well to attempt to instil an attitude of confidence and power in students' minds, but they will still lack a lot of the language experience and knowledge required to make a successful translation. How can I guide students in the right direction without crushing their spirits and making them feel dependent on my feedback? The most obvious solution to this problem is to use the often untapped resource of peer-feedback. Nicol (2010) collects ample evidence from research to demonstrate that assessing the work of their peers helps students to proofread their own future work, as well as making them more aware of the assessment criteria. He argues convincingly that written feedback needs to be reintegrated into a dialogic context so that students process it usefully, rather than merely filing it away and forgetting about it. If feedback remains monologic (the teacher speaks, the student listens) then it is unlikely that the student will act on the comments they have been given. But when they interact with feedback, students are more likely to take it on board. Nicol (2010) proposes several models for organising peer-assessment, which I hope to build into future courses:

- Students bring three copies of their work, with an identification number (rather than their name) and distribute these for feedback among the other students (pp. 509–10).

- Students guide their feedback by posing their own questions to the teacher, highlighting the issues they had with the work, or areas where they need clarification (pp. 507).
- The teacher distributes examples of work by previous cohorts so that students can discuss them in groups (p. 505).
- The teacher asks students to discuss their feedback in small groups and produce a collaborative action plan for how they can all improve (p. 508).

Peer-feedback cannot entirely replace the feedback given by the teacher, but it could help to create the kind of dialogic mindset that I believe could be very beneficial to students, helping them to see themselves as empowered to guide their own learning, and thus overcoming the 'student–teacher contradiction'. Reading and assessing one another's work could help to build group cohesion, enabling the students to see their class as a collaborative 'community of practice' (Wenger 1998) rather than as an assembled group of individual learners in competition.

Questions for the reader

How could you make feedback more dialogic in your own teaching?

Could peer-assessment perhaps be more integrated into your university course structure?

What strengths does peer-feedback have over feedback from a teacher?

What would a 'community of practice' look like in your own classroom?

7. Conclusion: R=T=dialogue

Considering dialogue as a model for teaching and learning benefits both teachers and learners, and will also help both to mentally integrate these concepts. When teaching is done dialogically, learning becomes more autonomous, as students have to engage directly with the problem at hand. When learners engage dialogically with a problem, they understand that it will be a process of trial and error – an exchange of ideas – and that negative responses are not indicative of failure in this experimental method. Rather, students can feel emancipated from their status as dependents, and learn that they already possess the know-how to make progress in their learning, if they simply carry on asking the right questions. The model of dialogue thus proves highly useful in developing forms of research-based education.

References

Cook, Guy. 2010. *Translation in Language Teaching. An Argument for Reassessment*. Oxford: Oxford University Press.

Freire, Paulo. 1996. *Pedagogy of the Oppressed*. Translated by Myra Bergman Ramos. Harmondsworth: Penguin. Original language publication 1968.

Greenall, Annjo Klungervik. 2006. 'Translation as Dialogue.' In Ferreira Duarte, João, Assis Rosa, Alexandra and Seruya, Teresa (eds) *Translation Studies at the Interface of Disciplines*, pp. 67–81. Amsterdam: John Benjamins.

Nicol, D. J. 2010. From monologue to dialogue: improving written feedback processes in mass higher education. *Assessment & Evaluation in Higher Education* 35.5, 501–17.

Prigogine, Ilya and Stengers, Isabelle. 1984. *Order out of Chaos. Man's New Dialogue with Nature*. Boulder, CO: Heinemann, New Science Library.

Vella, Jane. 2002. *Learning to Listen, Learning to Teach. The Power of Dialogue in Educating Adults*. Revised Edition. San Francisco, CA: Jossey-Bass.

Wenger, Etienne. 1998. *Communities of Practice: Learning, Meaning, and Identity*. Cambridge: Cambridge University Press.

Links to the R=T Framework

Tejas Joshi
UCL Institute of Education

- Ellen introduces dialogue as an under-rated and under-utilised facet of student–staff partnership. Her emphasis is on moving away from the traditional unidirectional teacher-to-student relationship of knowledge delivery and, by drawing on Freire's work, she proposes a participatory, dialogical process that fosters student participants as equal partners.

  The dialogue she advocates is not merely literal, as may often be perceived, but in fact connotes a metaphorical dialogue within the relevant discipline, such as the process of its development, which presents opportunities for exploration, systematisation and analysis, thereby culminating in the learner engaging in the development of knowledge and not simply receiving it from the teacher. Demonstrating this in the context of translation, which is an important component of language education, she suggests that significant and reflective research is required in order to identify the potential for embedding dialogue across disciplines.

- The challenge of insufficient communication, be it between students and staff, between departments, as well from the university has been emphasised time and again, and against this backdrop the 'R=T=dialogue' certainly seems to offer a valuable alternative. However, how does the concept translate into practice?

  Ellen's exemplification in the context of translation provides a formidable case in point, but it also indicates the requirement of a significant shift in mindset and practice from staff. This shift is in fact a necessary predecessor to working with student partners in all contexts, given that the relationship is traditionally unequal.

Second, what works as an effective dialogic practice for one discipline may not necessarily work for another, but this challenge presents another opportunity for student–staff partnership projects to delve into existing discipline-specific insights (for instance, dialogue in science education) and deploy them in their own contexts. In terms of larger scale curricular, pedagogic and assessment considerations, incorporating dialogic practices would demand extensive pilot research – an opportunity as well as a challenge.

Lastly, a consideration particularly relevant to dialogic interventions is their inherent complexity as an educational tool, understanding the niceties of which demands both student and staff partners to be significantly well-versed in the psychological and linguistic affordances of dialogue. When not considered, dialogue within student–staff partnerships is at risk of being either trivialised or, as Ellen puts it, be perceived in terms of its literal definition.

- In conclusion, the constructivist dialogic approach presents a platform for addressing the barrier of communication as well as providing opportunities for research-based student–staff partnerships. The key recommendation here is its value in promoting equality between the student and staff members by deploying the quintessential tool of communication, which is central to education.

The necessity of extensive research and critical reflection, both in terms of the very discipline as well as in pedagogically translating it into feasible practice, ensures contributions from both the staff and student members and in terms of opportunities, shows promise as a creative and innovative exercise for both stakeholders.

For a prospective research-based educator intending to participate in such a student–staff partnership, a starting point would be to reflect upon the extent of their reliance on dialogue in their own practice and in light of their own roles as a teacher, learner and educator. That in itself could lead to many emerging questions and motivations to be pursued further.

2.4
Interdisciplinary research-based teaching

Advocacy for a change in the higher education paradigm

Agathe Ribéreau-Gayon
Department of Security and Crime Science and Institute of Archaeology, UCL

with Professor David d'Avray
Department of History, UCL

Agathe's distinctive contribution to the case for research-based teaching is to link it with advocacy for interdisciplinarity. By its nature, an interdisciplinary approach is more likely to make students think rather than simply attempting to master a standard body of knowledge.

Professor David d'Avray

1. Introduction

According to the QS World University Rankings by Subject 2016, UCL is the top-rated university in the field of Education. Although this ranking mostly reflects the quality of research of UCL academics – not necessarily of their teaching – it certainly gives UCL academics, students and staff a privileged position from which to reflect on their own teaching, to suggest ways of further blending teaching with research – two inherent aspects of higher education that are too often considered in isolation. This raises the important question of how we can transform excellence in research on education into excellence in education itself. This chapter will explore to what extent the R=T initiative can be an answer to that question.

As a PhD candidate (Forensic Anthropology, Department of Security and Crime Science) and a teaching assistant, I am lucky enough to be a student, researcher and teacher all at the same time. This is an incredibly enriching position, one which has significantly developed my personal interest in the quality of education. My involvement in the R=T initiative further developed my awareness of the lack of suitability of traditional educational models – where research stands apart from teaching – for today's students' needs. I will therefore explore here the benefits of the R=T model to enrich education and curriculum, specifically addressing the challenges of boundaries. I will then examine two different types of boundaries: those between research and teaching; and those between traditional disciplines. I will suggest concrete ways to contribute to the blurring of these boundaries, to help with developing research-based education.

2. Towards R=T: blurring the boundary between research and teaching

Although nowadays most academics are expected to both conduct research and deliver teaching (all at the same time), it has been demonstrated that, in reality, research and teaching tend to be conceived, prepared and delivered separately. This rather arbitrary separation between research and teaching has created a lack of balance between research-time involvement and teaching-time involvement. A major issue is that research tends to be more valued than teaching within both academia and the scientific community. In that context, many researcher–teachers focus on delivering high-quality research rather than high-quality teaching. This issue has been criticised across Europe for a number of years because it has a direct negative impact on the quality of teaching delivered to students, and also because many academics feel that teaching distracts them from their research.

The approaches taken by researchers, students and teachers can be seen as somewhat incompatible given their inherent natures. A researcher is, by definition, in an empirical process, in a dynamic of discovery; their conception is that not everything is known so far, and nothing is finite. The natural tendency of a student, however, is to expect eternal knowledge, finite verities. The position of a teacher lies somewhere between that of the researcher and of the student. A researcher–teacher's attitude will depend on their personal involvement in the research: the closer they are to it, the more likely they are to convey to students that verities and science are in constant evolution, able to be shaped by students' active involvement. On the other hand, a teacher who is not directly involved in research will tend to refer to traditional bodies of knowledge that they will barely question, thereby transmitting this approach to their students. For these reasons, the expectations of researchers, students and teachers seem difficult to merge.

To bridge the gap between research and teaching, it seems sensible to suggest the development of a research-based education, where students and teacher are able to conduct research together in a classroom environment. This would free up enough time for the researcher–teacher to deliver both quality teaching and cutting-edge science, and for the learners to acquire the required knowledge and skills to be adequately prepared to conduct research themselves. The challenge is to find ways to blend R and T that work for both the teacher and the learners. Throughout his career, Professor David d'Avray, Professor of medieval history at UCL, developed several strategies to further blend research and teaching in his everyday work. To deliver research-based teaching he manages to constantly involve his students in his research – both Masters and undergraduates. In his experience, a good way to initiate first-year undergraduate students in research in medieval history is to engage with them around the analysis of ancient manuscripts. This activity, done in class, enables the students to conduct research on material that is crucial to historians, while developing their analysing, reasoning and critical skills through the observation of concrete evidence. Professor d'Avray transcribes and translates unpublished medieval documents for his undergraduates to study, thereby introducing them to source material as yet unstudied by scholars. This strategy provides students with a sound understanding of how to conduct research, shortly after entering university, which implies a very important shift in their conception of education compared to the environment of high school, where preparing students for research is hardly the primary objective. Professor d'Avray also runs courses relating to books for which he is doing research. In so doing, his students benefit from original research, while also allowing the teacher to build on the students' feedback in class to inform and improve his or her research. Professor d'Avray therefore creates an educational environment that relies upon both research-based teaching and teaching-based research, a rarely achieved balance between R and T in higher education to date. This is a great example of a successful way of linking R and T where learners are conceived as partners in both research and teaching by the teacher (Healey 2014). This educational strategy proves highly beneficial to the blurring of the boundaries between research and teaching, but also between teachers and students, another artificially set boundary.

Another issue when trying to implement research-based teaching in higher education is the existence of boundaries between undergraduate and postgraduate students. Indeed, my experience both as a student and as a PGTA has made me realise that within the broad category of learners there is a gap between the expectations of teachers for undergraduate and Masters students, because the latter are expected to conduct more independent research. This can create an imbalance between the teacher's expectation of their students and the students' expectations of doing research, and of being adequately prepared and supervised to do so. PGTAs can play a key role in facilitating the transition from undergraduate to postgraduate, and in helping both students and teachers reach their respective objectives. Thanks to their position, experience and age relative to the students, PGTAs (as students–teachers–researchers themselves) are uniquely positioned to act as a sort of 'intercessor' between learners and teachers, developing a deep and up-to-date understanding of the actual needs and expectations of the new generation of learners (Healey 2014). This is certainly the main asset of PGTAs, whose perspectives are different from those of students at undergraduate, Masters and even PhD level. Indeed, as a PGTA, I developed an integrated approach that effectively blends research and teaching by putting knowledge into historical perspective, and within its production context, to provide a comprehensive vision of a field (Morss and Murray 2005). From a practical perspective, an integrated approach can be easily implemented, by making sure that students are fully aware of the entire scope of skills, resources, facilities and expertise available (i.e. libraries and staff), not just those that are thought to fit their area of study or are available within their home institution. Even more important is that students use this wide range of information to make critical connections between fields and concepts. As a PGTA, I have noticed that some Masters students often miss this global vision. I then try to make sure that I personally inform students and direct them to relevant members of staff who can help, as early as possible in the academic year.

On a more theoretical ground, putting knowledge into context is critical to help students discover that research is inherently an ongoing process, that it evolves constantly and cannot, therefore, provide absolute and definitive answers to students' questions or to any topic discussed in the literature or media (Bell and Kahrhoff 2006; Walkington 2016).

This can be concretely achieved with object-based and problem-based learning activities in a classroom setting (Biggs 1999; Dolmans et al. 2005). Object-based learning is an educational approach based on the handling of an object that enables the creation of quick cognitive links between a tangible thing and intangible theories or concepts (Bonwell and Eison 1991; Bell and Kahrhoff 2006). This empirical process facilitates the understanding of, sometimes complex, theories by the handler of the object, and is therefore acknowledged as an effective way of learning (Bonwell and Eison 1991; Bell and Kahrhoff 2006). In object-based learning, the object is used as a way to concretely test some aspects of an approach as well as its challenges, via the intellectual process of midwifery, known as maieutics, where the learner 'gives birth' to knowledge they were not aware they had acquired. Maieutics has proved effective for deeply understanding a process or concept and also for keeping a long-lasting memory of it. This learning approach can be done with a great diversity of objects – from fossils, to maps, to paintings – and can thereby be applied to a wide range of fields. As part of my research-based teaching activities to Masters students in Forensic Anthropology, I use objects (such as bones and X-ray images) as a concrete starting point. We then use these objects to discuss, as a group, the methods, practices or paradigms from a range of disciplines (such as Justice, Medicine, Forensic Sciences, Archaeology, History, etc.) that used to be the norm in our field before being amended or refuted, but that contributed to inform – sometimes directly – the methods currently in use. This approach is usually very well received by the students, as evidenced by both what they say and their written coursework. It allows them to quickly incorporate a critical evaluation of the current methods and stimulates their ability even to suggest avenues for improvement. However, this integrated approach is not implemented to date in many fields, something I came across as an early-career researcher. For instance, I noticed that medical schools in mainland Europe only offer very cursory training in the history of medicine and, more importantly, they draw no conclusions from medicine's past practice into the way it is taught and applied today. This is regrettable, as teaching the history of medicine would definitely help students understand to what extent the body of knowledge in medical science has constantly evolved, and that what they consider to be a scientific truth today may actually be challenged tomorrow.

Despite being a very efficient way to deliver a research-based teaching, object-based learning is not always easy to set up, especially for certain subjects, class configurations (i.e. large groups in amphitheatres) or type of learners (i.e. various background and receptivity) (Cain

2010). Although well described in the literature, I believe the most efficient way to understand the challenges regarding the implementation of object-based learning in a classroom setting is to experience it personally, which I did from two different perspectives: as a teacher and as a learner. For example, for a particular activity in the context of a practical class, I asked the students to discuss in pairs a copy of an anonymised medical X-ray that I had used for my own research. I noticed that the activity was received differently according to the level of familiarity of the students with X-ray images, so that not every student was able to discuss the object in a way that would have facilitated their understanding of the problems I wanted to lead them to realise. I had a chance to experiment with some of these challenges myself as a learner by joining a workshop on object-based learning delivered in the UCL Art Museum. This experience from a learner's perspective made me realise to what extent cultural differences – including language, background (i.e. humanities vs. 'hard' sciences) and personality – and learning type (i.e. visual, spatial, auditory, etc.) play critical roles in the success of an object-based learning approach. Being aware of the logistical and intellectual challenges of object-based learning is of great help for the teacher to tailor their activities, as well as their expectations, in accordance with the diversity of their students.

I believe developing this integrated, active, research-based teaching approach is crucial for students to understand the limitations of knowledge and education, and for them to appreciate the research process. Beyond that, this approach is very important for encouraging the development of students' critical thinking as well as their resilience, two paramount skills in the building of their curriculum as well as their identities (Biggs 1999; Walkington 2016). This is something I have never been told by my professors or supervisors and that I discovered empirically, but which is a critical step toward prepare students to conduct research in the fields of their choice. I think this is another way to develop effective research-based teaching that enables students to adopt the expected conceptions to conduct research while being taught in class. I appreciate that this change in the conception of teaching represents a major shift compared to the school environment, where students are used to being given verities by their teachers. The process takes time, and should therefore start as soon as students begin university, thus leaving a legacy for the next generation of undergraduates that the first cohort of students – now postgraduates – will teach. Significant gains in developing effective research-education will be achieved if this transdisciplinary and transgenerational dialogue is initiated.

3. The blurring of traditional disciplinary boundaries: an effective way towards a research-based education

Blurring arbitrary traditional disciplinary boundaries will foster the development of a cross-disciplinary research strategy, where research and teaching are blended in a natural fashion. Because my background is an intimate blending of the Humanities (Archaeology and Anthropology) and Sciences (Biological Anthropology and Forensic Sciences), which I completed in both France and the UK, along with much professional experience abroad (i.e. internships and scientific collaborations), multi-disciplinary transnational dialogue is inherently part of my education, teaching and, in a broader context, identity. As a PGTA and a researcher now, I build on my own experience as a student as well as on the experience of inspirational professors I met to inform my daily practice, both in teaching and research. I am therefore trying to implement a cross-disciplinary approach in my capacity as a PGTA, at two complementary levels: internal – within UCL– and transnational. I am directly involved in interdepartmental courses, workshops, conferences and publications between the Department of Security and Crime Science, the Institute of Archaeology and the Department of Anthropology. I have also initiated several multidisciplinary research collaborations between UCL and universities abroad. These collaborations and networks have allowed me to discover theories and methods used outside the UK which I now use as teaching material on an *ad hoc* basis during my teaching, thereby expanding the traditional scope of the topic.

The importance of overstepping traditional disciplinary boundaries to facilitate the implementation of research-based education is acknowledged by several teachers, including Professor d'Avray. He supports extending the research-based approach he uses with ancient manuscripts to support learning in various other fields, by making *ad hoc* adaptations for the given discipline and resources available. Some might argue that this cross-disciplinary research strategy is mostly applicable to 'humanities' because of their intrinsic nature. However, I am confident this approach is also applicable to the so-called 'hard' sciences, for which the educational model is traditionally considered as consisting of a first phase (first-year undergraduate) of acquiring the methods, but with very little actual research. From my own experience, this conception mostly relies on *habitus* and can absolutely be adapted to the hard sciences, by following the example of humanities and immersing students in research right from their first year, as Professor d'Avray has done for several years with his students. From my perspective as an early researcher–teacher in both the humanities and sciences, I am convinced that the implementation of such an interdisciplinary approach requires taking a step back from one's field and to start working *on* it – not just *in* it. It is important to bear in mind that the shift in the educational paradigm may take some time. It is therefore all the more important to address the issue and to spread the word, as the UCL ChangeMakers and Connected Curriculum are doing. In this view, it is crucial to try applying new methodologies with first-year undergraduates, to allow sufficient time for these new approaches to blossom throughout the students' curriculum. The blurring of artificial, traditional boundaries between disciplines will lead to a critical change in the education paradigm that will be hugely beneficial to both learners and teachers.

Professor Peter Abrahams, of the Warwick Medical School, has developed a novel multidisciplinary educational approach for his students, who benefit from a wide range of innovative, user-friendly, technology-based methods and tools (such as applications for mobile phones and tablets, online platforms, as well as songs). Because this educational strategy provides diversified resources and approaches, it effectively supports students' learning, including doing research. Linking technology, education and research works very well in stimulating learners' attention and curiosity, as well as ensuring a long-lasting memory of a given topic, a phenomenon also reported in the literature (Ballantyne and Knowles 2007). Even more interestingly, this educational strategy enables students to play a key role in the development and improvement of teaching materials. They can tailor these to their own needs thanks to their up-to-date skills in technology, and they thereby inform Professor Abrahams' practice and enable him to develop his own technological skills. In so doing, a mutually beneficial, balanced student–teacher relationship is built (Healey 2014). Professor Abrahams' practice is a fantastic example of a successful transdisciplinary approach that effectively facilitates the delivery of research-based teaching.

Another inspirational and successful example of cross-disciplinary research-based teaching is the Centre for the Forensic Sciences (CFS) at UCL. The CFS is a research-based education initiative directed by Dr Ruth Morgan (who is also my PhD supervisor). It was established in 2010 with the aim of delivering cutting-edge, research-based teaching in a range of disciplines under the large umbrella of the forensic sciences (geosciences, chemistry, genetics, statistics, etc.). The novelty of this educational strategy relies on the development of cross-disciplinary classes that blend together disciplines that, traditionally, have not necessarily been linked together in higher education. For example: archaeology with forensic sciences; psychology with forensic anthropology; or even architecture with crime science. In parallel to teaching time, multidisciplinary, research-based workshops, seminars and conferences are also run throughout the academic year. These regular events are fantastic opportunities for students (of all levels) and staff to engage in stimulating dialogue with speakers from both research and practitioner backgrounds (i.e. police officers, crime-scene technicians, lab technicians, forensic pathologists, etc.) who represent a variety of disciplines both across and outside UCL, in the UK and internationally. The CFS demonstrates how it is concretely possible and enriching for both learners and teachers to work within an international, multidisciplinary environment while maintaining a good balance between research and teaching-time involvement. The suitability of this cross-disciplinary, research-based educational model for today's generation of learners is evidenced by the ever-increasing number of students at the CFS and the success of its flagship and highly distinctive multidisciplinary MSc degree in Crime and Forensic Science, which clearly meets the need for strong research-based training. Overstepping traditional boundaries, including in the hard sciences, is a valid model applicable to a variety of fields, and one which also fosters the development of new, stimulating fields.

PGTAs can play a crucial role in the implementation of a cross-disciplinary educational approach. A concrete example is the one-hour workshop at the UCL Teaching and Learning Conference, which I co-led with a fellow graduate teaching assistants (GTA). It gathered a very diverse panel of GTAs from a range of nationalities and backgrounds, in subjects as diverse as geography, English, German, biochemistry engineering and forensic anthropology). Discussions included the need for solutions to better understand one another's approaches, and to find ways to adapt them to a particular group or subject, in the common interest. The workshop demonstrated the power of interdisciplinary dialogue to inform one's teaching, by merging approaches from the humanities and hard sciences. Thanks to their ability to directly contribute to the implementation of novel areas for collaborations between researchers, teachers and students, in disciplines that do not necessarily have a long-term history of integrating one another's approaches, GTAs can play a key role in blurring the boundaries between student and teacher, as well as between traditional disciplines. GTAs thus represent a great hope within higher education for implementing research-based teaching, for a change in the higher education paradigm that calls for all stakeholders (academics, GTAs and the students themselves) to engage in a constant, balanced and constructive dialogue.

4. Conclusions: R=T – a common endeavour for a common concern

GTAs can play a key contributory role in helping to bridge the gap between research and teaching, and between students' and teachers' expectations when it comes to implementing research-based teaching. In this view, interdisciplinary work that involves different stakeholders in higher education is key to merging research with teaching, which in turn will contribute to creating a more suitable academic model.

Concretely, research-based education can be implemented by employing a number of suggestions that I have experienced myself – both as a student and a GTA. These could be developed as a common endeavour between students, teachers (including GTAs) and researchers (see the box on recommendations).

First, it is critical that students acquire research acumen by being involved in research projects the moment they start university. This will develop their professional, personal and intrapersonal skills that are critical in the building of students' identity. Developing students' interest and skills for research during class time can be facilitated by creating stimulating cross-disciplinary environments. A fantastic benefit of this approach is that it can be applied to almost any field. In this view, interdepartmental classes (i.e. archaeology and statistics; ecology and social anthropology), seminars, workshops (such as object-based handling in museums for both students and staff), research projects and collaborations must be encouraged. Involving collaborators from abroad can add enormous benefit, not only to improve the cohesion of these multidisciplinary projects, but also to develop students' awareness of other approaches that they may find helpful to support their learning – as I experienced at UCL with the R=T initiative. Cross-disciplinary educational strategies can prove greatly beneficial in preparing students to conduct research and, beyond that, to develop a more balanced relationship between students and teachers so that they learn from one another. While in theory these integrated, multidisciplinary approaches are supposed to be applied already in higher education, in my experience, for the most part, they tend to remain ideal goals, still to be achieved to date.

These suggestions, based on first-hand experience in higher education, will foster a new academic model based on a more homogeneous blend of research and teaching, stepping forward towards achieving excellence in education.

Implementing research-based education: recommendations

- Involve students – including first-year undergraduates – in hands-on research projects directly relevant to their teachers' research, for them to acquire the empirical nature of the research process.
- Suggest object-based and problem-based learning approaches to facilitate the development of students' critical minds.
- Create interdepartmental seminars, conferences, events, research projects and collaborations to facilitate cross-disciplinary education.
- Invite external speakers, including from abroad, to share their experience and views on research.
- Develop internships and professional placements, including abroad, to broaden students' conception of their field and topic of interest.

References

Ballantyne, N. and Knowles, A. 2007. Enhancing student learning with case-based learning objects in a problem-based learning context: The views of social work students in Scotland and Canada. *Journal of Online Learning and Teaching* 3, 363–74.

Bell, D. and Kahrhoff, J. 2006. *Active Learning Handbook*. Saint Louis, MO: Webster University.

Biggs, J. 1999. What the student does: teaching for enhanced learning. *Higher Education Research & Development* 18, 57–75.

Bonwell, C. and Eison, J. 1991. Active Learning: Creating Excitement in the Classroom. ASHE-ERIC Higher Education Reports.

Cain, J. 2010. Practical concerns when implementing object-based teaching in higher education. *University Museums and Collections Journal* 3, 197–201.

Dolmans, D., De Grave, W. S., Wolfhagen, I. and Van der Vleuten, C. 2005. Problem-based learning: Future challenges for educational practice and research. *Medical Education* 39, 732–41.

Healey, M. 2014. Students as partners in learning and teaching in higher education. Workshop. http://www.mickhealey.co.uk/workshops-offered/sotl-change-and-partners/students-as-partners-in-learning-and-teaching-in-higher-education. [Accessed October 2017].

Morss, K. and Murray, R. 2005. *Teaching at University: A Guide for Postgraduates and Researchers*. London: Sage.

Walkington, H. 2016. Pedagogic approaches to developing students as researchers, within the curriculum and beyond. Higher Education Academy. https://www.heacademy.ac.uk/sites/default/files/resources/walkington-pedagogic-approaches.pdf. [Accessed October 2017].

Links to the R=T Framework

James Claxton
Department of Physics and Astronomy, UCL

- For me, the key message of Agathe's chapter is that object-based learning has a greater effect on students' learning than conventional methods, such as lecturing. Object-based learning fits into research-based education since the students are in contact with current research and interacting with its equipment and methods). The chapter also refers to research-based education as having longer lasting effects on retention of knowledge: having been in contact with objects, students can remember the concepts behind them far better than when being told them. This can also be stimulating for staff, as they can see how the students adapt and respond to this different learning style. The chapter highlights the success of interdisciplinary work and how this has boosted interest in students' programmes of study.

- The benefit of object-based learning is increased student engagement: when free to learn actively alongside staff, students have a better feel for their discipline and how research is conducted. Students working with staff would have a wider awareness of the real-world applications and opportunities in their field, as well as being able to consider what they want to do with their future, with a better understanding of the differences between their study and a career as a researcher. Interdisciplinary events and projects would give students an insight into industry, into how real-world projects are conducted, and how interdisciplinary fields of study are developing.

  A significant challenge of object-based learning is that for students to be in an environment where they have free access to laboratory equipment and research materials requires space, funding and staff time so that students can study materials at their own pace and level of curiosity. The challenges of interdisciplinary events and collaboration stem from the traditional siloing of departments and fields of study: insufficient communication between departments and different approaches to research-based education.

- I believe the key principle for any staff–student partnership moving towards research-based education is that both sides must benefit from and feel appropriately rewarded by and incentivised for participating. A student has a great incentive to work alongside a staff member: they rapidly gain valuable experience and benefit from the staff member's up-to-date methods and skills (staff attend conferences and read current literature which can be passed on through observation rather than teaching). Staff who are working much more closely with students would feel a greater sense of accomplishment when they have a more decisive impact on their students' skills and abilities. Staff could also receive awards for investing in students and encouraging them along their growing careers.

  This is a key aspect of any staff–student partnership: both sides must feel they are learning from each other and being appropriately recognised for their work.

2.5
Institutes for all

Learning from the Institute of Making

Frances Brill
Department of Geography, UCL

with Professor Mark Miodownik
Institute of Making and Department of Mechanical Engineering, UCL

I enjoyed reading your chapter, and thanks for your insightful analysis (and support) of what we do. Although we have had new knowledge, many journal research papers and spin-out companies emerge from the Institute of Making, I am equally proud of the failures: they say a lot about our culture of uninhibited exploration and playful exuberance.

Professor Mark Miodownik

1. Introduction

The Institute of Making (IoM) is a UCL initiative that opened in 2013, where students and academics from different disciplines engage in research in a shared space, often collaboratively. In its own words it has a 'programme of symposia, masterclasses and public events [that] explores the links between academic research and hands-on experience, and celebrates the sheer joy of stuff'. It runs as a research club and has both real international business and policy impacts.

The MakeSpace is a physical place for members of the institute to put their ideas into practice, to explore what they want and, in doing so, make student-to-teacher and peer-to-peer learning part of the day to day. This is revolutionary in the natural sciences: here is a space, outside of normal labs, with high-tech equipment that undergraduates, post-graduates and staff can all use at the same time. It is an arena where any distinction between teaching and research blurs, and consequently the boundary between teacher and student is also challenged.

The IoM is run by Professor Mark Miodownik, a material scientist and engineer who, as one UCL colleague pointed out, has the character and charm to attract students. For him, teaching is about creating an environment where students can have creative and productive dialogues. His approach to the institute is very student focused; it is a space for student ideas to flourish. Interestingly, he stresses the importance of an interdisciplinary approach, which he believes is only effective because of the strength of the individual departments across UCL. When students from different backgrounds come together, they inspire one another, they have different parts of the making experience to offer, and everyone can learn. In this way the research and teaching integration also begins to make teachers out of students, for other students.

The distinction between research and teaching is heavily entwined with the division between teacher and learner. As many academics said during the panel discussion at the R=T Launch Event, at which Professor Miodownik described the institute's work, there is a need to move beyond this binary understanding of the lecture hall. In situations where the division blurs, everyone can learn from one another, and it becomes easier to integrate teaching with research practices. The learning process must be beneficial for all. The IoM succeeds because it does just this and creates a culture of curiosity.

The biggest challenge to learning in this way is marking and feedback. In regular lecture halls, lecturers teach to a list and so prevent students from exploring their ideas in the truly open way the IoM does. For Mark, this regimented nature, the way teaching is assessed and the need for output-orientated courses, can all inhibit research-focused teaching. These issues were echoed by academics from all disciplines, with more and tighter circles for student–teacher feedback offered as a solution. It becomes about making the feedback informal and ensuring the student is enjoying the learning process. However, this challenges the very core of how British higher education currently functions. For Mark, the 'tick-box' approach required to meet National Student Survey targets and ensure teaching is of a sufficient 'quality' homogenises the students and acts as the antithesis of student/research-based teaching. We need a continual dialogue and for students to get stuck in, and to research – to pursue their passions.

This chapter addresses what we can learn from the IoM, with a particular emphasis on using it as a method for integrating research and teaching. Highlighting the way it can be applied in a Human Geography context, I illustrate the way interdisciplinary elements such as 'urban' can be emphasised in new 'institutes' going forward. Addressing the challenges of space, and finding a way of measuring progress, I argue for more field trips, which are assessed through portfolios rather than exams. Taking the idea of the R=T initiative forward, it becomes apparent that institutes are effective tools for creating a research-orientated learning environment capable of integrating all years of undergraduates, postgraduates and academics.

2. More is better

The IoM has been a clear success in UCL, with discussion at the launch event concluding that one way to take forward a research-based education model was to 'make more institutes': a range of different interdisciplinary sites, each with a unique, research-led focus. In this section I draw on my experiences of participating in the roundtable discussion at the launch event and from existing interdisciplinary groups to show that while there are problems with copying the IoM model exactly, it has the potential to be a place where people of different backgrounds come together within a department or field of research to learn together.

Thinking from my own, Human Geography perspective, the idea of institutes intuitively makes sense. For example, it would be possible to develop an institute around urban research creation. Specifically, reconciling the institute model with the work of the interdisciplinary PhD group 'Stadtkolloquim', there could be an 'Institute for Urban' where students from across the university are encouraged to engage with urban processes and understandings. In the case of UCL, with the research and practical elements of the Bartlett Faculty of the Built Environment, there would be a clear 'leading department'. However, students from all disciplines, including Engineering, Geography, English and Slavonic and Eastern European Studies, have already presented at the PhD group, and there is no reason why they would not get involved with a broader institute. This would also offer a way to integrate already-existing organisations into one space, offering the chance for them to engage with one another rather than exist in isolation.

When asked, 'what does R=T mean to you?', Mark answered that it means creating a space where people from different backgrounds can come together with their ideas in a research-focused space. But if creating the space is possible, what will attract the students? One of the big appeals of the IoM is access to the latest equipment, which students would otherwise not have the chance to use. In this respect, the institute idea might not work in all disciplines, but the idea of 'access' to something new or something 'exciting' could perhaps be expanded upon. Technology is continually evolving and is ever more present in the classroom; building on this, virtual spaces that mimicked the environment of the IoM could be created. An effective virtual environment such as, for example, 'Slack', which has proven successful in the business world, might present a similarly successful space for students to opt into, and engage with academics. Responding to a presentation at the 2016 UCL Teaching and Learning Conference, Professor Jason Ditmer of UCL Geography described how he had already started a slack space for the department. However, it is about making this space fun, granting access to otherwise difficult-to-reach parts of 'Geography'.

More broadly from the discussion, two issues with the institute approach became evident. First, logistics and estate management, with universities unlikely to have unlimited, unused space meaning that finding an area that could always be set aside could be problematic. This is especially true for lab-based work, where estates management strictly divide research and teaching areas. Looking forward to new buildings and new spaces, Professor David Price, UCL Vice-Provost (Research), spoke of the possibilities for UCL East. Dealing with this issue more generally requires a great understanding of the estates' teams' motivations for the divisions. Is it just a traditional, institutional way of operating, which can be altered, or is there a more fundamental, unavoidable reason for the split?

Second, the institute idea rests on the premise that in their spare time, students will opt in to research. The nature of having an opt-in research space means that those who want to stretch themselves on the course or those who prefer research to content-learning will have the chance to excel. This is great for those who come to university curious to learn more. But for those students who, like me, realise only when they do a dissertation in their third year that they would have enjoyed research the whole way through, the opportunity can easily be missed. The other negative consequence of an opt-in programme is that it privileges those who live closest to university or who do not have the time constraints of a part-time job. Furthermore, for those who do extracurricular activities, their time is already limited. It becomes necessary to work hard on the recruitment process and address how students can be encouraged to try it out. One approach, as the IoM trialled this year, is to offer free trial membership. Another would be to run an early seminar session from the institute. However, this would most likely result in department-specific institutes, something that goes against the very nature of the model.

Clearly the institute model could be effective, if implemented in a way that encouraged active engagement from the beginning of a student's degree. With enough space, as campuses expand, creating 'fun' environments where the 'doing' of a subject is integrated with learning is possible.

3. Get out there and do it: creating an identity

The second area I wish to explore is fieldwork, and how this too can be viewed as an effective tool to engage teaching and research in a way that begins to challenge the student–teacher binary. Addressing the pros and cons of fieldwork, I explore how it can be used to create a student 'identity'.

Field trips, such as those used by UCL Archaeology, which gear students towards becoming archaeologists, are essential in creating rich, research-led environments. Reflecting on this in the context of the broader function of the university, it becomes easy to see the benefits of immediately setting the tone of a course: a week-long trip or event to show what being a biologist or being a historian might mean in practice directs students towards being a member of a discipline, rather than learning that discipline. The benefits of overcoming the student–teacher binary identified as part of the institute can thus be used in other forms of learning.

There are issues with fieldwork though, especially for those subjects with high 'basic skill' requirements or health and safety issues. As Professor Liz Shephard of UCL Biosciences asserted at the launch event, research in her field requires a basic set of skills, which must first be taught. The natural answer to this is to teach the skills through the research process, find a level of research (however limited this may be) that can be done based on prior knowledge, and begin with that. At the same time, a natural concern for others are the health and safety implications of immediate fieldwork, but health and safety remains an issue for everyone doing research, at all times. The best way to tackle it is head-on and teach students about the immediate potential issues in this respect as well: research is a complex process that is not just about the immediacy of the experiment or the data collection, but rather the broader decisions and preparations that go into fieldwork. Why not get students to go out there and get stuck in to all aspects of research from the start? As research shows, to be most effective, 'learners must be actively engaged in learning' to achieve deep understanding (Barkley et al. 2005, 10).

Geography is a discipline traditionally associated with trips (Sauer 1956); in my case various British hostel trips where we battled daily with what felt like a year's worth of rain to go and walk up what appeared to be Everest, admiring where glorious glaciers used to exist. For me, geography at school was all about the adventures, the exploration and learning in the field. In a learning environment in which, by comparison, economics was about memorising eight bullets points and linking them to form the 'perfect essay', geography offered salvation because of its research, because as students we were encouraged to find a topic we wanted to know the answer to and to go out and find the answer. It created a very active learning environment, since it was not only a place to perform research but to learn about new concepts or theories (Pawson and Teather 2002). At university this does not need to just be the case for geography: all disciplines can inspire their students through fieldwork and exploration.

A great advantage of fieldwork, as with the institutes, is exposure to other students doing different levels or types of degrees. Pedagogical studies show that the best undergraduate education includes deliberate and extensive interaction between students of all levels and with staff, in an active learning environment (Orndorff 2015). From these relationships 'role models' are formed, as Professor Anthony Smith, UCL Vice-Provost (Education and Student Affairs), argued in his closing statement at the R=T Launch Event. Fieldwork offers the chance for students from different points in their degrees to come together; PhD students who want a chance to teach can lead elements of the course, while Masters students who want more exposure to research environments can do their own research, at a more advanced level, with the undergraduates. This creates partnerships across departments where students see how research can develop and lead to further research opportunities and degrees, as well as an opportunity to stretch the students at the top of the class by challenging them to engage with postgraduates. It can also lead to further partnerships. To offer one example from my own experience in geography, an undergraduate student who was taught and assisted in his research project on a field trip by a first-year PhD student subsequently collaborated with her the following summer, the results of which fed into his third-year dissertation and her PhD thesis.

This is not to say field trips are for all subjects, or that they are not without their own set of problems. Once again, they are often expensive and time-consuming to organise; there can be questions around logistics and how to engage students in a wide range of topics within just a few days' worth of projects. If the point of research-led teaching is to foster the students' innate curiosity, part of fieldwork should be allowing them to pursue their personal project, but this is not always possible. The answer is managing expectations: if students know what to expect of the experience and they understand that the idea is to prepare them to be a member of their discipline, this will help to shape the way they approach it.

There is also the fear of losing sight of the broader objectives, and of fieldwork instead simply mimicking the classroom, becoming another means of achieving a pre-defined series of objectives for meeting certain pre-defined levels of 'success'. While in many cases fieldwork has been shown to get students more involved and more active in their learning, it can also take the fun out of the activity itself, thus reducing research and enquiry to just another means to an end (Hupy et al. 2005). Hupy (2005) suggests that the answer is to bring in an element of competition, and that by using this 'within a field setting proves an excellent means of teaching geographic tools, techniques, and principles' (Hupy 2005, 134). Such an approach echoes the institute model: in these situations, the students get an unprecedented chance to shine and 'be the best', not through tests but though ingenuity and genuine and deep engagement with their subject.

The alternative would be to flip the idea on its head: instead of having a week pre-course for fieldwork, have an intensive week pre-course for the basic skills, loading students with the necessary knowledge to then allow the remainder of the curriculum to be taught through research. It is about challenging the underlying premise of higher education. Teaching should not just be about imparting knowledge, a transfer from teacher to student. Instead, it should be about discovery and learning from one another and from the situations the students are put in. As Mark reminded those present at the launch event, teaching is about creating the perfect environment to foster knowledge development.

Field trips can be exhilarating: they can be a space in which students and academics finally breach the binary and where a student realises just how much of a 'Historian' or 'Chemist' they really are and could be. They are a place where students from different years and at different points in their academic environment have the chance to learn and research together – just as the IoM offers on-site. In this respect, field trips could be a solution to some of the problems of institutes. On the other hand, they raise problems with funding, they can require skills that students lack before the trips begin, and the experience could reinforce disciplinary boundaries rather than move towards the interdisciplinary approach the IoM advocates and creates.

4. When it all goes wrong – and how to fix it

The field trip and institute-based approaches to learning are very effective in integrating a research agenda into the teaching process. They blur the boundaries between teacher and student and foster a more creative and engaging learning experience. However, aside from their individual problems (which have potential solutions as outlined above), they are both subject to three key challenges: how to assess the student's performance, weekly variation and broader applicability.

Research is not always successful and this is an important part of the learning experience. However, given the output-focused nature of higher education and the need to continually assess a student's progress through formative, summative and exam-based assessments, when research fails to prove a hypothesis or goes completely wrong, how can we assess the student during field trips or in an institute setting?

Instinctively, the answer is to design assessment that measures how well the student dealt with the failings, what caused them and how the research methods were applied or not applied. But in some situations, marking criteria are prohibitive, often requiring data collection or successful experiments for analysis and conclusion marks. The reality is that even when some failures are arbitrary or beyond the control of the student, there is a subconscious acknowledgement of their failings, as well as a sense of failure on their part. Students are under increasing pressure to 'succeed', and so in output-focused curricula, research can place undue pressure on students, for whom things outside their control dictate their grade and feeling of self-worth.

A viable and effective alternative to traditional methods of assessment is portfolio-based, as research shows across disciplines (Defina 1992; Yancey 1999; Hamp-Lyons and Condon 2000; Harris and Sandra 2001; Song and August 2002; Chang, 2008). At the IoM, Mark Miodownik uses portfolios, as they can constantly evolve, recording student activities and research. Portfolios ensure that all stages of the process can be assessed equally and that, even when things go wrong, students have all the marks they would have for the events prior to it, and can illustrate the choices they make going forward to get the remaining marks. Developing a portfolio is also a great way to reflect on the process as the student develops, and can encourage them to pursue something 'beyond' or 'out of the box'.

There remain problems with portfolios though, as shown in both the reality of the IoM and existing research. Studies evaluating the effectiveness of portfolio-based assessment for postgraduates in medical schools in the UK show there are a number of very practical elements that must be considered, primarily the need for strong institutional support (Tochel et al. 2009). Furthermore, portfolio management and assessment is time-consuming and requires the academic to constantly observe progress, checking in with the student and ensuring they are updating it as they go along. This is where Graduate Teaching Assistants (GTAs) could come in and be used for weekly checks, making sure the student is on track. Again, this speaks back to achieving a more effective faculty where there is cross-degree and more student–teacher interaction: in this case giving GTAs more responsibility and allowing them to be effective 'go-betweens'.

One potential problem is weekly variation in both students' and teachers' timetables. The nature of ten-week terms with different people doing different courses, affiliate students and interdisciplinary programmes, creates huge week-by-week variations. This is further exacerbated by personal commitments: weekly away football matches, for example, or working up to an art exhibition that requires extensive organisation in the final few days. Therefore, asking students to contribute every week could be an issue. This could be solved with consistent, periodic marking, instead of weekly check-ins. If the students had half-termly checks by the course convener, giving everyone some flexibility, issues surrounding termly fluxes in workloads would be overcome. Another problem is the intensive nature of checking a portfolio. Since it is part of an ongoing project, it would require the academic to check and return it almost immediately and, again, they too have other commitments and are often used to working to different deadlines.

The portfolio approach could be a great solution for core courses. It would force a more research-focused, student-orientated approach to learning and reduce problems with experimental failure. It requires a change of mindset, though, with both academics and students needing to prioritise the continual updating and research involved with this course over others, which perhaps should be the case with core courses anyway.

5. Taking it to the next level

Research-based teaching, which inspires students to excel, to pursue discovery and to look for answers, can have incredible impacts beyond their degree. As the IoM has shown, it can lead to company formation, new products being made and new grants received. We need to take this as an example of how students can drive change within and beyond the university.

There remains a central challenge to the institute approach, and that is the dilemma posed by having a research space that exists outside the taught curriculum, and therefore has limited impact on the wider university teaching environment. Can the portfolio approach discussed above and the example set out by the IoM, be reconciled with growing pressure on output-focused results to create a programme where the student has the chance to explore ideas that interest them in a safe, learning environment? Previously at UCL, students have worked throughout their second year to contribute to a departmental project: each year a new cohort engages with the project and eventually there is published output where every student involved is a named author. This necessitates a research-focused learning situation, which waits until the student has learned basic skills in their first year but without disturbing their final-year dissertation. Crucially, it also gives them something to show for it at the end: they can hold the publication and know they were part of it.

Alternatively, the project could be run across different years, so for the duration of a student's degree they are engaging with one extended research project. In the first year this could be structured around a basic grounding or understating that gives them the necessary skills to do more research, perhaps similar to the MPhil year for a PhD (i.e. probationary period of many doctoral programmes in the UK): a vital part of the research process, but one that would not require a huge amount of prior knowledge. The issue that arises is the breadth of disciplines and changing interests: university is also about developing as a person and exploring interests, and students are likely to change their preferred area of study during a three-year course. Furthermore, the breadth of subjects that students might want to pursue could make supervision or structuring classes around it challenging. Building on this, these research projects could be structured around the departments' stated research clusters. In this way students could add to broader disciplinary debates, stay on top of current academic thought and help shape it themselves.

6. Conclusion

Looking forward, the model provided by the Institute of Making is a viable option for many institutes. For those with the space and the enthused academics, it is a way to show students that learning can be fun, and for students with different backgrounds to learn to respect one another's respective skill set. In this way the IoM offers some important point for any R=T learning situation: the student–teacher binary must be broken down; students of all disciplinary backgrounds can add to a project; and anyone can be involved in research, if they want to be.

Going forward, the most important thing is to take these lessons and learn from them. In this chapter, I have tried to demonstrate how there are ways of addressing the potential flaws, and finding a way of making institutes accessible and attractive for students, irrespective of incomes, academic dreams and extracurricular activities.

References

Barkley, E. F., Cross, K. P. and Major, C. H. (eds). 2005. *Collaborative Learning Techniques: A Handbook for College Faculty*. San Francisco: Jossey-Bass.

Chang, C. C. 2008. Enhancing self-perceived effects using Web-based portfolio assessment. *Computers in Human Behavior* 24, 1753–71.

Defina, Allan A. 1992. *Portfolio Assessment: Getting Started*. New York: Scholastic Professional Books.

Hamp-Lyons, L. and Condon, W. 2000. *Assessing the Portfolio: Principles for Practice, Theory, and Research*. Cresskill, NJ: Hampton.

Harris, S. and Sandra, M. 2001. Portfolio use in two principal programs. *Rural Educator* 23, 19–23.

Hupy. J. 2005. Teaching geographic concepts through fieldwork and competition. *Journal of Geography*, 131–5.

Hupy, J. P., Aldrich, S. P., Schaetzl, R. J., Varnakovida, P., Arima, E. Y., Bookout, J. R., Wiangwang, N., Campos, A. L. and McKnight, K. P. 2005. Mapping soils, vegetation, and landforms: An integrative physical geography field experience. *Professional Geographer* 57, 438–51.

Orndorff, H. 2015. Collaborative note-taking: The impact of cloud computing on classroom performance. *International Journal of Teaching and Learning in Higher Education* 27(3), 340–51.

Pawson, E. and K. Teather. 2002. 'Geographical Expeditions': Assessing the benefits of a student-driven field-work method. *Journal of Geography in Higher Education* 26, 275–89.

Sauer, C. O. 1956. The agency of man on the earth. In Thomas, W. L. (ed.) *Man's Role in Changing the Face of the Earth*, pp. 49–69. Chicago: University of Chicago Press.

Song, Bailin and August, B. 2002. Using portfolio to assess the writing of ESL students: A powerful alternative? *Journal of Second Language Writing* 11, 49–72.

Tochel, C., Haig, Alex, Hesketh, Anne, Cadzow, Ann, Beggs, Karen, Colthart, Iain and Peacock, Heather. 2009. The effectiveness of portfolios for post-graduate assessment and education: BEME Guide No 12. *Medical Teacher* 31, 299–318.

Yancey, K. B. 1999. Looking back as we look forward: Historicizing writing assessment. *College Composition and Communication* 50, 483–503.

Links to the R=T Framework

Lauren Clark
UCL Institute of Education

- One key element of this chapter is how fieldwork can foster the development of a professional identity, by interacting with more experienced members of the discipline (PhD students, academics). Frances mentions that by engaging in fieldwork early on in their educational career, students could see what it is like to be a member of a discipline, rather than just learning the discipline. This kind of identity development could also happen in an institute setting; however, the cross-disciplinary nature of the institute could equally prevent the reinforcement of disciplinary boundaries – a potential downside to identity development. A further key message is that students will become aware of how what they are learning in the classroom, the lab, and in fieldwork is important to their future and to the mastery of their discipline. This helps to encourage students to engage more with their studies, especially on issues that might not seem as engaging (such as safety protocols or ethical concerns).

- The use of fieldwork and institutes as a way to master research skills embodies all of the key opportunities in the framework. Fieldwork (1) promotes interdisciplinary work; (2) provides a space for innovative research through collaboration with other staff and students from other disciplines; (3) promotes the development of research skills early on in student careers; (4) challenges the student–teacher dichotomy and helps staff and students to learn from each other; and (5) helps make the relevance of what students are learning more apparent by emphasising connections with the real world.

  The main challenges lie in the lack of resources, especially time and funding, and in the case of institutes, space (3). Another significant barrier is that of the current approach to curriculum and assessment design in British Higher Education (5). Student-led research in the Institute or in the field can be difficult to assess and give feedback on, making it problematic in the current system. Frances suggests using portfolio-based assessment, but this requires an even larger and on-going time commitment from academics, as well as a change of mindset. However, I believe the benefits of integrating institute projects and fieldwork into courses far outweighs the cost to students and academics, and the time/work burden can also be shared by PhD students (as suggested by Frances).

- Challenging the traditional relationship between staff and students is essential for all research-based education that involves student–staff partnerships. In my opinion, this is an overarching principle from the framework that needs to be appreciated and addressed. In order for research-based education to be successful, educators and students need to be willing to push the boundaries of what is 'normal', what is easy to assess, what takes the least amount of time and effort, and what they take for granted as being the right way to do things. Higher Education is not just about getting a qualification, or getting a grade – it is about gaining knowledge and experience. Educators should have that in mind when they design courses and programmes. As Frances says, 'Teaching should not be just about imparting knowledge, a transfer from teacher to student. Instead it should be about discovery and learning from one another and from the situations the students are put in'. Encouraging more equal student–staff partnerships can inspire both staff and students to be more creative and passionate about their work.

2.6
Creating space for active learning
(Opportunities from) using technology in research-based education

Eirini Gallou

UCL Institute for Sustainable Heritage, and The UCL Bartlett Faculty of the Built Environment

with Professor Peter Abrahams

Warwick Medical School, University of Warwick

This chapter deals with the challenges of using technology to enhance the education process and the student learning experience – not just to replace the teacher by technological or digital gimmicks. The secret of this process is to base it on the student's active participation in the development of their own learning tools. Eirini rightly stresses the possible trap of replacing the old human teacher with the new computer machine but notes that the actual thinking process needs to be different and actively involve the student in the development of this new digital material. Examples are given of interactivity in science, medicine and architecture where the new learning process might engage sounds, vision and 3D processing, and even 'hot-off-the-press' 3D printing. Other disciplines have used video of speeches, sounds from music, or scenes of theatre productions, all of which can be made into serious gaming programs with interactive responses which cause the student to get actively involved in the end product of their discipline within a real-world environment. As she mentions, hands-on learning in an experimental manner, even using the student as a peer teacher, is the aim of using all the tools of technology to make a stimulating exciting interaction – which often will take many times longer than just preparing a simple lecture. However, the rewards for both student and teacher are greater, especially if applied through an experimental learning cycle as illustrated by Eirini.

As a professor well past my 'sell-by date' and a 'digital immigrant', it is intellectually tough keeping up with all the new advances in technology, so using one's young 'digital native' students to help develop these new programs for their own education makes common sense. The teacher becomes student but the student becomes self-teacher or peer teacher, adding to their layers of knowledge. It is a win–win situation for all within higher education.

Professor Peter Abrahams

1. Introduction

The R=T initiative has offered me and many other students the opportunity to get involved in discussions around research-based education at UCL through a series of masterclasses, connecting researchers and teachers with the student experience. The theme of the R=T Tech event – the use of multimedia and online platforms – forms the basis of this chapter, which looks at exploring innovative and effective ways to link technology, education and research.

The thoughts that follow are inspired by the presentation by Professor Peter Abrahams of Warwick University, who shared his thoughts on research-based education in the digital age through examples of his own teaching in anatomy and medicine. They also seek to express some of the ideas from the subsequent panel discussion with UCL staff and students, and of course incorporate personal reflections based on my own experience in engineering and museum studies.

My current PhD research, in the interdisciplinary field of sustainable heritage, places me at the intersection of humanities and STEM studies, challenging my practice as both a student and future teaching assistant, caught between two different value systems. It is through the lens of this interdisciplinary background that I explore the question posed at the start regarding the potential of technology to enhance active learning in higher education.

2. The technology challenge: creating new forms of experience and enabling active learning

Both the power and weakness of technology lie in the way it can be used. As with any tool created by humans to improve a way a process can be realised (usually by replacing labour with mechanics), it can certainly augment the time a lecturer can focus on the material itself, rather than making the material more easily accessible or perceivable for the students.

Twenty-first-century blended learning models advocate a mixed use of traditional and new teaching and learning modes, combining face-to-face with online learning. However, the power of the new modes of learning is attenuated due to the limited opportunities that the existing built learning environment infrastructure can offer (Mitchell 2003).

It has been argued that misuse of technology in a classroom can suppress or hinder student learning (Grasha and Yangarber-Hicks 2000; Koehler et al. 2007; Koehler and Mishra 2009). Therefore, instructors need to think about the relevance or appropriateness of using a particular technology in their classroom so that the focus remains on manipulating ideas rather than technological tools (Brown et al. 2004; Kuda-Malwathumullage 2015).

The dilemma remains in setting the limits of how to utilise technology in higher education. Its role can undermine traditional lecture techniques, the human power of which cannot be easily contested.

On the one hand, some researchers argue that technology is merely a tool for accomplishing teaching and learning goals for instructors and students (Grasha and Yangarber-Hick 2000; Miller et al. 2000). Others advocate incorporating technology into teachers' knowledge base, generating a special knowledge (Koehler et al. 2007; Koehler and Mishra 2009). In any case, the debate is not around replacing tutors but about supporting their role – in the way a device may support how we accomplish a task.

Technology-enabled active learning (TEAL) is an innovative approach applied at the Massachusetts Institute of Technology (MIT), providing a successful alternative to the potential of technology to enhance active learning in universities.[1]

TEAL describes a research project in MIT Physics freshmen classes, aiming at delivering greater learning gains than the traditional lecture format through the use of interactive engagement (which first appeared in the 1990s). A variety of assessment techniques used by TEAL have proven the effectiveness of interactive engagement across a range of student backgrounds. The teaching methods used in the TEAL classroom managed to double the average normalised learning gains for low-, intermediate- and high-scoring students when compared to traditional instruction. The method followed in such a class typically incorporates lecture, recitation and hands-on experiments in one presentation.

Instructors deliver twenty-minute lectures allowing filtration with discussion questions, visualisations and pencil-and-paper exercises. Students' learning is reinforced by using animated simulations designed to help them visualise concepts and carry out experiments in groups during class.

This successful, pioneering example in physics has affected similar teaching curricula. Looking at the broader picture, since MIT first launched the concept in 2003, some emerging TEAL models have proliferated outside of the US (for example, CDIO (conceive, design, implement, operate) in the Faculty of Engineering, University of Melbourne; the doctoral engineering design studio at the University of new South Wales), which are still in the early stages of evaluation.[2] Although the original TEAL model was launched to rejuvenate the teaching of Physics 1 at MIT, subsequent versions of it have proliferated in disciplines such as geology, chemistry, engineering, education and architecture. It is in engineering that the most advances have been made, and this is largely because of the need for engineers to have a wide range of competencies that cannot be assessed solely in the examination room. This observation highlights the fact that opportunities are not equally distributed in different disciplines. Some environments can offer a more fertile ground for technology-enhanced learning to flourish.

Having discussed these basic challenges and the TEAL model suggestions, its role in enhancing active learning can now be delineated by considering a number of case studies from different disciplines.

3. Enhancing active learning through technology: some case studies

I include examples in this section from teaching practice to clarify ways of employing technology for enhancing active learning. There are two major sources of inspiration. First, the work of Professor Abrahams: the ideas presented in the Masterclass can be thought of as inspiring and exemplary for the discipline of medicine. Second, my personal experiences in creative and cultural studies both in and outside UCL (specifically, museum studies, UCL's Institute of Making (IOM), as well as my background in architectural engineering). These examples are meant to provide a canvas for comparing initiatives with the lessons learned from TEAL, and to juxtapose the differences between disciplines and priorities in teaching and learning served by technology.

3.1 Examples from Professor Abrahams's work

These three examples from Professor Abrahams's practice illustrate ways technology may enhance active learning in the classroom and out of it within a research-based curriculum.

First, through his postgraduate teaching work, Professor Abrahams uses 3D printing to create models of human organs.

The building process helps in deconstructing the nature of the organs, increasing the possibilities for students to learn anatomical features prior to building the model. In addition, students can implement their existing knowledge of anatomy through actively engaging with the process of creation, exploration, inquiry and object-based learning. Finally, it allows more abstract and difficult medical/scientific concepts to be explained through the use of a physical object, so can be particularly useful for teaching postgraduate medical students. This sequence resembles the circle of experiential learning presented here earlier in theory, in a well-linked prototype.

Technology is used as an incubator for interconnections between different stages of the learning process.

Second, Abrahams combines some of the skills and research methods applied in different disciplines. The interdisciplinary nature of the project and the insertion of research aspects (for example, research knowledge on improving current digital production of organs) familiarises students with new skills, providing a real-life and active experience. Thus, it increases the opportunities for different types of students to engage with the inquiry-based process and thus increase their learning by participating in this experiential learning activity. This case also suggests ways to incorporate students as partners in education: getting postgraduate students to create educational material is a rather illuminating example of how students can make the best research workers. The material can be then used for teaching purposes and reflect the expertise coming from the faculty itself, enabling a higher appreciation of the research realised within the institution and transcending disciplines. Students benefit from taking the researcher's role, with all it entails. Interdisciplinary research subjects and collaborations are fostered.

Technology is used as an incubator for interconnections between different disciplines and levels of the curriculum.

Third, Abrahams' work illustrates another way of applying technology in facilitating teaching, and promoting active learning the classroom.

X-rays, CT scans and angiograms are three ways of visualising human anatomy. Real anatomic sections, matched together, can help to provide a holistic understanding of the human body for medical students. The students can test themselves, participate by entering games combining the three technologies, and then compare how different parts of the human body look on an X-ray or a CT scan – a rare opportunity to learn through an innovative way.

To take this further, a teacher could provide a structured way of assessing this knowledge beyond the classroom. For example, by making an iTunes book, a teacher can enable access from anywhere, increasing the independence of students and possibly expanding the audience. Another part of Professor Abrahams' work points out how using multimedia experiences could assist in explaining difficult- to-grasp medical concepts to students. For example, by creating songs and employing lyrics with medical terminology, he experiments with stimulating students' minds and leaving them with unforgettable memories. He is creating an invisible process through which experience is turned into knowledge over a larger period of time through assimilation. This practice enables active experimentation and students 'learning by doing': students create songs themselves and then practise them immediately, having a concrete learning experience (i.e. how two stages of experiential learning are connected, following D. Kolb's model).

Technological means are used to enhance visualisation of hard-to-grasp concepts, making knowledge accessible in many ways. Multimedia's ability to create stronger learning experiences is used beneficially. Variation fosters creativity, increasing students' progress.

These examples showcase multimedia as a means of interactive engagement in the class. But is this applicable to all subjects? It would be interesting to consider whether other disciplines could provide similar case studies focusing on activities that could be embedded in the traditional classroom. As an engineering student, I am aware how creative practices can bring something intriguing into class and stimulate participation from less active students. Technology can certainly provide variety in the means to achieve that.

The role of the tutor, however, remains crucial in providing cohesion between the information imparted and the experiences the students engage with. As Professor Abrahams explained in the R=T Tech event:

> You have to think: how can I make this memorable? By bringing in everything that is around the subject, not [trying] to teach the didactic bits – they can go and get them [from] the web. Make it a story, make it an exciting story. Because as a teacher . . . your passion, your enthusiasm actually does more than any fact you can get to the student. Ever.

The element that needs to be emphasised is the passion of the tutor when encouraging his students to experiment with technological means and be creative in classroom. It is the first spark to support initiatives that the curriculum may encourage further, like co-creating material for the classroom, combining evaluation and teaching.

Where the teacher's role may also prove powerful – in the process of employing technology-based learning activities – is in linking disciplines, creating new opportunities that would direct research efforts towards harnessing the skills of specialised (research) students to enhance the learning of students in a variety of other disciplines.

And the role of students? Students can encourage or ask for such projects and gain a collaborative role in managing such partnerships. Active learning gains more power this way, projected out of the classroom and into the arena of research.

Of course, an assumption underpinning these kind of initiative is a well-linked institutional network of facilities that supports student–staff collaboration. Two examples from UCL Museum Studies initiatives are illustrative and offer a perspective from another discipline.

3.2 Examples from UCL Museum Studies

The UCL Museums & Collections (M&C) department offers many opportunities for applying object-based learning, especially in faculties linked with the museums; Museum Studies and the Institute of Education principally organise courses based on M&C's cooperation. The role of information and communications technology (ICT) in museums allows, for example, interactive displays to present tailored information to audiences and permit virtual access to artefacts held in museum stores. MA Museum Studies students familiarise themselves with both real-life practice and the latest research by using conservation technology as a means to understand the properties of various objects within the UCL M&C.

For example, the recent student exhibition, 'We Need to Talk: Connecting Through Technology' (created by MA Museum Studies students at the Institute of Archaeology and displayed at the A.G. Leventis Gallery from May 2015 until April 2016), provided multiple opportunities by having technology as a theme. It gave students an active role in exploring and presenting technologies that people have used to communicate with each other in different periods of time, reflecting on their discipline and practice using this diachronic approach. The project's Twitter page[3] shows how state-of-the-art technological applications in documenting archaeology were presented and proves how the subject gave a lot of people the opportunity for creative teamwork (i.e. images and material produced, such as wearable tech). In a research-intensive university such as UCL, collections have to keep pace with cutting-edge innovations and new discoveries. Objects on their own help to develop the important skill of drawing conclusions based on an examination of evidence, paying attention to the limitations and reliability of that evidence. They are also ideal for generating group and class discussion.

Technology can be used as a theme for connecting disciplines. It provides opportunities for interdisciplinary research for all levels (undergraduates and postgraduates), expanding the skills students gain by being an active part of those projects. It can provide knowledge on the latest scientific applications, increasing interest and inspiration for the further research accomplishments of young student–researchers.

The second example from UCL Museum Studies is a 2016 exhibition that was co-organised by the IOM, UCL research personnel and researchers and students of Museum Studies and Chemistry on the use of materials. The exhibition illustrated the double use of materials: for industry and for the scientific research-enabled cooperation of different disciplines (Chemistry department, Museum Studies, History of Technology). At the same time, it proved to be engaging for wider audiences. The educational aspect of this exhibition was supported by providing real objects for viewing – from the IOM collection and some of the faculties' own machinery/historic tools, items normally inaccessible to the public. Scientific explanations of the processes of material treatments were combined with lay-language descriptions, providing an opportunity for the participants (research students) to practise an important aspect of a researcher's role: public engagement and knowledge-sharing.

Technology can be the initiator of partnerships and a useful tool for realizing public engagement by researchers and students. Employing research results and presenting them efficiently to wider audiences, they exchange roles with their teachers creating knowledge instead of consuming it.

A third interesting project featured recently in UCL's object-based learning webpage is from the Department of English Language and Literature. Dr Chris Laoutaris used the UCL Art Museum to help his students understand Shakespeare plays outside the closed context of their own field, accessing the museum's online anatomy pack.[4] His experience underlines the multiplicity of existing opportunities and material within UCL that can be combined in new, imaginative ways, stimulating more than one of the five senses of students. Audio museum guide material can be combined with anatomical drawings and text reading in the classroom. The impact of such initiatives' could be extended through experimentation by the teaching assistants participating in them, and by encouraging the use of the latest technological improvements to equipment used in art and heritage conservation.

Technology can provide multi-sensorial experiences by increasing the means by which information is acquired during teaching and thus increase the chance of creating memorable classes.

Realising these initiatives as exhibitions underlines the role of partnerships in turning ideas into reality. The exhibitions are a means of engaging the wider university community with the interdisciplinary research-based projects being undertaken – and inspiring students.

3.3 A final example

Finally, as a comparative example, I would like to quote my personal experience as an architectural engineering student.

Disciplines like engineering have become increasingly digitised over the last decades, with newly designed research programmes based on technological advances promoting a digitised way of teaching. This teaching mode may differ in many ways from that adopted by more traditional universities – those that foster the historic valuation of the built environment over practical skills. In this sense, architecture provides a good example of embedding technology in teaching and enhancing active learning. Advances in 3D printing and laser-cutting technologies have informed the way both professionals and academics perform their duties, and given rise to the more interactive teaching found in design studios. Students get hands-on experiences in laser-cutting labs, increasing their inquiry-based knowledge assimilation. At the same time, opportunities are provided to share skills, to become technical instructors and develop both academically and professionally.

However, students and staff all have to be vigilant. In an era of constant adaptation, it is not only the means of teaching that change. The disciplines themselves are continuously being redefined through that process.

4. Conclusion: what about all together?

The themes/conclusions drawn from the case studies show multiple ways and benefits from applying technology to assist active learning in different disciplines. They also showcase technology's power in enhancing aspects of research-based learning in the curriculum, such as interdisciplinary and cross-disciplinary learning.

Students and staff will always have distinct motivations and rationales around working together. The differing perceptions of one another's roles and tasks surely affects their motivation and their active engagement in the process of teaching and learning. Technology-based learning activities could act as a unifying platform for dealing with differences between professors and students, enhancing not only learning but also communication and collaboration.

Building on the R=T initiative and the UCL Connected Curriculum, voices coming from both sides should be heard. We can only benefit from the use of technology if it is used as an interactive 'in-between' zone, as a common teaching language between different disciplines, and also as a means familiar to both teachers and students – a platform that will enable role-exchanges within universities. Looking towards long-term changes in teaching and learning, the successful application of technology within the curriculum requires us to embrace change while also respecting tradition. This means we need dialogue if we are to reach the desired balance for both students and teachers.

Notes

1. See http://web.mit.edu/edtech/casestudies/teal.html
2. See: http://www.oecd.org/education/innovation-education/centreforeffectivelearningenvironmentscele/45565315.pdf
3. https://twitter.com/IoAExhibition15
4. http://www.ucl.ac.uk/teaching-learning/case-studies-news/object-based-learning/anatomical-drawings-shakespeare

References

Brown, A. H., Benson, B. and Uhde, A. P. 2004. You're doing what with technology? An exposé on 'Jane Doe' College Professor. *College Teaching* 52, 100–4.

Grasha, A. F. and Yangarber-Hicks, N. 2000. Integrating teaching styles and learning styles with instructional technology. *College Teaching* 48(1), 2–10.

Koehler, M. J. and Mishra, P. 2009. What is technological pedagogical content knowledge? *Contemporary Issues in Technology and Teacher Education* 9, 60–70.

Koehler, M. J., Mishra, P. and Yahya, K.. 2007. Tracing the development of teacher knowledge in a design seminar: Integrating content, pedagogy and technology. *Computers and Education* 49, 740–62.

Kuda-Malwathumullage, C. P. 2015. Impact of technology-infused interactive learning environments on college professors' instructional decisions and practices. MS (Master of Science) thesis, University of Iowa. http://ir.uiowa.edu/etd/1867 [Accessed 16 June 2016].

Miller, J. W., Martineau, L. P. and Clark. R.C. 2000. Technology infusion and higher education: Changing teaching and learning. *Innovative Higher Education* 24, 227–41.

Mitchell, W. 2003. 21st Century Learning Environments. Presentation at a workshop on new learning environments at Queensland University of Technology in conjunction with K. Fisher.

Links to the R=T Framework

Christine Plastow

Department of Greek and Latin, UCL

- Eirini's chapter explores the key role of technology in approaching research-based education, in promoting engaged and active learning. Technology can be implemented to make research activities interactive, and in some cases, such as 3D printing, to allow students to interact physically with research objects. This allows staff to make their own research more accessible to students as well as encouraging students to participate actively in the research process, and even in some cases to create teaching materials for future classes. Students can take on a tutor's role among their peers, leading research-based learning activities. Staff and students become researchers working together with objects and technology to create learning through research, moving away from the traditional model of teacher as active provider of knowledge and student as passive recipient. Technology should not replace traditional learning methods, but be used alongside them, in order to augment engaged and active learning and create a more fulfilling experience for staff and students.

- The implementation of this message faces several challenges. As outlined in the joint framework, a lack of resources may be an issue: technology can be expensive and funding difficult to secure, particularly in fields where it is not viewed as 'essential' such as in my own field of Classics. As Eirini mentions, some fields will be more receptive to advances in technology than others. Students may require training to use new technologies which would necessitate additional teaching hours, and there may be the danger of damage to expensive equipment.

A primary benefit of the message would be the reduction in planning time for staff able to rely on technology for a portion of their teaching, allowing them to focus more on content and research-based learning. The active and engaged learning encouraged by technology transfers out of the classroom, promoting greater academic engagement and enthusiasm for the subject and learning and research more generally. The use of practical technologies keeps students and staff at the cutting edge of their fields, and prepares students for careers where these technologies are used every day. The use of new technologies leads to innovative research which is beneficial for staff as well as students, giving them wider opportunities for their own research.

- Staff and students should work together to find successful ways to engage with new technologies, as appropriate to their own field of study. Staff can facilitate students in working with technology in ways which not only promote focused, engaged research-based education, but also allows both students and staff to reflect on learning methods, and encourages students to take on the role of the tutor among their peers. Staff should make technology-based research accessible to students, and students should be willing to learn to use it productively and engage with the benefits it offers. The emphasis should be on the partnership throughout the process: although the staff member may lead the group, the students should be encouraged to engage in the selection and implementation of technology in research as well as its use, to promote a more inclusive and productive research-based learning environment.

2.7
Learning-oriented assessment

Sayara Saliyeva
Department of Chemical Engineering, UCL

with Professor Jeremy Levesley
Department of Mathematics, University of Leicester

Sayara's work is a valuable addition to the argument that research and teaching are symbiotic in higher education. In particular, it focuses on how the development of research skills in students requires a change in assessment practices. It argues that assessment strategies that encourage learning, rather than just measure learning, are crucial to the development of the research-focused graduates required in the knowledge economy. It explains why the engagement of all stakeholders in student outcomes (e.g. students, academics, governments, employers) will lead to processes that develop life skills rather than narrowly focused 'academic' skills. It introduces stratified assessment as a paradigm in which threshold capabilities can be recognised.

Professor Jeremy Levesley

1. Introduction into the R=T context

Currently, in higher education systems across the world, as a remnant of the industrial economy, we can observe an imbalance in the favouring of research over teaching (Shin et al. 2015). Over the decades, governmental encouragement for high-impact research has resulted in the establishment of institutional policies where both the promotion and evaluation of academics are mainly concerned with research output indicators. In turn, this has shifted academic staff's interest within the education sector, devoting more time to research and less time to teaching activities. This has led to complaints from students, and has especially become an issue for UK higher education institutions since the recent rise in tuition fees. This, in turn, raises a fundamental question: are universities citadels for research or teaching?

Hattie and Marsh (1996) indicated the need for developing and improving synergy between research and teaching. Almost two decades later, the UK Government green paper, 'Fulfilling our Potential: Teaching Excellence, Social Mobility and Student Choice' (BIS 2015a), set the scene for the biggest shift in the national framework for higher education in England for a generation, outlining the proposal for the Teaching Excellence Framework (TEF). It was acknowledged by the Higher Education Academy that there is a need for institutions, particularly research-intensive universities, to reconsider their commitment to improve the student learning experience. By recognising teaching as the core of academic work, and to maintain and improve the quality of teaching, students are encouraged to take advantage of universities' cutting-edge research.

Griffiths (2004) developed a framework identifying the types of links between teaching and research, and this was further developed by Healey (2005) and Jenkins et al. (2007). The research–teaching/learning nexus as experienced by students can be research-tutored, research-based, research-led and research-oriented. In a research-led environment, students' learning is mainly concerned with subject knowledge informed by research findings. The course content mainly consists of the current disciplinary research interests of staff, and teaching is focused on information transmission. In the research-oriented environment, students' learning is about research processes, with the emphasis on knowledge production and development of a research ethos through teaching. In the research-tutored environment, students' learning is via group discussions and evaluation of research findings, taking a critical-thinking approach. In the research-based environment, students' learning as researchers is predominantly designed around inquiry-based activities in a dialogue teaching mode.

Research-based learning enables opportunities for meaningful learning by encouraging students to take part in the research process of their discipline and engage actively and creatively with questions and open-ended problems. It is broadly acknowledged (J M Consulting 2000; Elton 2001; Aitken and Tatebe 2014) that 'R benefits T' and the research–teaching nexus should be incorporated into university mission statements and/or strategic plans and curricular if the quality of students' learning is to meet the needs of the knowledge economy.

2. The importance of assessment and feedback

This chapter looks at the 'assessment' part of the issue. The *Oxford Learner's Dictionary* gives the following definition of assessment: 'an opinion or a judgment about someone or something that has been thought about very carefully' (Oxford University Press, 2016). Assessment has a direct effect on students' futures by affecting many aspects of their education, including student grades and further progress. But the validity and reliability of assessment are often challenged (Bloxham 2009) and the mix of its purposes (e.g. certification, feedback to students and teacher, students' learning motivation, diagnostics level of understanding and course reputability) makes it hard to put into perspective.

Originally assessment in higher education consisted of formative assessment comprising peer/critic review and discussion. As the education system in the last century underwent a shift from elite to mass education, being driven to satisfy the economic imperative of the Industrial Revolution (Robinson 2010), higher education objectives focused on training the managers of industry and giving researchers the means to find new materials to feed into the engine of progress. This, in turn, caused the deviation from a learning-centred focus, instead pushing examinations and various forms of summative assessment to the core of higher education, serving the purposes of certification and selection.

These led to our current situation, where there is an over-emphasis on the measurement of learning often at the expense of the assessment for learning (Price et al. 2008). 'Assessment defines what students regard as important, how they spend their time and how they come to see themselves as students and then as graduates' (Brown et al. 1997, 12). It must be acknowledged that our current system of assessment, which focuses on marks and grades, is not working. A greater emphasis on assessment *for* learning, rather than an assessment *of* learning, is required to achieve a holistic sense of learning. Clearly, there is a need to change the method of assessment if we want to change what and how students learn.

3. Assessment embedded in learning

Havnes (2013) argues that assessment in learning needs to include the institutional, cultural and epistemic cultures and contexts. Hammerness (2006) holds the view that the key problems of assessment embedded in learning are fragmentation of the knowledge base; theory and practice; and research-based and experience-based knowledge. This is in opposition to the heterogeneous and integrated nature of knowledge that is a requirement from employers as well. Havnes (2013) also argues that there should be a particular focus on assessment practices and students' learning from the perspective of what matters in professional practice beyond higher education. But, at the moment, such courses are the exception rather than the rule.

Furthermore, the question is how could assessment aid students' learning and the development of professionalism by supporting the learning of curricular components and also serve to connect different modules, subject areas, contexts, theories and practices to provide holistic learning? The gap is caused by both professional practice problem-solving and academia being focused on knowledge at the core of learning objectives. Subject knowledge should act as a tool in professional practice. It should be integrated as part of in-class activities via perception, interpretation and assessment of multi-layered problems. Knowledge should undergo the shift from being an object of learning to becoming a tool for attending to 'the true object' of professional practice (Havnes 2013). Thus, the assessment should be fit for purpose, linking assessment methods that are designed to meet students' learning needs. Generally, there is a need for alignment between teaching, learning and assessment (Biggs 1996). In other words, we need to pay attention to assessment in curricular development.

McPhun (2010) defines integrated assessment as 'providing an engaging and creative learning platform that closely links to the reality graduates will experience in the workforce: a process that combines and blends the learning outcomes from multiple topics into a series of streamlined, realistic, employment-focused activities; effective ways to synthesise topics into a coherent and contextualised framework using complementary skill and knowledge sets' (McPhun 2010, 1). This requires assessments to take place throughout the programme, allowing the student to apply newly gained knowledge and develop competencies. Explicit subject and procedural knowledge-measurement should be blended into seamless assessment components that occur genuinely from multiple sources, including lecturer observation, documentary evidence, panel feedback, and peer and self-assessment.

Students undergoing integrated assessment perform qualitatively at a different level, since they are exposed to an open-ended development and are working on multiple objectives matching real-world requirements (Heywood 2000). Creativity and 'outside-the-box thinking' focus on graduate success. This should address the problem identified by Burgess (2007, 5): 'It [the UK honours degree] cannot describe, and therefore does not do full justice to, the range of knowledge, skills, experience and attributes of a graduate in the 21st century.' To develop such a programme, one should identify common topics or skills, complementary knowledge or performance outcomes and opportunities for integration.

Eraut and du Boulay (2000) define working competence as 'the ability to perform the tasks and roles required to the expected standard', that is, skills or knowledge leading to improved performance. The competence evidence collected by the assessor is challenged against the benchmarks provided by the unit standards that are matched to the national professional institutions' qualifications and requirements of the industry. It is based on the sum of all these integrated assessments that one can be recognised as competent (or not). Two key components of competency-based assessment are skills and competencies.

Skill is a task or group of tasks performed to a specified level of proficiency, which typically involves the manipulation of tools and equipment, or expertise that is knowledge- or attitude-based. Competency is a skill performed to a specified standard under particular conditions. One can be given many opportunities to demonstrate skill, and the assessment process should allow for capturing and recording such demonstrations (Witty and Gaston 2008).

4. Stratified assessment

'. . . with our ambitions for the Connected Curriculum come the need to ensure that our assessment practices shift to respond to the new emphasis on students learning through research' (UCL 2016, 9). As a response to this call of the UCL Educational Strategy 2016–21, a new facet incorporating research-based learning into integrated assessment might be implemented via the approach of 'stratified assessment'. This concept was initially presented by Jeremy Levesley (2016) and was inspired by Bloom's taxonomy (Anderson et al. 2001). The idea behind stratified assessment is that it comprises a small number of levels. All students have an opportunity to attempt all levels of the assessment, although students can opt out after each of the levels if they are satisfied with the result achieved.

The first level of the assessment is designed to distinguish on the basis of pass or fail. A student is eligible for a third-class mark by passing an easy test on the basic topics covered in the module, which students can do on their own by reading a module core book. This level is mainly a knowledge-base check, to establish the extent to which students have understood the research findings (i.e. research-led learning).

The next level up within the assessment checks students' ability to flexibly apply knowledge. This barrier distinguishes the 2.1 and 2.2 classification mark. This level requires not only a knowledge-based understanding but also cognitive competencies (e.g. performing complex analysis) to the extent that students can construct knowledge in the subject (i.e. research-oriented learning). A set of online preparatory sample questions can be designed and made available to the students to practise for this level of the assessment.

The final level of the assessment, aiming at the first-class mark, requires students to have an in-depth understanding of the subject knowledge, often beyond the scope of the curricular. One should be able to demonstrate a requisite variety of competencies. This level involves answering open-ended questions quite often in a real-world context. Hence, it requires synthesis across the degree, broader understanding around the subject and beyond. This level of assessment involves critical evaluation and inquiry-based (research-tutored and research-based) learning. In this way, the stratified assessment approach engages students as partners in their education and as co-producers of knowledge that corresponds to dimension six of the Connected Curriculum.

It is advisable for each student to attempt the level of the assessment that is near their zone of discomfort. Thus, the stratified assessment approach has a potential to improve the experiences of both students and staff. For academics, it reduces the pressure to set a single test so that a majority of the cohort meet the overall assignation of marks to the assessment. Assessment outcomes are more fair and reliable compared with conventional assessment.

Currently, UCL has an overarching comprehensive moderation of marking policy that informs the procedures for marking students' work. This aims to ensure the consistency of marking, including the proper application of the assessment criteria, across students and modules. Moderation checks whether the overall assignation of marks to the full set of assessed work for an assignment is appropriate in the context of the marking of other sets and of the academic standards for the award. Hence, stratified assessment has the potential if not to completely eliminate the need for moderation and scaling (which is a costly procedure) but at least to reduce the need for it.

All students are kept motivated, no matter what their background or level of understanding in the subject area, as there is none of the usual alignment with mid-range students. Those who are struggling to keep up with the material might decide to attempt only the pass/fail level, while the students with outstanding performance are kept motivated by the open-ended nature of the last part of the assessment.

On the downside, this approach might cause differentiation among the students and unreasonable levels of competition. While stratified assessment practice can be considered for piloting, we should also attempt to address the issues associated with such a change of practice.

5. Stakeholders of higher education

When looking at higher education as a business, the stakeholders would be students, potential employers, government and higher education institutions themselves. All of them are directly affected by how research materials and skills are taught at universities and thus how our society shapes its future. When deciding whether to pursue a degree at a higher education institution, a prospective student hopes that it will give them the chance to study a subject that interests them and boost their career prospects and earnings potential. In the UK, this becomes even a bigger dilemma given the recent rise in tuition fees.

It is evident that graduates earn significantly more than non-graduates over the course of their careers (BIS 2015b). However, choosing a degree programme that develops employability skills as well as provides subject knowledge, and which is offered by a university that has a good reputation with employers, greatly improves a student's chances of landing a prestigious job (Chris Phillips interviewed by Hilpern 2008). Thus, in the knowledge economy, as the level of information technology employed within industry increases rapidly, the teaching–research nexus becomes important for future graduates' employability opportunities. According to Jenkins (2004) students value learning in a research-based environment; however, Zamorski (2002) emphasises that they can also feel excluded in many ways.

Scott (2002, 13) has argued: 'Not only are they [students] engaged in the production of knowledge; they must also be educated to cope with the risks and uncertainties generated by the advance of science.' Potential employers would like universities not only to convey the subject knowledge to the students but also to help them develop a set of skills essential for the world of business. Moreover, the subject knowledge should be cutting-edge so that a graduate leaves the university familiar with innovations in the field that would empower them with an extra 'tool-kit' that they can use in their professional careers. The skills obtained via research-based learning are the ability to define, plan and execute projects that require motivation, independent thinking, self-assessment, target-setting, energy and focus on finishing complex and difficult tasks (Professor James Knowles interviewed by Hilpern 2008). Therefore, curricula need to prepare students for careers where the science is complex and where its application to society is also complex.

The Government, in turn, wants higher education institutions to provide high-quality teaching and research and produce highly skilled graduates and postgraduates who will maintain society's sustainability. To this end, higher education's regulatory framework is designed to protect students, foster innovation and help maintain and develop the UK's global reputation for HE excellence. Higher education institutions are expected to be more professional in their teaching, more productive in research and more entrepreneurial in everything.

6. Feeding in the NSS perspective

The students' perspective can be seen from the National Student Survey (NSS): final-year student feedback from UK universities capturing their perceptions about the quality of the course and the institution in general. The results are used to compile university league tables (Lenton 2015). In theory, the NSS is a good idea; however, poor implementation misleads and has the potential to severely compromise the standard of education by reducing very different courses at very different universities to a simple set of metrics. With increased tuition fees, students are seen as customers who must be kept happy, and the NSS is now effectively a customer satisfaction survey. Recently, 200 student representatives signed an open letter supporting a boycott of the NSS, a symbol of the marketisation of education and of the survey itself as a flawed instrument that provides little information regarding the quality of education (Bonnar and Kelly 2013). Nevertheless, via the NSS, students make their voices heard about the things that matter to them.

7. Concluding remarks

None of the stakeholders is satisfied with 'business as usual' as a way of running higher education. There are apparent reasons to postpone universal implementation of research-based learning, but this will require a review of institutional-wide policy and practices to curricular design and development. Thus, before any such changes occur, a consultation should take place, gathering the viewpoints of all stakeholders involved in the higher education process.

Buckley's (2011) investigation into staff and student perceptions of the relationship between research and teaching observed that the two groups had different expectations. Therefore, there is a need for a shared understanding of what research in teaching is and how it should be achieved.

Research-based education is key to ensure that students are taught in an engaging and challenging manner; that their subject knowledge is kept up-to-date; and that their research and evaluation skills are developed to better equip them for the challenges of their future careers. Programme designers should work to clarify the links between the tasks students complete on an assessment and the competencies those tasks are designed to measure. This should include assessment design that would be embedded into learning. 'Stratified assessment' has the potential to improve the assessment experiences of both students and staff.

References

Aitken, G. and Tatebe, J. 2014. *Recognition of Teaching Excellence: Discussion Paper*. Auckland: University of Auckland.

Altbach, P. G., Reisberg, L. and Rumbley, L. E. 2009. *Trends in Global Higher Education: Tracking an Academic Revolution*. Paris: UNESCO.

Anderson, L. W., Krathwohl, D. R. and Bloom, B. S. 2001. *A Taxonomy for Learning, Teaching, and Assessing: A Revision of Bloom's Taxonomy of Educational Objectives*. New York: Pearson.

Biggs, J. 1996. Enhancing teaching through constructive alignment. *Higher Education* 32, 347–64.

BIS. 2015a. *Fulfilling our Potential: Teaching Excellence, Social Mobility and Student Choice*. London: HMSO. https://www.gov.uk/government/uploads/system/uploads/attachment_data/file/474266/BIS-15-623-fulfilling-our-potential-teaching-excellence-social-mobility-and-student-choice-accessible.pdf. [Accessed 10 June 2016].

BIS. 2015b. *Graduate Labour Market Statistics January – March Q1 2015*. London: BIS.

Bloxham, S. 2009. Marking and moderation in the UK: False assumptions and wasted resources. *Assessment and Evaluation in Higher Education* 34, 209–20.

Bonnar, L. and Kelly, S. 2013. *From Below Average to Above Average: Six Years of Reflecting and Responding to the National Student Survey*. Glasgow: University of Strathclyde.

Brown, G. A., Bull, J. and Pendlebury, M. 1997. *Assessing Student Learning in Higher Education*. London: Routledge.

Buckley, C. A. 2011. Student and staff perceptions of the research–teaching nexus. *Innovations in Education and Teaching International* 48, 313–22.

Burgess, R. 2007. *Burgess Group Final Report: Beyond the Honours Degree Classification.* London: Universities UK.

Elton, L. 2001. Research and Teaching: Conditions for a positive link. *Teaching in Higher Education* 6, 43–56.

Eraut, M. and du Boulay, B. 2000. *Developing the Attributes of Medical Professional Judgement and Competence.* Brighton: University of Sussex.

Griffiths, R. 2004. Knowledge production and the research–teaching nexus: The case of the built environment disciplines. *Studies in Higher Education* 29, 709–26.

Hammerness, K. 2006. From coherence in theory to coherence in practice. *Teacher College Record* 108, 1241–65.

Hattie, J. and Marsh, H. W. 1996. The relationship between research and teaching: A meta-analysis. *Review of Educational Research* 66, 507–42.

Havnes, A. 2013. Assessment in Higher Education: A CHAT Perspective. In Wells, G. and Edwards A. (eds) *Pedagogy in Higher Education: A Cultural Historical Approach.* New York: Cambridge University Press.

Healey, M. 2005. Linking research and teaching exploring disciplinary spaces and the role of inquiry-based learning. In Barnett, R. (ed.) *Reshaping the University: New Relationships between Research, Scholarship and Teaching.* Maidenhead: McGraw-Hill/Open University Press.

HEFCE. 2015. *National Student Survey results.* http://www.hefce.ac.uk/lt/nss/results/2015/. [Accessed 10 June 2016].

Heywood, J. 2000. *Assessment in Higher Education: Student Learning, Teaching, Programmes and Institutions.* London: Jessica Kingsley Publishers.

Hilpern, K. 2008. Does a degree guarantee you a good job? *The Independent.* http://www.independent.co.uk/student/career-planning/getting-job/does-a-degree-guarantee-you-a-good-job-795996.html. [Accessed 20 May 2016].

J M Consulting. 2000. *Interactions between Research, Teaching, and other Academic Activities: Report for HEFCE.* Bristol: Higher Education Consulting Group.

Jenkins, A. 2004. *A Guide to the Research Evidence on Teaching–Research Relationships.* York: Higher Education Academy.

Jenkins, A., Healey, M. and Zetter, R. 2007. *Linking Teaching and Research in Disciplines and Departments.* The Higher Education Academy. https://www.heacademy.ac.uk/sites/default/files/186_linkingteachingandresearch_april07.pdf [Accessed 10 June 2016]

Lenton, P. 2015. Determining student satisfaction: An economic analysis of the National Student Survey. *Economics of Education Review* 47, 118–27.

Levesley, J. 2016. Peer-assisted learning and assessment design. Masterclass presented at UCL, London.

McPhun, H. 2010. *Integrated Assessments – Engaging Ways to Enhance Learner Outcomes.* Wellington: Ako Aotearoa.

Oxford University Press. 2016. *Oxford Learner's Dictionary.* http://www.oxfordlearnersdictionaries.com/definition/american_english/assessment. [Accessed 19 April 2016].

Price, M., O'Donovan, B., Rust, C. and Carroll, J. 2008. Assessment standards: a manifesto for change. *Brookes eJournal of Learning and Teaching* 2, 1–2.

Robinson, K. 2010. *RSA ANIMATE: Changing Education Paradigms.* TED talk. https://www.ted.com/talks/ken_robinson_changing_education_paradigms. [Accessed 10 June 2016].

Scott, P. 2002. High wire. *Education Guardian* 8.

Shin, J. C., Arimoto, A., Cummings, W. K. and Teichler, U. 2015. *Teaching and research in Contemporary Higher Education.* Dordrecht: Springer.

UCL. 2016. *Education Strategy 2016–21.* London: UCL.

Vygotsky, L. S. 1978. *Mind in Society: The Development of Higher Psychological Processes.* Cambridge, MA: Harvard University Press.

Witty, E. and Gaston, B. 2008. *Competency Based Learning and Assessment.* Ellerslie: ETITO.

Zamorski, B. 2002. Research-led teaching and learning in higher education: A case. *Teaching in Higher Education* 7, 411–27.

Links to the R=T Framework

K. M. Nabiul Alam
UCL Institute of Education

- The chapter highlights the importance of understanding students' learning experiences in a competitive employment market. As the level of information technology employed in the knowledge economy industry increases, the teaching–research nexus becomes important for graduate employability. Sayara stresses that a review of institutional policies and practices around curricular design and development is required prior to making any changes. A consultation should gather viewpoints of all stakeholders, including students, potential employers, government and higher education institutions themselves on how to shape the academia of the future.

- The biggest challenge lies in developing a common understanding between stakeholders about student–staff partnerships, due to the differences in knowledge, skills, experiences and personal circumstances. Interdisciplinary and cross-departmental communication is central to the fair exchange of ideas and views. Giving proper recognition (e.g. letter of recognition, mentioning contributions in university publications and celebrating successes through celebratory events) would help to ensure staff and student motivation. All the aforementioned strategies are equally applicable to introducing a learning-oriented assessment system by reaching agreement on a system of assessment at the department level and by exchanging ideas and views across departments and universities.

- In my opinion, it is time to challenge traditional collaborations between staff and students. This can be made possible by encouraging open communication between staff and students across university departments, and across universities within the UK and the wider world. Databases of research staff and students would allow likeminded people to communicate directly, exchange ideas and develop themselves. Finally, sharing research into innovation in assessment, such as the learning-oriented system discussed by Sayara, individuals and institutions can both gain new knowledge and work to improve students' experiences of assessment and feedback.

2.8

Large-group teaching

Problematics, pedagogics and partnerships

Preeti Vivek Mishra

UCL Institute of Education; now at Department of Education, University of Delhi

with Professor James Davenport

Department of Computer Science and Department of Mathematical Sciences, University of Bath

Academics, individually and collectively, are clever people and, faced with a new situation, will address it ingeniously. Being human, when faced with an old situation, they will tend to address it the same way as before. When faced with a very similar situation, they will adapt the previous solution slightly. Preeti's chapter challenges us to realise that the changes in Higher Education, both qualitative and quantitative, mean that 'How best to teach' is a new situation that requires ingenious solutions, not just adapting the old ones.

Professor James Davenport

> ### Box 1: Sample this!
>
> - Between 2004/05 and 2013/14, net staff numbers at UK universities grew by 49,475. Sixty-eight per cent of this growth is attributable to an increase in academic staff.
> - Despite these increases in academic staff numbers over the period, student–staff ratios remain at a level similar to 2004/05, at sixteen to one, thereby indicating increased student numbers.
>
> Source: Universities UK 2015

1. Context

Increasingly, the economics of neo-liberal education perpetuates systemic and structural compulsions which require us to stop, think, critically reassess, challenge and/or calibrate our role and pedagogic practices as academics.

The continuing discourse of education as a tool for socio-economic vertical mobility has seen an influx of students into higher education institutions. Scott (1997), inter alia, identifies this as a reason for the 'massification' of higher education (HE). Interestingly, the last decade has seen a surge in full-time students entering both first degree as well as postgraduate taught and research programmes. Part-time enrolments for each have, however, witnessed a decline in the same period (Universities UK 2015). This continual rise in the number of students has direct and pressing implications for the processes of learning and teaching in HE.

Academic discourse concerning the quality of education has identified a favourable pupil–teacher ratio as one of the key components of an effective and fulfilling teaching–learning experience. However, unlike the hugely researched, debated and discussed issue of pupil–teacher ratios for school education (OECD 2014), the discussion around the same with reference to HE has been scant in public and policy discourse.

This is not to imply an absence of discussion. When it does occur, the nomenclature used is that of student–staff ratio (SSR) (Universities UK 2015). The SSR is designed to show the total number of students per member of academic teaching staff, and is calculated from the student and staff full-time equivalent figures (HESA 2016). For a long period of time now, the British HE system has relied on the SSR to gauge the adequacy of the human resource available for teaching (SRHE 2012).

Yet, the issues of calculating the SSR and the implications of using it in HE are more nuanced and complicated than for the pupil–teacher ratios used in school education. Given the complicated matrix of HE created by the various modalities of teaching and learning – face to face and online, full-time and part-time, taught and research-based programmes, etc. – the quantification and calculation of academic staff's teaching engagements is decidedly layered and non-linear. In HE, the SSR rarely translates into a teacher-taught ratio, and thus has limited pedagogic bearing. The SSR of 16 in Box 1 rarely translates into scenarios where teachers walk into lecture rooms with just 16 students awaiting them!

Why is the HE teacher–student ratio so important? To answer this, we need to look at the very aims of HE, which are, in turn, defined by the ever-evolving realities of the HE landscape. The subsequent sections in this chapter attempt to sketch this landscape as it largely exists today, and explore related issues in large-group teaching.

2. Higher education: an appraisal

The aims of HE have been contested substantially. In particular, Barnett's (1990) expositions on the emancipatory aim of HE has received much attention (Aviram 1992). Barnett posits that self-understanding and self-empowerment are the key elements in emancipation. HE, Barnett argues, must strive to facilitate a state of intellectual independence as well as a discipline-transcending reflection for all students. For Barnett, HE is so named because it necessarily calls upon higher-order skills like analysis, synthesis, imagination, criticism and evaluation. It involves critical reflections on the disciplinary knowledge gained as well as critical self-reflection.

White (1997) questions the philosophical underpinning of Barnett's arguments and highlights the contradistinction between a discussion on the aims of school education and what he refers to as post-compulsory education designed for autonomous agents. He invokes the principle of 'consumer sovereignty' to denounce a paternalistic imposition of an emancipatory aim on HE. Yet, White meets Barnett midway by acknowledging that through HE 'students should be encouraged to reflect on the philosophical and sociological horizons of their own specialism and its relationships to other specialisms, especially with a view to an enlargement of their own self-understanding and capacity for autonomous action' (White 1997, 14).

Aviram (1992, 183) argues that the aim of HE to be 'an educational mission transcending the enhancement of various individual and social practical interests' is repeatedly undermined by, first, the external pressures on the modern university to establish its pragmatic utility and, second, by the practising academic's declining faith in a larger educational mission. Universities are under sustained pressure to prove their continuing relevance. The conceptualisation of the knowledge society has been a key driver in rephrasing the expectations we have of universities. The CHERI report (2007) elaborates on the changing nature of the university, wherein the premium on the production of 'relevant' knowledge has led to questioning of the centrality of the teaching–research nexus characteristic of the 'traditional' academy. The early signs of the 'movement from the "traditional academy" with its stress on basic research and disciplinary teaching to the "relevant academy"' (Locke 2007, 3) are only now becoming evident. They bode an increasingly fragmented reality within HE. The fragmentation is evident in the differentiated typologies of institutions, as well as academic/research-role profiles. Whereas on the one hand, an epistemological–pedagogical rationale for integrating research and teaching is being exhaustively discussed, the reality is foreclosing the possibility for its realisation. As Locke (2005, 101) points out, 'the separation of research and teaching is itself the result of policy and operational decisions made over some time to distinguish the way these activities are funded, managed, assessed and rewarded.'

Similarly, the predicament of academics themselves has been a topic of sustained interest. Kinman and Jones (2003) assert that academics are reeling under increased job demands, while their job satisfaction and levels of support have declined in recent years. Others have shown that the job satisfaction among academics is much lower when compared to the UK workforce as a whole (Metcalf et al. 2005). The reasons for this state of dissatisfaction vary from pecuniary reward to the qualitative and aspirational aspects of the job. Importantly, academics derive more satisfaction from research. Teaching, though perceived in a positive light, is not the most important reason for their becoming an academic (Kinman and Jones 2004).

The evolving picture is one of an increasingly business-like HE sector with ever-growing student numbers (Kinman and Jones 2003). The demands of the knowledge society lead to increasing differentiation and a 'service station concept' of university (Aviram 1992). The situation is exacerbated by mounting pressures on over-burdened academics to balance teaching, research and administrative responsibilities (Kinman and Jones 2003; CHERI 2007). A casualty of these pressures is the reduction in the quality of, and available real time for, student–teacher interactions.

The related phenomenon of the massification of HE is also relevant here. Scott (1997, 15) notes that since the 1960s, HE has become increasingly socially pervasive and has moved beyond its marginal status. This has resulted in, *inter alia*, an increase in student intake, which has in turn exerted increased demands on institutional and staffing provisions within HE.

The debates on whether emancipation is a suitable aim for students in HE, or whether the conceptualisation of a knowledge society has rather done a disservice to education at large, are ideological in nature, and will find takers on both sides. However, other issues, like the impact of teacher motivations and expanding class sizes on the effectiveness of teacher–learner interactions, may be more readily amenable to a consensus.

The undeniable reality remains that the debates and issues continue to interact dynamically to shape, arbitrate and delimit the aims of HE in general. At the same time, they make it less likely that the professed aims of HE, in real-time educational interactions between students and teachers, can be achieved.

The take away from the discussion above remains that in the day-to-day experience of a university academic who walks down a corridor towards a lecture hall for her next class, the macro-reality of HE produces constraints that seem immediately non-negotiable. One such constraint – whether face-to-face or online – is burgeoning class sizes.

The next section draws upon (i) my experience as an academic and (ii) the masterclass dialogue to deconstruct the notions of, and delineate some challenges arising from, large-group teaching.

3. The reality and casualties of large-group teaching

Box 2: How do you boil a frog without letting it know? (and what is the connection?)

Prof. James Davenport posed this question based on an urban legend (Gibbons 2002) to the attendees of an R=T Masterclass on the theme of large-group teaching. The solution had an eventual analogical import relevant to the theme.

See if you can figure out the connection as you read his solution!

Place the frog in water at room temperature. Put the pan on the stove and very gradually increase the temperature. As the process is designed to be painstakingly slow, the frog remains oblivious of the marginal temperature increase, till of course it is very late for the poor frog to redress his predicament! (but, see Gibbons 2002).

Schools have classrooms.

Universities have lecture halls!

Assuming the intentionality of language orchestrated through specificity of words, the semantic difference between a room and hall is instructive. It tells us something about the reality of class sizes in HE!

I am a teacher–educator and a pedagogue by practice. As a mid-career academic, I have taught large groups. At the same time, as an academic dealing with education as a discipline, the concerns about what transpires in teaching–learning scenarios is my primary intellectual preoccupation. Therefore, to me, a class size of 45 – which I often end up teaching with resentment on the Bachelor of Education programme at the Department of Education, University of Delhi – definitely qualifies as a large group. I was therefore taken aback upon being told that the class sizes in some of the undergraduate courses at the University of Bath, as well as UCL, could go well beyond 200!

My first reaction, bordering on disbelief, led me to think about what qualifies as being a large group in a formal education space?

My reasoned response was that any number which renders individual students 'identity-less silhouettes' in a class is large, and is sacrilegious to the very aims and pursuit of education, either emancipatory or functional. Put simply, a large group is one which constrains the proactive engagement of every student in the process of learning and impedes the teachers' ability to enable such proactive engagement on logistic grounds.

What, then, is the threshold beyond which the group size is sacrilegious to the very aims of education?

This, I reckon, is a matter for a non-linear investigation. I am of the view that the futility of an arbitrary proclamation of a magical number – say beyond 30 (the commonly used threshold for differentiation between large and small samples in statistics) – is self-evident in education on at least two grounds: first, an educational interaction has human beings as its actors. It forecloses the possibility of a nomothetic, homogenising and universal dictum on a magical number across educational scenarios. The definition of what comprises a large group will thus organically evolve from the particularities of the teacher and taught.

To give an example, if the class comprises of non-native speakers for whom the instruction in, say, English is a jeopardising rather than enabling variable, creating an added layer of educational challenge in comprehending and engaging with the content at hand, then probably a class size of 25 may already be large enough to render the achievement of any semblance of effective teaching–learning experience questionable. Language is only an illustrative case in point; the students' prior knowledge and cognitive readiness for the content comprise some others pertinent variables. The particularities of the teacher and the learners are multifarious and are best left to a reflective practitioner to observe, delineate and consider.

The content under consideration is another key parameter in determining what may constitute a large group. I will refrain from resorting to disciplinary categorisations in arguing this. Rather, I posit that irrespective of disciplines, it is the nature of the content (ranging from, for example, statement of facts to descriptive exegesis on observed phenomena, to critical and deconstructive analysis of theoretical postulations) which must be the reference point to determine what comprises a large group. So, whereas a customary overview of the course at the beginning of the term, or an enlisting of theorists to be read during a course may be well received, even in a large group, a critical overview of the historical evolution of a concept may not.

Once again, as subject specialists, it rests upon our shoulders to figure out which content demands a more intimate learner–teacher interaction and which, if any, may be suitable for large-group teaching.

Having said this, I revert back to the earlier point about the non-negotiability of the restraints of large class sizes. The above discussion is not predicated on a utopian hope about the teacher choosing at will what class size to teach. Instead, it is aimed at signposting some points to help the sensitive practitioner undertake a reflexive audit of the reality that she faces and the challenges it may entail, thereby enabling her to work towards effective pedagogic strategies to address the reality and counter the inherent challenges.

Teaching a large group, when 'large group' is defined in relation to the matrix of student, teacher and content specificities and demands, is a daunting task in more ways than one.

For the learners, the forced expectation that they will acclimatise to the reality of studying in a large group may significantly challenge the socio-psychological as well as cognitive competencies of new entrants to HE, who were accustomed to studying in relatively smaller groups during their school years. Professor Davenport pointed to this in his Masterclass discussion, noting that he feels 'sorry for people [learners] negotiating the challenges of transitioning from small groups to inordinately large groups.'

The issue of acclimatisation is relevant for teachers as well. Especially challenging is the dichotomous experience of being taught in smaller groups during their own student years and then having to teach large groups as academics. A teacher who has experienced the large group as a student is better equipped, at least at the outset, to appreciate students' learning predicament and the challenges facing them in a large group. However, this challenge is surmountable by reflective teachers willing to visualise and empathise with their students' predicament, and engaging in a dialogue about collaborative strategies to redress the challenges of large groups.

Specifically, large-group teaching can impinge on the nature and extent of an individual student's engagement in class. Given the burgeoning teacher–student ratio and the declining average time available in a scheduled class to encourage the proactive participation of every student, the challenge to design a meaningful learning experience for all involved becomes imminently pressing.

Professor Davenport alluded to the legend of 'boiling a frog' (see Box 2) in this context. He recalled how academics sometimes fail to take into consideration the consistently increasing numbers of students in their class, thereby also failing to devise pedagogic strategies to address the changing demographic of the class, until finally the damage done to the learners, as well as their own reputations and calibre as academics, is irrevocable. However, and thankfully for us, Gibbons' (2002) debunking of the urban myth shows that frogs are not inevitably doomed and do manage to turn the tide.

Large groups pose yet another challenge, albeit arising from an unexpected quarter. A pragmatic solution to support the increased number of students in HE has been to devise a system of tutorial support. There has been a differentiation of roles between lecturing and tutoring. For some, there has been a wishing away of the challenges of large-group teaching, predicating it on the premise that allocating a relatively smaller number of students to individual tutors would offset the lack of quality interaction in the lectures, and that the student learning experience will be significantly augmented and enriched. However, the rise in the number of students has meant that there has been a commensurate rise in the number of tutors. This has led to the challenge of establishing and sustaining parity, in instructional support as well as the quality of assessment and feedback received by students.

The phenomenon of large groups has also thrown up assessment-related challenges. First, the challenge of maintaining consistent grading of student assignments for formative as well as summative assessments remains as valid a concern as ever. Apart from the increasing demands on individual time and effort, assessment for large groups also requires an extended investment of time and effort in inter-examiner coordination to ensure grading parity.

Another pressing challenge is that of designing effective in-class formative assessment strategies. A large group makes it difficult for teachers to ensure that most students participate in in-class formative strategies like discussion activities. This is pedagogically unsound, as researchers have found that students enjoy the opportunity to reflect, consolidate knowledge or work on a problem (Weaver and Cottrell 1985; Stead 2005; both cited in Foster 2013).

Similarly, a key component of a teacher's in-class formative assessment effort is to look out for non-verbal cues indicative of students' dipping concentration and interest levels or discomfort with the content being transacted. Often these cues initiate impromptu strategies for further elaborating and clarifying the lesson's content and concepts. Higher numbers of students in a class will increasingly restrict a teacher's ability to engage with the non-verbal cues that students unwittingly demonstrate throughout a lecture.

Yet another challenge is to provide in-class feedback to students on their queries, observations and responses. The greater the number of students, the easier it is to practise being equitable by providing little or no feedback to everybody, rather than providing detailed feedback inconsistently. In everyday lived reality, the ticking clock can add to the pressure of content delivery and doubly jeopardise the will and candour for extensive feedback.

The above-mentioned set of pedagogic challenges may severely jeopardise the teaching–learning experience. Any attempts to avoid the fate of the boiled frog will be predicated on devising effective pedagogic strategies to address these challenges. The next section attempts as much, drawing upon my pedagogic reflections and on the interactions with Professor Davenport.

4. Teaching large groups: pedagogic innovations and reaping the collective dividend

Philosophers of education have arduously explicated the difference between education, teaching and instruction. I have come to believe that in the context of formal classrooms, teaching, to be worth its salt, should be taken up in the spirit of education. I therefore embed the subsequent discussion on a willed supposition of an ontological synonymity between teaching and education in the formal educational setting. It is in this spirit that I use the term 'teaching' hereafter.

To me, both the relevance and legitimacy of teaching large groups effectively derives from an appreciation of the difference between instruction and teaching; with me rooting for the latter. I see instruction as predetermined, linear, factual, emphasising physical and/or cognitive skill development, and easily replaceable. Teaching, on the other hand, is dynamic, dialogic, interactive, rarely mechanical, and aimed at holistic development. The solution to how to teach effectively in a large group derives, in the first place, from the very aims of teaching itself.

In line with our earlier discussion on the aims of HE, teaching in HE must aim at nurturing a spirit of critical inquiry towards oneself and one's discipline, paving the way for an intellectual inclination for disciplinary transcendence, a quest for interdisciplinarity, and an ability for reasoned and autonomous action. This articulation necessitates an experience-based education that enables reflective and critical capabilities and facilitates a meaningful and creative appropriation of one's disciplinary specialisation. The end aim, which I recognise is an ongoing one, is to use knowledge meaningfully in the world we inhabit. Given these aims of HE, research must become a key component of our pedagogic repertoire. I attempt an explication of how this may be done in the context of large-group teaching.

As a teacher–educator, I can hardly over-emphasise the need for a teacher to be more than a master at content delivery. Yet, I start with content delivery for its primacy and sheer obviousness in the discourse of what teachers do.

At the outset, content delivery is a pedagogic misnomer on two counts; first, it connotes the existence of a fixed rather than dynamic content, which is delivered 'as is'. I argue that the dynamism of content derives from the synergetic interactions of the teacher and the learner. That is why no two classes are ever alike in a teacher's experience, even when repeating the same curriculum year after year. Second, the term 'delivery' masks the proactivity of the 'recipient' (and I use the term half-heartedly), who is hardly passive. Classrooms impose physical passivity upon learners through the structuration of space, but mental passivity can only result from a collaborative failure of the teacher and the learner. Mental agility implies that individual recipients engage and negotiate the content ideographically. Importantly, research-based education can be a key ally in countering the physical passivity by changing the definition of what comprises a classroom. In addition, problem-based, scenario-specific research can be used as a valuable pedagogic strategy to keep students mentally agile and invested by positioning them as problem-solvers and innovators.

With further reference to content delivery in large groups, we must recognise that the knowledge society, riding on the omnipresence of technology as a tool for knowledge sharing, has increasingly meant that content – as an assortment of theories and facts – is ever within the reach of the initiated student. The knowledge society's challenge to content delivery is one beyond packing it all in a lecture; it is about deconstructing the content, questioning its sacrosanct status and contextualising it against the modes of knowledge production that created it in the first place. This mandates a diminishing reliance on linear lecturing. Paradoxically, large-group teaching is perceived as being notoriously appropriate for precisely this: linear lecturing! Encouraging students to stay abreast of the latest research in their field, as well as assuming the role of paradigm-defying critical researchers through micro-projects, can be a useful strategy to enable them to relook at the dominant knowledge analytically and muster the courage to challenge it.

Professor Davenport points out that the concern over technological advancements rendering a teacher's role irrelevant can actually be countered by deploying technology as a pedagogic ally. To elaborate: first, advancements in technology have enabled web platforms like Moodle, which can facilitate 'flipped' classrooms and create academic spaces and an intellectual ethos for critical reflections.

In addition, the internet has become a tremendous and ever-evolving resource repository, allowing teachers to assume the additional role of a 'resource curator'. Engaging students as co-curators of knowledge can be an interesting way of researching a chosen topic. Research in this case would take form of collecting material, cataloguing it against the dominant paradigms of the discipline and evaluating it. This will enable students to critically engage with a topic of their choice.

Lecture podcasts from across the globe, well-researched documentaries and archival resources are just an internet search away for the curious teacher–student team. These resources allow teachers to counter the linearity of the lecture and make learning a research-rich, multi-sensory, interest-provoking and engaging experience.

However, the above discussion is not to denounce the value of a well prepared and presented lecture. A lecture – laced with critical engagement of the content, interdisciplinary anecdotes, academic trivia, a subtle dose of humour and consistent attempts at keeping the students involved – is an equally successful pedagogic strategy. However, the lecture must not be a didactic exercise, but should build upon the intellectual explorations of the students discussed above.

In a similar vein, whereas the assessment-related challenges of large-group teaching are pertinent, they too are addressable. Effective assessment must be predicated on the ontological and epistemological aims of teaching itself. At the outset, it should be recognised that the faculty is rarely trained for large-group assessment methodologies. Professor Davenport refers to assessment as the 'untaught black arts', because teachers are never really inducted into or oriented to an institution's assessment and marking practices.

The situation is particularly challenging with regards to teaching a large group which jeopardises opportunities for engagement and learning for some students. The institutional failure to create a conducive learning environment cannot be allowed to translate into the academic failure of students. Large groups thus create an ethical reason to adopt formative and enabling assessment. To illustrate, formative assessment can take the form of mobile quizzes and 'clickers'; flipped classrooms can create space for peer-to-peer feedback further augmented by feedback from the teacher.

Additionally, the systematic creation of study groups and a regular discussion schedule earmarked for study-group interaction can significantly enrich student understanding. The groups can feedback representative comments in the discussion. However, there has to be a commensurate effort from the faculty to engage regularly with the group comments.

Group work has an added advantage of developing the soft skills so often glossed over in large-group teaching. Groups must be balanced for the various forms of heterogeneity. Negotiating this heterogeneity itself presents an opportunity for reflexivity, appreciation of differences, and academic, cultural and, in some cases, generational tolerance. It also serves to provide a regular space for the cultivation of such soft skills as coordination, effective communication, conflict resolution, teamwork, time management and negotiating complex group dynamics. These opportunities go beyond subject-embeddedness and contribute to what is expected from education for life. The soft-skill dimension can introduce 'authentic learning' to the class, as it enables students to nurture the social–personal skills which will remain relevant beyond their immediate contexts (Newmann et al. 1996).

At a macro level, HE has attempted to counter the institutionalisation of linear lecturing and the related challenges of large-group teaching by ingeniously creating an augmenting mechanism of teaching and tutorial support in the form of teaching associates (or assistants) and tutors. Together, the lecturer, teaching support staff and the tutors are capable of creating a collective dividend for the student from a large group, as well as for each other.

Professor Davenport draws upon his pedagogic experience to note that this arrangement is determinedly beneficial for students as they engage with 'more than one sort of teacher doing more than one sort of teaching'. For them the whole experience can be more than the sum of the parts. Similarly, given the melange of pedagogical experiences that the team members bring to the discussion desk, lecturers, tutors and teaching assistants all stand to benefit from interacting with each other.

However, this triangulation of academic engagement must be requires caution with respect to parity in academic rigour, as well as in assessment criteria. Further, this 'teacher collective', if I may call it so, must not be relegated to a hierarchical tier system. Finally, there is also an inherent threat that the classroom becomes synonymous with information transfer, and tutorial support with personalised learning, which must be consistently avoided. The collective must work with formal and democratic communication channels, a shared sense of responsibility and accountability, a participative approach to curriculum and intra-institutional policy design.

I have so far attempted to illustrate some of the challenges of large-group teaching and made some suggestions for addressing them through, *inter alia*, designing research opportunities in which students can get involved. Yet, far from providing a checklist for large-group teaching, the intent has been to explicate my ontological and epistemological approach towards engaging the individual students who make up the large group. The specific problems and solutions I have chosen to discuss are hardly exhaustive. Nonetheless they stem from an understanding of HE as a key opportunity for students to develop the academic courage to be critical, original and active members of their class and subsequently of society. This necessitates an institutional ethos where students' voices and participation is continually sought, collectively laboured over and ceaselessly cherished, cohort after cohort.

To wind up the discussion, I attempt a further exploration of the possibilities offered by research-augmented teaching for engaging with large groups of students.

5. R=T in the context of large-group teaching: further explorations

Increasingly, the educational discourse has been dotted with themes of authentic learning, transformative education, constructivist education and so on. Each of these stresses the need for connecting learning with the 'real world'. Driscoll (2005) emphasises that if the learning process is separated from its applications in the real world, the knowledge earned from it will remain inert and unused beyond the classroom.

I share the sentiment behind these appeals, which derive their intellectual conviction from the aim of education itself. Formal education must be inspired by the need to establish the relevance of the curriculum, vis-à-vis the real world beyond the classroom.

Relevance does not imply correspondence or adherence. It may and must entail criticism and critiques too. HE, as an exit point to the real world for many, must strengthen its focus on nurturing the capacities for finding correspondences as well as critiques of the disciplinary theorisations, vis-à-vis the everyday lived experiences of humanity. An important channel through which to induct students in this way of approaching disciplines is by establishing a dialectic relation between research and teaching.

In a similar spirit, Locke (2005) furthers a number of arguments in favour of integrating research and teaching. These include preparing students for the super complexity of a pluralist world, developing an attitude of lifelong learning and critical enquiry, and keeping students abreast and engaged with the latest developments in their chosen field of professional practice. He further highlights the academic, professional and curricular enrichment that an R=T approach entails for practising academics (Locke 2005, 119).

Each of the above comments stresses the need for not discounting R=T; the challenges of the large group notwithstanding. Instead, large-group classes are viewed in a befitting and enabling context, to try and establish the R=T equivalence. I argue that, despite those who do not supporte an integrated approach to research and teaching complaining that there are not enough people 'to staff research activity throughout a mass HE system' (Locke 2005), the institutional arrangements for teaching large groups allow the benefits of the teachers' collective to be enjoyed. This allows for a collaborative intellectual engagement focusing on designing a specific pedagogic project that can foreground research in teaching as well as assessment modalities.

Second, the multitude of research specialisations within the teachers' collective significantly broadens the ambit of research areas that can be weaved into the learning–teaching contexts. It also allows for a more diverse research mentorship. Further, it can create an institutional space where students can be regularly engaged in research projects as short-term collaborators. The association can also take form of long-term engagements as team members.

Again, whereas there have been arguments stressing the need to break the link between R and T, citing its adverse effects on individual learning, I argue that a being in a large group of students, especially within HE, allows learners to reap a demographic dividend arising from interacting with peers from varied nationalities, previous disciplinary backgrounds, formal and informal work experiences, academic interests, as well as linguistic and cultural skill sets. In the context of R=T, this allows the flexibility to conceptualise multiple and diverse group projects across a varied range of content areas. Interestingly, the latent multi-dimensional heterogeneity of the large group also allows the opportunity for a rigorous investigation of a chosen research problem, from diverse socio-cultural, geo-political and linguistic-ethnic vantage points.

From the point of view of students in a large-group setting, R=T is also desirable given the research finding that students positively value 'the link between teaching and research because it places particular weight on meaningful exchange, based on equal measures of mutual respect and trust' (Deakin 2006, 84). This takes me back to the initial concern about rendering individual students as identity-less silhouettes in a large-group classroom. The R=T approach allows for foregrounding the individual students – their interests, strengths, capabilities and learning needs – thereby creating a space for idiographic pedagogy within the constraints of the massified HE.

Finally, integrating research in the teaching experience, above and beyond its intrinsic academic rationale, can also address the challenges of formative as well as summative assessment thrown up by large-group scenarios. The assessment can be based on group work with clearly defined criteria of the nature of the engagement of group members, collectively and individually. The engagement with research can be designed in the form of evaluations of existing research on the basis of disciplinary understanding, conceptualisation of a research project addressing specific academic areas, simulated bidding for grants through drafting a relevant research proposal or project outlines, and making group presentations of a bid or peer evaluations of a proposal on the basis of the understanding of content as well as the research methodologies, etc.

Notwithstanding the above, I do wish to restate that I regard the teaching of large groups as a system-enforced condition, which is bereft of a sound academic or pedagogic logic. I do maintain, however, that despite the neo-liberal massification of HE, there is always room for pedagogic innovations. I argue for strategies that can find strength in numbers by reaping dividends of, on the one hand, teacher collectives comprising various teaching support staff, and, on the other, the immense heterogeneity characteristic of student cohorts enrolling in HE.

The underlying motivation behind these academic interventions and innovations must be to establish a conspicuous interface between the content and the real world. In doing so, teachers must rely on their own reflexivity, the dividends of ever-expanding technology, and the immense potential of research to inform and invigorate teaching.

References

Aviram, A. 1992. The Nature of university education reconsidered (a response to Ronald Barnett's *The Idea of Higher Education*). *Journal of Philosophy of Education* 26, 183–200.

Barnett, R. 1990. *The Idea of Higher Education*. Oxford: Oxford University Press.

CHERI (Centre for Higher Education Research and Information). 2007. The changing academic profession in the UK: Setting the Scene. http://www.universitiesuk.ac.uk/highereducation/Documents/2007/ChangingAcademic.pdf. [Accessed 25 April 2016].

Deakin, M. 2006. Research led teaching: A review of two initiatives in valuing the link between teaching and research. *Journal for Education in the Built Environment* 1, 73–93.

Driscoll, M. P. 2005. *Psychology of Learning for Instruction*. Toronto, ON: Pearson.

EDUCASE. 2012 Flipped Classrooms: Educase Learning Initiative. https://net.educause.edu/ir/library/pdf/eli7081.pdf [Accessed 26 April 2016].

Foster, E. 2013. Teaching large groups. CADQ Guide. https://www.ntu.ac.uk/adq/document_uploads/teaching/137815.pdf [Accessed 26 April 2016].

Gibbons, W. 2002. The Legend of the Boiling Frog is Just a Legend. http://srel.uga.edu/outreach/ecoviews/ecoview021118.htm [Accessed 26 April 2016].

HESA. 2016. Technical Definitions: Student:Staff Ratios. https://www.hesa.ac.uk/component/content/article?id=2937#SSR. [Accessed 26 April 2016].

Kinman, G. and Jones, F. 2003. Running up the down escalator: Stressors and strains in UK academics. *Quality in Higher Education* 9, 21–38.

Kinman, G. and Jones, F. 2004. *Working to the Limit*. London: Association of University Teachers.

Locke, William. 2005. Integrating research and teaching strategies: Implications for institutional management and leadership in the United Kingdom. *Higher Education Management and Policy* 16, 101–20.

Locke, William. 2007. *The Academic Profession: Changing Roles, Terms and Definitions*. London: Centre for Higher Education Research and Information.

Metcalf, H., Rolfe, H., Stevens, P. and Weale, M. 2005. *Recruitment and Retention of Academic Staff in Higher Education.* Research Report 658. London: DfES.

Newmann, F., Marks, H. and Gamoran, A. 1996. Authentic Pedagogy and Student Performance. *American Journal of Education* 104, 280–331.

OECD. 2014. Education at a Glance: Country Note – UK. https://www.oecd.org/unitedkingdom/United%20Kingdom-EAG2014-Country-Note.pdf. [Accessed 25 April 2016].

Scott, P. 1997. The crisis of knowledge and the massification of higher education. In Barnett, R. and Griffin, A. (eds) *The End of Knowledge in Higher Education* (Institute of Education series ^A152285). London: Cassell.

SRHE (Society for Research into Higher Education). 2012. Handle with care – why the student: staff ratio may be a misleading indicator. Conference abstract. http://www.srhe.ac.uk/conference2012/abstracts/0172.pdf. [Accessed 25 April 2016].

Universities UK. 2015. *Patterns and Trends in UK Higher Education*. http://www.universitiesuk.ac.uk/policy-and-analysis/reports/Documents/2015/patterns-and-trends-2015.pdf. [Accessed 25 April 2016].

White, J. 1997. Philosophy and the Aims of Higher Education. *Studies in Higher Education* 22, 7–17.

Links to the R=T Framework

Harry Begg
Department of Political Science, UCL

- Student–staff partnerships in research-based education can take many forms, and Preeti emphasises how each class and course will require a bespoke approach from course convenors. Teaching no longer takes place solely in lectures or tutorials; rather, partnerships are formed through a variety of staff–student interactions, including tutorials, seminars and lectures. The quality of such partnerships does not simply come down to student-to-teacher ratios, and such a statistic may mask the reality of the quality of teaching and learning. Research-based education in the context of large class sizes can result in a spirit of critical enquiry, and large classes should not necessarily be seen as a negative.

- Large class sizes are difficult settings for teachers, and experiences of these partnerships may push their teaching skills to the limits. For example, there is a challenge in staff being able to pick up on non-verbal cues from students (e.g. lack of understanding), which may be easier in a tutorial setting. Feedback is also a problem, and individual feedback is nearly impossible. The further problem that this creates is that students may become passive recipients of knowledge rather than active learners.

  However, if conducted effectively, these partnerships in large class sizes have considerable potential. Students can be positioned as problem-solvers and innovators if they are given tasks to complete in small groups; this develops soft skills such as teamwork, and it promotes active learning. With the mass of information available to students via the Internet, staff can fulfil the role of 'knowledge curators', complementing and if necessary redirecting their students in the learning experience. Large group classes provide the possibility of non-linear learning if the traditional start–middle–end lecture is reformulated. While traditional assessment changes with large group sizes, new forms of assessment like quizzes and peer-to-peer feedback can take its place. Finally, there is a demographic benefit to large group learning, where students interact with multiple peers from diverse backgrounds to triangulate their understandings.

- This chapter offers a model for large-group learning which challenges the traditional linear-style lecture. In my opinion, it would also be important to consider how didactic lectures can and should be an important part of the learning experience. Some of my most memorable learning experiences have been where teachers have espoused their most passionate and heartfelt beliefs. There is a lot of information 'out there' for students to absorb, but argumentation (particularly in the liberal arts) is a key aspect of the teaching and learning experience. A diverse student environment in a large group can highlight areas of both agreement and difference. Debates and didactic discussion points can help invigorate the learning experience and bring out the passion of students.

2.9

Engaging students in research with 'real-world' outputs

Making an impact outside of the lecture theatre

Dallas Roulston

Department of Microbial Diseases, UCL Eastman Dental Institute; now at Middlesex University

with Professor Rachel McCrindle

School of Systems Engineering, University of Reading

I really enjoyed reading your chapter. Connecting students with research and external audiences through real-world outputs has many benefits, and it is great to see how you are making a strong case to promote this approach.

Professor Rachel McCrindle

1. Introduction

Universities have long been thought of as places where students are provided with the knowledge essential to become a valuable part of the workforce. In such a knowledge-focused environment, the course content (lectures, practical demonstrations, etc.) is often initially designed to provide the student with the knowledge necessary to understand the subject matter. Assessment is subsequently devised to evaluate whether the student, typically individually, can retain and recall this core knowledge. To better prepare students for life after university, knowledge *must* be accompanied by the ability to apply the knowledge in the real world. To enhance the design of the curriculum, one should initially focus on the tasks required to both understand the subject matter and apply and demonstrate the appropriate skills. These skills should be used to shape the assessment, and, further, the assessment should shape the course content and provide the students with the skills necessary to complete the assessment. As opposed to the traditional assessment tools, students may be tasked with undertaking a research project or assignment, possibly as part of a small group, in which the students produce an assessable output. To greatly add value to the students' outputs, it may be desirable to focus on outputs directed towards, and with impact to, external audiences. Learning through research is the major concept underpinning the UCL Connected Curriculum initiative.

> Students choose a university in part because they want to be where knowledge is created, not just imparted. (Arthur 2014)

The focus of this chapter is on exploring how the implementation of a curriculum focused on learning through research at all levels of education, which connects students with external audiences through real-world outputs, has many benefits. Engaging students with research involving real-world objects not only motivates students, it offers an introduction to valuable and desirable research skills, instils a variety of skills highly attractive to employers, provides students with the ability to apply their subject knowledge to real-world scenarios and generates impact outside of university. We will explore a number of examples of how students tasked with a project have produced an output with real-world impact. We also hear from Rachel McCrindle, Professor of Human and Computer Interaction at the University of Reading, to whom I spoke during an R=T Masterclass.

2. Links to the UCL Connected Curriculum

The central dimension considered is Dimension 3 of the UCL Connected Curriculum, 'Students make connections across subjects and out to the world', which pertains to connecting with external audiences and creating an impact in the real world. This is in line with 'UCL's commitment to making an impact for good in the world and explore concepts of global citizenship' (UCL 2016). Furthermore, students gain a multidisciplinary approach to their research.

Another aspect discussed in this chapter includes Dimension 5, 'Students learn to produce outputs/assessments focused at an audience', which focuses on the production of outputs through a programme and the connection with external audiences. In learning through research and enquiry, students develop skills and generate an impact further afield than the lecture theatre. Finally, we consider Dimension 4, 'Students connect academic learning with workplace learning', in which programmes allow students to further connect with external audiences through workplace exchange or placements during the course of study. Through this connection, students gain a number of skills that may not be acquired through a more traditional university education. These skills include project management and business acumen.

3. Personal perspective

During my undergraduate degree, in medical laboratory techniques, a majority of the course work was taught through lectures and laboratory demonstrations. These activities focused on performing the tests employed in medical sciences laboratories. However, they were taught as bite-sized chunks focusing on a particular test and often lacked any connection between them. Moreover, the understanding of the tasks was taught at first principles and did not reflect the real-world environment. This 'first-principles' approach allowed a solid understanding of the technique: comprehending how each test worked and the steps involved in performing it. This may seem the ideal way to gain the knowledge to understand, and therefore perform, the test in the real world. However, when I first stepped into a medical sciences laboratory, knowledge of the theoretical aspects was there but application in the real world was lacking. Test kits, reagents and protocols differed and many methods were automated. Although I understood the principles of the test, I needed further training to perform each test in the real-world environment. I was fortunate enough to work in a laboratory during my study and having that real-world experience was invaluable to understanding the subject matter. It may be ideal to consider involving the employers of graduates in curriculum design. For example, many of my graduating peers went to work in medical science laboratories. By approaching these employers and working with them to understand the skills they look for in their future employees, we could design a curriculum that provides students with these skills. By establishing interactions with employers, we also initiate and foster that connection with the real world.

4. Real-world outputs with real-world impact

If students are tasked with undertaking a research project and therefore learn through enquiry, they will inevitably produce an assessable output. Most student outputs are only observed and assessed by a small number of people and therefore possess limited impact. If these outputs were aimed at a wider, external, audience this impact has the potential to be amplified. The production of real-world outputs allows students to connect with peers, industry and the end user. Focusing on one, or more, real-world outputs also teaches the students a number of desirable skills and the ability to apply the knowledge learnt to real-world scenarios. Professor McCrindle stated that we could consider real-world outputs as 'anything which has any impact and adds value outside of the classroom'.

Other examples of outputs may include the publication of articles in peer-reviewed journals, oral and poster presentations at conferences

Case study 1 Chlorine, an element of controversy

An extraordinary example of students producing real-world output occurred within the Department of Science and Technology Studies at UCL between 2000 and 2005, and eventually led to a fascinating real-world output. Chemistry historian Dr Hasok Chang devised an innovative educational experiment: 'Students usually write essays with standard answers to standard questions. I thought it would be more interesting to have them do some original research, but we wanted to produce something that was publishable and wouldn't just gather dust in a pile. That's when we came up with this idea of inheritance.' Dr Chang set his class the task of producing a dissertation on the history of a single chemical element, chlorine, from its discovery in the 1770s to the present day. Subsequent students were provided with the works compiled from the previous students' work, and were tasked with advancing and improving the works. Following five cohorts of undergraduate students, the compilation of the works resulted in a monograph, published in 2007 by the British Society for the History of Science.

Science and Technology Studies, UCL

and exhibitions or public events, as well as the dissemination of content online in the form of blogs or videos. Furthermore, the value of the role of social media in the dissemination of information should not be underestimated. It could be envisaged that these outputs could change policy and evidence-based practice or even change our understanding. As PhD students and academics, we are likely to be encouraged or we are expected to produce these types of outputs (see, e.g., *Nature* 2015) and therefore it seems logical that undergraduate students should experience these activities at an early stage in their academic career. Additionally, many employers outside of an academic career require these types of activities as an obligation of the post. Other outputs may include the design, development and production of a product, such as the games created during one of Professor McCrindle's software engineering modules. In these, software engineering students develop games that not only teach the participants about software engineering but also allow the students to learn through the process of creating the games (see Case study 2). Professor McCrindle has developed an innovative software engineering module for approximately 200 first-year students at the School of Systems Engineering. The students are from a wide range of disciplines, including computer science, information technology, cybernetics and robotics. The software engineering module is compulsory for students as it is an integral skill in whichever field they pursue.

To further motivate her students, each year Professor McCrindle holds the Software Engineering Brilliance Awards, or SEBAs. In addition to more formal assessments, the students present their work to real-world partners and academics, competing for awards in various categories. 'When the students win one of the awards, it is considered rather prestigious and the students add it straight to their CV as it shows that they were the best in class', Professor McCrindle explained. Another example of real-world outputs include those produced by her human–computer interaction students who work in conjunction with a global web development company to experience how web development projects are undertaken in the real world: from initial conception of an idea, through marketing and design, to a fully implemented and documented solution. A number of her final-year students have also developed a variety of medical devices, which are designed and produced to improve the lives of patients suffering from debilitating conditions and therefore have real-world impact.

Case study 2 Do you want to make a game?

Rachel McCrindle, Professor of Human and Computer Interaction at the University of Reading, discusses the use of gamification in her software engineering module. As part of the module, students are tasked with producing a game in which they learn about software engineering. This learning could be embedded in the game 'board', in other objects associated with the gameplay (such as question cards) or in the ethos or mechanics of the game. In designing the game, the students learn about the software engineering process: planning, designing, developing, testing, adjusting and re-testing. But why teach software engineering in this manner? 'Software engineering is a real chicken-and-egg situation for the students', Professor McCrindle said. The students need to know the underpinning concepts, theories, knowledge and tools before they use them on a project. However, they often do not appreciate the true value of them until they have used them on a project, and ultimately on a real-world project or placement. Through working on a project, students become more engaged as they 'take ownership' of the project. This is increased by working as part of a team. Along with the knowledge and application learnt through the gamification process, the students also acquire a number of other useful and desirable skills, including working as part of a team, project management skills, research skills and 'soft' skills such as communication skills, problem-solving, decision-making and creativity. Students also have to be able to react when things go wrong and have the ability to adapt to changes during the process. Because students are more prepared for the real-world environment, they often obtain placements. 'When students return from their placements or other projects, the students state that they found the knowledge and the ability to apply it really useful,' said Professor McCrindle. Therefore, through implementing a pedagogy based on real-world outputs, the students have an impact outside the lecture theatre. In subsequent years, students take the project further by applying the knowledge and skills learnt to other projects and in some instances producing and marketing systems as well as interacting with industrial partners. The external partners work with the university staff to lecture the students and set assessments which reflect real-world scenarios. This interaction creates a collaborative and sometimes multidisciplinary approach with a focus on 'real-world outputs' that breeds 'real-world skills'.

Software Engineering, University of Reading

5. Research = Teaching = Real-world-ready students

I'm sure that at one time during your schooling you asked the teacher, 'Yes, but when am I ever going to use this in real life?' Through implementing a research-based education, this question may become a thing of the past as the students are able to see the application of the knowledge they are learning. By establishing an environment where students learn through research and inquiry, students are more enthusiastic. They take ownership of their project and develop a vested interest in obtaining the knowledge required to push the project forward and apply their skills to improve the project and, eventually, the final output. This ownership is often seen in Masters research and PhD projects. It would be highly attractive for undergraduates to follow a similar path. The students are also able to see that the outputs they are producing have real-world impact.

The term 'research' can be widely different depending on the field of study. However, the act of research is the basis of progress in every field. To this end, each and every field will have outputs relevant to the real world. Some may be generic across all disciplines, for example the publication of articles, books and online content such as blogs and vlogs (video blogs). More specifically, research in the sciences may influence evidence-based practice in fields such as medicine and engineering, while outputs in law and political science could impact policy makers. Through research, students also have to reflect on many of the factors experienced in the real world. These may include working as part of a team, working under time or budget constraints and the ability to produce outputs and communicate the work to a variety of audiences from diverse backgrounds.

By engaging students in learning through research, with a focus on real-world output and interactions with real-world partners, the students gain a variety of skills that prepare them for life after their degree. Taking the project from conception through design, production, implementation and testing to the final output requires creativity and adaptability. Whether remaining in academia or in the wider workforce, the skills that students gain are desirable and attractive to employers.

6.1 Technical skills

By undertaking a research project and producing real-world outputs, students will acquire valuable technical skills. To have the ability to produce such an output, students must understand the knowledge and processes required to complete the task and communicate the results.

6.2 Communication

Through real-world outputs, students demonstrate that they are able to communicate the findings and outcomes of their research. They must also learn how to adapt the communication of their research to a varied audience. For example, audiences in industry may be more interested in commercial aspects while academic audiences may be more focused on learning outcomes. Working as part of a team also requires the ability to communicate effectively in a clear, concise way through verbal and written interaction, as well as the ability to listen to team members. These interactions may require students to negotiate with and persuade others.

6.3 Teamwork

One of the most important skills sought by employers is the ability to work as part of a team. During my discussion with Professor McCrindle, she stated that she could not emphasise this enough and that, increasingly, employers are looking for people who can work in diverse and international teams. Working as part of a team provides students with a number of desirable skills. To be an effective team member, students must be able to communicate effectively. Within the team environment, working on a project together, students must be able to compromise and speak up to have their voice heard. For the project to succeed, students must share effort and credit, and this may throw up issues when it comes to assessment of the project. Traditionally, assessment is focused on the individual, whether in examinations or performance in practicals. Working as an individual is counterproductive in the real-world environment where most jobs involve teamwork. Prior to assessment, Professor McCrindle asks her students to sign a groupwork contribution sheet, stating whether each member of the team has contributed equally. If so, the project as a whole is assessed and each member of the team receives the same grade. If not, the assessment and mark is adjusted accordingly. Other skills that students gain through teamwork, and which employers find desirable, include the ability to manage a project and delegate tasks, build positive working relationships, take responsibility for actions, work to a deadline and manage time and budget constraints.

6.4 Leadership

To complete the task at hand, students within a team need to keep themselves and others motivated, requiring good leadership skills and the ability to communicate effectively. These skills are desirable in almost every job. Being able to contribute to a group discussion requires the self-confidence to speak up, sometimes in potentially confrontational situations and, if only recently employed, as the least experienced person in the room.

6.5 Project management

During any project, students acquire the ability to manage a dynamic project. Therefore, they must remain organised, keep the team motivated and task-focused, and work under constraints. These may include time pressures – such as how much time each member has to contribute, working to deadlines and hitting key targets in a timely manner – as well as budget constraints. The ability to understand risk management and cope with and learn from negative outcomes are also highly desirable skills for employers.

6.6 Business acumen

By interacting with industrial partners, students gain an alternative perspective, thinking about the business aspects of their output, how their industrial partner operates and how they compete within a dynamic marketplace.

7. Designing the curriculum

Applications of theoretical material in real-life scenarios make content easier to understand, and the relevance of content is demonstrated by real-life application. When I teach my students about microbiology, I design the practical sessions to reflect the real-world experience as much as possible. This may include the collection, handling and processing of real specimens in a real-world environment. The students work in small groups and much of the work is self-directed. Through research and enquiry, the students are able to gain knowledge and technical skills. When students make mistakes, they are also able to observe and understand the consequences, both to the results and, inevitably, the patient. This real-world process increases engagement and improves laboratory skills, core knowledge and the application of that knowledge. The feedback I have received has reflected this. When designing the curriculum based upon the acquisition and application of knowledge and the production of 'real-world outputs', the focus should initially be on assessment. Moreover, the assessment, or an aspect of the assessment, should be focused towards 'real-world scenarios'. It is important to consider whether assessment is to be undertaken individually or as part of a group. Individual assessment appears to be the current preferred method. However, working individually seems counterintuitive when considering life outside of university. The majority of professions require employees to work within a team.

Professor McCrindle's advice to those considering implementing a curriculum focused on real-world outputs was to start small and not be too ambitious. She said that these things often grow, and grow at a fast rate. For example, blogging often starts with an audience of just a class of students and spreads further afield. Further advice includes grasping the opportunities that come along, but if it is not what you want to do, don't do it. More opportunities will come along. And finally, value networking and collaboration: real-world partners are an important aspect of the real-world experience.

8. Problem-based learning

Problem-based learning is a student-centred learning experience (Barrows 1996). Being student-centred in nature, the focus of instruction is shifted from the lecturer to the student. Problem-based learning was initially utilised in medical schools, but its use is now more widespread. In traditional learning, students are taught the content they need to know to pass the course, they memorise that content and then a question or problem is set to check whether this knowledge has been retained. In problem-based learning, the focus is instead on solving an open-ended problem. Students work in small teams. To start the process, the students define current knowledge, identify areas where current knowledge is lacking and plan how and where to find the information needed. Therefore, it is the students who drive the learning process. The facilitator, referred to as the tutor, supervises, directs and provides support during the process.

Using problem-based learning, students gain flexible knowledge of the subject, problem-solving and effective collaboration skills, self-directed learning, and intrinsic motivation (Hmelo-Silver 2004). Problem-based learning and working in a team requires innovation, creativity and collaboration to find the best path. One of the benefits of problem-based learning is the ability to expose the students to complex thinking. In the real world it is often less about getting to the desired conclusion, and more about getting there by the optimum path.

9. Challenges and barriers

There are a number of challenges and barriers to implementing teaching through research with real-world outputs. The major issue is in student management, especially where students have a variety of backgrounds and abilities. However, the level of student management required tends to diminish as students gain in experience, so it is more of an issue earlier in their studies. Students work in teams and, as such, assessment needs to be adapted to consider the dynamics within a team. Students also work closely with external stakeholders, which may include industrial partners or volunteers. In these cases, the students need to understand the professional aspects of working with these users.

10. Real-world partners – don't go it alone

To gain a greater perspective of the real world, it is ideal to have industrial collaborators. In the sciences and engineering, industrial partners are often linked with research. This relationship should ultimately be synergistic in nature. Students work closely with industrial collaborators and must develop communication skills with these external partners in a professional manner. In partnership with the research councils, industrial partners take a leading role in the development of research projects as well as providing further funding, training and support. These include the UK's CASE studentships (formerly known as collaborative awards in science and engineering), which are collaborative training grants that provide students with a first-rate, challenging research training experience. They allow graduates to undertake research, leading to a PhD, within the context of a mutually beneficial research collaboration between academic and partner organisations, such as research funding bodies. During CASE studentships, research students undergo a placement with the industrial partner, developing real-world skills. They gain experience of an industrial research environment, as well as business-related training, for example in project management, business strategy and/or finance – expertise not provided in the academic environment. Students are also able to gain access to equipment and facilities that may not be available in their university, and develop a range of valuable skills that enhance their future employability. An important point to consider is how this pertains to less industry-intensive fields of study. The sciences and engineering have always been well connected with industry. But when you consider faculties such as law, political sciences or education, the terms 'industry' and 'industrial partners' probably do not fit. Perhaps a more favourable term is 'real-world partners'.

11. Knowledge Transfer Partnerships

An important idea that Professor McCrindle discussed was Knowledge Transfer Partnerships (KTPs). She has been an advocate of such partnerships for over two decades, undertaking projects in collaboration with small and medium-sized enterprises, global corporations and charities/social enterprises across a wide range of markets and domains. The KTP programme is part-funded by the UK Government, and is one of the UK's largest graduate recruitment programmes. It is designed to encourage collaboration between businesses and universities, allowing businesses to increase productivity, innovate and flourish. Each KTP consists of a business in the form of a private enterprise, public body or voluntary agency, a knowledge base in the form of a university, other higher education institution or research organisation and a recently qualified graduate, referred to as an associate. Initially, industry is connected with a university to solve a key strategic challenge identified by the company. The university and business then jointly submit a grant application to Innovate UK and if successful an associate is employed to work on a specific project. Many universities have a dedicated KTP contact or centre. The aims of each KTP programme are to facilitate the transfer of knowledge and technology and increase the spread of technical and business skills within the business, stimulate and enhance business-relevant research and training undertaken by the knowledge base, and enhance the business and specialist skills of a recently qualified graduate (Innovate UK 2015). As a part-government-funded programme, a business entering into a KTP programme contributes a considerable proportion of the project costs

(33–50 per cent), with the government contributing the remainder. Average annual project costs are approximately £60,000. This includes the associate's salary, as well as a travel budget, personal development budget, academic input and expertise, and administrative support. In a KTP, the academic institution employs the associate who works with the industry partner. The graduate, in conjunction with their academic/industrial supervisors, brings new skills and knowledge to the business or develops them as part of the project. Following the completion of a project, approximately 60 per cent of graduates in a KTP are offered a permanent job with the industrial partner. Furthermore, it has been shown that businesses taking part in KTP increase their annual profit and create new positions. The academic partners are able to produce on average more than three new research projects and two research papers from each project.

12. Conclusion

Throughout this book we have been exposed to many examples of how we can improve teaching through encouraging students to undertake research. By involving students in research they acquire the subject knowledge, often in a self-directed manner. However, they also obtain the skills to conduct research, analyse data and manage projects. And by working in small groups, reflecting the mode of working in most real-world jobs, students also gain valuable leadership, negotiation and communication skills. These skills are, of course, highly desirable for a career after education. Embarking on research, meanwhile, can prepare graduates for a frequent requirement being asked of those in industry: that they disseminate their work to a wider audience. In academia, the term 'publish or perish' has been coined to reflect the pressure on academics to continually disseminate their research. The most considerable part of this process is peer review. In more traditional assessment, for example marking an essay, the only person likely to read the essay (apart from the student) is the assessor. By exposing output to the real world and therefore to a wider audience, the peer-review process opens up a dialogue between the author(s) and their peers and may require them to defend their findings. By encouraging students to undertake research as part of the learning process and produce output to a wider audience, we are able to produce students who not only know their subject area but who are capable of applying that knowledge in real-life scenarios.

References

Arthur, Michael. 2014. From research-led to research-based teaching. Research, 30 April. http://www.researchresearch.com/news/article/?articleId=1343435. [Accessed 24 October 2017].

Barrows, Howard S. 1996. Problem-based learning in medicine and beyond: A brief overview. New Directions for Teaching and Learning 68, 3–12.

Biotechnology and Biological Sciences Research Council (BBSRC). n.d. Industrial CASE Partnerships (ICP). http://www.bbsrc.ac.uk/skills/investing-doctoral-training/case-partnerships. [Accessed 7 July 2016].

Hmelo-Silver, Cindy E. 2004. Problem-based learning: What and how do students learn? Educational Psychology Review 16, 235–66.

Innovate UK. 2015. Knowledge Transfer Partnerships: what they are and how to apply. Last updated 7 July 2016. https://www.gov.uk/guidance/knowledge-transfer-partnerships-what-they-are-and-how-to-apply [Accessed 24 October 2017].

Nature. 2015. 'Publish or perish.' Nature 521, 159.

UCL. 2016. 03 Students make connections across subjects and out to the world. https://www.ucl.ac.uk/teaching-learning/connected-curriculum/learn-more/dimensions-accordion/students-connect-across-subject-disciplines-and-out-to-the-world. [Accessed 7 July 2016].

Links to the R=T Framework

Joe Thorogood
Department of Geography, UCL

- Dallas discusses the importance of making research a vital component of the teaching process from the perspective of a senior academic, and demonstrates how this seems to have yielded positive results. There are three key elements that emerge from this chapter. First, the many skills that students stand to gain from research-based teaching and their immediate applicability to careers beyond education. Second, an emphasis on some form of tangible output that the student can use within a CV to demonstrate the benefit of the partnership. Third, the importance of involving industry (or third parties more broadly) in the student-led research process.

  The student–staff partnerships discussed in the chapter are therefore more of a three-way partnership, which start with staff and students, but aim eventually to include partners outside of academia. Tangible outputs are a useful and important part of distinguishing these partnerships from industry-led workshops, careers sessions and other sessions that students may already attend.

- This chapter focuses predominantly on the hard sciences, but, as a potential benefit I see wider applicability in the social sciences that goes some way to solving the challenge of the potentially narrow appeal of research-led partnerships involving industry. How, for example, might a religious studies student benefit from an industry partnership? Do such students find themselves dissuaded from taking part in research-based education when the outputs that researchers in their field produce tend to be abstract, esoteric publications? How can industry help all students to learn skills that will help them with their degree and career plans? The danger is that certain disciplines may feel alienated, or disinclined to develop such partnerships due to a perceived lack of relevance to their discipline, or a lack of confidence in finding ways of making them relevant.

This chapter focuses less on the outputs themselves, and more on the process by which these are reached (e.g. the gamification of the research process). While this area does require some technical knowledge, industry could provide these skills on a rudimentary basis to many types of students. Judging the success of a partnership on the skills, as opposed to the final output itself, would be a good hook for making the idea of industry partnerships applicable more widely to different students in disciplines that do not engage with industry in the same way that students in the sciences or engineering disciplines might.

- The traditional relationship between staff and students needs to change. This principle resonates with the skills created by student–staff partnerships in many ways. First, certain skills will be unavailable to both staff and students if the boundaries are not probed. How, for example, will students learn to write academic publications, understand the underlying rules about journal selection, write for appropriate audiences and develop advanced referencing skills if staff are hesitant about working in exactly these skills together with their students? Furthermore, academics will learn valuable editing and collaborative skills from joint-authored work that they would not necessarily access when working with other staff. Creativity in publications stems from experimentation in style and structure, and involving multiple student authors will inevitably lead to research that is different, both theoretically and structurally. A good example of this is:

Cook, I. J., Hawkins, H., Sacks, S., Rawling, E., Griffiths, H., Swift, D., Evans, J., Rothnie, G., Wilson, J., Williams, A., et al. (2011). Organic public geographies: 'making the connection'. *Antipode* 43(3), 909–26.

2.10

Connecting graduates with the real world

Transferring research-based skills to the workplace

Jawiria Naseem
UCL Institute of Education, now at University of Birmingham

with Professor Lora Fleming
Medical School, University of Exeter

Coming from a research-intensive and non-reflective tradition of 'see one, do one, teach one', it is a thought-provoking pleasure to read and ponder Jawiria's reflections on the opportunities and challenges of incorporating research into teaching to better prepare students in Higher Education for jobs in all walks of life. I also find it very humbling but also comforting that pedagogic techniques, which I thought I had developed carefully and creatively over 30-plus years of interacting with students around research-intensive learning, are part of Jawiria's established 'toolkit' as an early-career teacher and researcher! I only wish I had had access to such reflections and pedagogy during my own lifelong career as both a student *and* a teacher!

Professor Lora Fleming

1. Meet the myth of the knowledge economy

Get a degree to get a job! This is a mantra I lived with during my seven years in higher education leading up to the submission of my doctoral thesis. With a PhD under my belt (of degrees), I was ready to hit the ground running and finally experience my mantra to the fullest. But believe me, I did not get very far in the race; more realistically, let's say that I was never part of the race. I still remember my first job application post-PhD for an early-career academic position, and the feedback I received: 'You are not qualified for the role'!

So what went wrong for me? Too many hopefuls with PhDs, not enough roles, scarce research funding opportunities, priority to income-generating and experienced candidates (yes, even for early-career roles) – the list goes on! I then rephrased my mantra to meet the reality of the world I had entered blind-sided to: 'Get a degree and *hope* for a job!' My experience is far from being unique. Degrees alone are not sufficient in an increasingly competitive market, despite the continuous (dis)belief in the knowledge economy.

With its emergence in the late 1900s, the concept of the knowledge economy reflects the centrality of information and technology in modern societies (OECD 1996). Each country's competitiveness in globalised labour markets is bound to the skill and qualification level of its labour force (Lauder et al. 2012). In exchange, education, especially gained at university level, is perceived to be a gateway for personal material success. Individuals equate university qualifications with 'a better paid, more interesting and high-status job' (Brown et al. 2003, 111). Although very appealing, this idea of the knowledge economy is a myth.

The 2008 economic recession created a very precarious future for young people, including those who left the educational system with higher educational qualifications (McDonald and Thompson 2016). Within the UK, graduates soon became the largest group among the unemployed and up until 2012, the number of unemployed graduates kept rising (McDonald and Thompson 2016). Those who did find jobs (both academic and non-academic) have demonstrated flexibility and creativity. For example, many graduates enter the job market in roles for which they are overqualified, roles that do not match their subject expertise or even personal interest (Foley and Brinkley 2015). What is more, securing a job does not necessarily mean job quality. Short-term contracts, part-time work and hourly contracts are the norm. Lowering their immediate employment expectations allows young graduates to add work experience and start building their careers. In academia, however, lowering expectations can have further negative repercussions as this attitude to work can be interpreted as poor CV and job performance (Gill 2014). This instability reflects the existence of a non-linear life course, where young people need to be ready to accept jobs *not* for life, and to engage with an ever-changing and demanding job market (especially with the rapid innovation in technologies) (Heinz 2004).

This precarious job market is coupled with a range of other factors. Add a shortage of jobs to the high supply of graduates, and you will get a well-known formula: advantaged employers. Recruiters expect much more from potential employees than academic skills and knowledge. They will look at the employability of graduates, that is personal attributes, and the added value on a CV, such as engagement with charity organisations and other stakeholders, relevant work experience gained during studies, additional training and/or qualifications (e.g. Brown et al. 2003; Andrews and Higson 2008; Tomlinson 2008). Employers' expectations, however, can affect certain groups more adversely, landing them with additional challenges. PhD holders, for example, may be expected to show evidence of publications, successful grant history and international experience. Women, in particular, might also experience the pressure of starting a family (Tomlinson 2008). Yet, adding value to their CV illustrates personal qualities, initiative and commitment, which make a candidate standout. Employers appreciate such added value, since it can be seen as evidence of the practical skills employees need to conduct their day-to-day job responsibilities effectively.

So where do these changes leave higher education institutions? The expansion of higher education in the 1990s marked a decisive shift from vocationalism to the knowledge economy. Higher education responded to this economic change by becoming a mass education sector responsible for ensuring national economic development as well as for delivering prosperity to individuals. Yet is it important to remember that the (initial) aims of this massification (i.e. an increase in university participation) as set out by the 1997 Dearing Report[1] portrayed a very different picture. Increased HE participation was meant to enable young people to develop intellectually, to gain higher skills, and to participate more fully and creatively in the knowledge economy, which relied on highly qualified workers with professional skills and knowledge (not gained through secondary education only). What we ended up with was too much focus on the knowledge economy (e.g. delivery of productive graduates to the job market) and a lack of appreciation of the actual skills and knowledge of graduates. This contributed to the marketisation of higher education (Furedi 2011).

The change in status of the higher education sector – from a learning provider to an instrumental provider – created an environment where prospective students started to act like consumers when choosing their degree and university, especially with the drastic rise in tuition fees in

2010 (Furedi 2011). Molesworth and his colleagues (2011) argue that HE institutions started 'selling' their services, focusing on the financial benefits their students would gain after graduation and showcasing the high percentage of their graduates who did find jobs within six months of leaving university (yet never elaborating exactly what these jobs are). Employability had become the top priority. The 'selling' point became less about students developing intellectually, and more about gaining employability skills and a marketable qualification, with degrees matched to profitable job markets. The students (and their families) want a return on their (minimum of) £27,000 investment– and who can blame them (Tomlinson 2008)?

If graduates invest so much (both financially and otherwise) in their studies, why do they have to secure adding non-academic value to their CV, whether they want to work in or outside academia? Put differently, how can students make use of the skills and knowledge they gain during their studies towards their employability? My answer to this is: through intentional research-based teaching and learning.

2. Research-based education equals building employability skills

The relationship between research (contribution to knowledge) and teaching (sharing of knowledge) is one that is often defined by a binary divide (Schapper and Mayson 2010). For some academics, research is often perceived to be a barrier to quality teaching, while others believe that researchers enhance the courses taught. Different disciplines also require different approaches for the construction of knowledge (and I will come back to the distinction between sharing and construction). Disciplines are grouped under two main labels often known as 'hard' and 'soft' areas. 'Hard' disciplines generally refer to the natural sciences whereas 'soft' disciplines refer to the social sciences (McGrath 1978). Some course content can be very straightforward ('hard' disciplines such as mathematics), while others are open to interpretation ('soft' disciplines such as sociology). Hence, the potential links between research and teaching can vary from one group of disciplines to the other, and so the extent to which research can be integrated also differs. Either way, inquiry-based learning or research-led teaching has become the way forward for developing employable graduates (e.g. Healey 2005; Brew 2010; McLinden et al. 2015; Ziniel and Ghalib 2016; Murray et al. 2017).

In the midst of these longstanding divides, what remains clear are students, their learning and perspective. The majority of students believe that research-active teachers offer a valuable learning environment (McLinden et al. 2015; Ziniel and Ghalib 2016; Murray et al. 2017). Research-based teaching means that the curriculum is designed around inquiry-based activities that require the direct involvement of students in research by positioning them as researchers (Murray et al. 2017). As such, research informs teaching and vice versa. This relationship is to help students learn (student-focused) rather than to teach students (teacher-focused) (Hannafin et al. 2013). This subtle distinction calls for a different mode of student–teacher interaction, one that challenges traditional boundaries and pedagogy.

In this scenario, teachers and students work together in the production of knowledge through active participation, rather than act as, respectively, providers and passive recipients of its transmission. Unbalanced power relations change into an equal partnership that benefits both teachers and students. Teachers, for example, can engage in pedagogic research wherein they work towards adopting and implementing the best teaching methods that would meet students' needs, encourage their learning, and enhance their experience. In doing so, teachers evaluate their own practice (for example, by ensuring that teaching meets learning outcomes and/or through student feedback), embrace new methods when appropriate, and are aware of the scholarship in the field of teaching and learning. Research-active academics are able to share their motivation and interests with students and develop the curriculum, which further contributes to the quality of the teaching and learning experience. The teaching–research nexus thus creates mutually enriching and supportive academic roles (Ziniel and Ghalib 2016).

The research-based education approach also has several benefits for students. Exposure to scholarly activity enhances students' role through the depth of learning and understanding of the subject and course content. Students get access to up-to-date knowledge (preferably from a range of researchers and not simply dominated by the teacher's work). This fosters students' intellectual development, and provides them an opportunity to get an insight into the research process (e.g. planning, data collection methods, analysis and ethics).

I am not saying there are only benefits in research-based education (I discuss challenges later), and, undoubtedly, the extent of student engagement in the research process will vary from one discipline to another. Yet, a first-hand research experience (even a limited one) is the very foundation that teachers can utilise to build their students' employability skills. Research skills can be broadly grouped into three categories (with some overlaps): research design, research methods and research data. These sets of skills add to the functional skills and expertise required to do a given job effectively. The following sub-sections provide a non-exhaustive list of skills (and personal attributes) that can be gained through research-based teaching and inquiry-based learning activities.

2.1 Research design

Research-design skills relate to strategic aptitudes required in solving problems at work. These can enable a graduate employee to identify and review a problem, generate solutions to the problem and then create new opportunities. Specific skills are:

- attitude of inquiry (reviewing existing research, questioning facts rather than simply accepting them);
- resourcefulness (foresight, gathering information);
- innovating (coming up with research ideas);
- understanding logistics (rights, permission, ethical approval);
- seeing the work through to completion (developing a work plan and reflecting on changes).

2.2 Research methods

Research-methods skills relate to connecting academic/technical knowledge expertise to objectives. These skills can enable a graduate employee to process, organise and apply their knowledge to successfully undertake their role. They include:

- project management;
- resourcefulness (adapting to real challenges and opportunities);
- communication and listening skills (engaging in peer feedback and discussion);
- team work;
- leadership;
- social skills.

2.3 Research data

Research-data skills build on research-methods skills, since they relate to goal achievements through engagement with work partners. They include:

- critical thinking (analysing data);
- listening (discussing findings with supervisor, colleagues, mentors);
- social skills (collecting data with research participants, gatekeepers, key informants);
- presentation and communication (disseminating research findings);
- confidence (gained through contributing to knowledge).

These research skills and personal attributes are generic; that is to say they can be transferred and applied to a range of situations including the workplace beyond academia. Skills can be acquired and attributes can be developed across all academic disciplines (with some more readily integrated than others depending on the curriculum design and subject).

Having set out an overview of transferable research skills, I will now discuss practical methods that teachers can implement to connect students with the real world, especially those undertaking non-professional degrees.

3. How to transfer research-based skills to the labour market: practical lessons for teaching staff

It should not come as a surprise if I say that there is a clear divide between how university degrees are grouped. On the one hand, there are all the professional degrees (e.g. engineering), and on the other the non-professional degrees (e.g. history). Professional education is designed to meet the needs of a particular occupation so that all students in these programmes acquire the necessary skills throughout their studies to perform their day-to-day job responsibilities effectively. For example, teacher trainees undergo both theoretical (lectures, seminars) and practical training (placements). Practical training is especially productive as it gives students an opportunity to engage with their future workplace. University teaching is mostly focused on problem-based learning (which is a form of inquiry-based learning). Problem-based learning promotes both active and collaborative learning and builds students' skills as independent learners, including their ability to think critically, an important employability skill (Allen et al. 2011). This means that students learn by solving a problem through thinking strategies and applying their subject-specific knowledge. For example, medical students are exposed to real patient cases to enhance their clinical cognitive competency.

Traditionally speaking, non-professional education offers very limited opportunities for students to experience the real world during their degree time. However, since the 2010 move to higher tuition fees, universities battle to attract students (*The Economist*, 2017). Many university programmes have been re-designed to include an optional fourth year (although this remains subject-specific) in undergraduate degrees. Often known as a 'sandwich year', this gives students a chance to do a work placement (internship, voluntary work, research) or even study a year abroad as an integral part of their degree. Students are thus able to build their CV by adding valuable work/life experience.

Although considerable attention has been given to the study format in non-professional degrees, teacher pedagogy and module design have not been exploited to the fullest in their potential to enhance student employability. The skills listed in Section 2 can be built throughout the full length of study by re-thinking the traditional course design. This includes departmental staff's research activities (even those of the teacher), lectures, seminar activities and assessments. These should all be driven by research content, process and problems.

3.1 Lecture

Typically, a university lecture runs between one and two hours, with the aim of covering four to six subject-specific points. Some academics include short activities while others prefer to have a teacher-focused format (where the teacher speaks for a lengthy period of time) before moving towards student-led activities. There are a number of ways in which lecture materials could be enhanced to be more research-based. The extent to which research material could be included would vary according to the discipline and the particular subject of a given lecture.

- Lecture material should involve research data from the teacher's own and others' research to ensure that students are positioned at the cutting-edge of research (and hopefully be inspired by different approaches to research).
- Lectures can be broken into speaking and 'stop-and-think' times. 'Stop-and-think' times are short, inquiry-based activities that can include, for example, a question posed by the teacher regarding a

specific point of the research (data) presented. Students then work individually or in small groups to come up with an answer. The teacher needs to adapt a student-centred style and act as a facilitator or delegator. These roles are useful in developing students' capacity for 'self-direction and autonomy' (Grasha 2002, 140). In addition, this short shift from teacher-focused to student-focused learning calls upon specific cognitive skills such as critical thinking, communication skills and/or group work in a fast-paced environment. (It can also help 'wake up' students at 9am on a Monday morning!)

- The teacher can use visual communication to generate discussion in non-textual ways to put across ideas such as graphs (secondary data findings), pictures (ethnographic research) and objects. Object-based learning is often implemented in museum or archaeology studies and can provide an innovative and unique, hands-on learning experience (Hannan et al. 2016). This pedagogy can also be applied to a range of other disciplines and contexts (see the case study discussion on object-based assessment below). This approach provides students an opportunity to examine the evidence and to draw conclusions.

- Lectures can be made interdisciplinary. Inviting guest speakers or staff from other departments and people working in NGOs, the business sector and government brings students a valuable diversity. Students are able to engage with people with different experience and skill levels (e.g. early career versus experienced staff), as well as from different ethnic and social backgrounds, helping to raise students' social awareness.

3.2 Seminar activity

Lectures are often combined with an hour-long seminar in small groups. Seminar work offers students an opportunity to discuss the lecture points in detail, ask for clarification and become an active participant.

- Group research projects can be used as a major form of pedagogy. The project can run over one term, building on the course content, or be a weekly/fortnightly project to prepare work for a given seminar. In addition to learning together, students will engage in a range of other research-related activities such as the organisation of the workload, information gathering and the dissemination of findings in the form of a presentation to the seminar group or in writing.

- Oral presentations can be innovative by using tools such as Pecha Kucha, a presentation style aimed at keeping information fast-paced and concise. Students can present up to 20 slides for up to 20 seconds each, giving a maximum presentation time of 6 minutes and 40 seconds. This pushes students to synthesise work and prioritise discussion points. It also hones their presentation skills, encouraging them to present information clearly and concisely to a particular audience.
- Seminar activities can also be prepared a week ahead by giving students a task such as literature searches on a specific topic or a question that will form the basis of the group discussion. This can be coupled with individual short presentations of findings to the rest of the group.
- Debates can encourage students to formulate and articulate particular arguments (requiring them to research different topics/questions), and can facilitate interaction between two or more groups.

3.3 Assessment

Assessment in research-based teaching can contribute to two points: first, it allows the teacher to evaluate students' knowledge; and second, it can become the basis for examining whether or not the key skills focused on during the term/course/module have been acquired by the students. The latter point requires teachers to approach assessment in an innovative way (Biggs and Tang 2011).

- Term assessment can be a short research project linked to enhancing community life (e.g. researching a particular aspect relevant to the local community). In doing so, students could connect with their/local neighbourhoods, akin to voluntary and charity work. Students then have an opportunity to spend a considerable amount of time in the 'real world'.
- Assessment can be research-based. For example, an event reported in the news can be used as a basis for a comparative discourse analysis involving at least two news sources.[2]
- Peer-assessment (often used to transfer assessment ownership to students) can be used to enhance writing skills (e.g. structure, grammar and proofreading) as well as constructive critiquing and critical-thinking skills.

Becoming part of research projects sets up a workplace culture and environment (both academic and non-academic) where people collaborate on common goals. This requires sharing information, communicating, reflecting on the team's work and taking responsibility for one's own tasks and objectives. Building learning environments beyond the classroom can therefore provide research opportunities for students. For example, involving students in the research of departmental staff can contribute to their work experience and enhance their social as well as other key skills such as team work, the ability to follow guidelines and working under management. Student seminar activities can be made an integral part of a research project of a member of staff.

Business partners can also be involved ('business' understood in broad terms). For example, student research projects (e.g. the fourth-year project and/or final-year dissertation) can be linked to the needs of a particular business. This will build relationships between the HE institution and local businesses, and give students the opportunity to engage with the job market and develop their research skills (such as reviewing the literature and data collection, which are skills transferable to the workplace). This 'real-world' experience and networking also provides an opportunity for future internships with community groups, government or industry.

I am well aware that some of the above points will require detailed planning and time, involvement of staff across the university and, most importantly, a willingness to bring about change for the sake of student employability. However, many of these elements can be implemented at a personal level. Teachers can start preparing their students for the workplace by becoming an intentional research-active teacher. This means that teachers design courses/modules specifically to equip students with the research skills that are transferable to the workplace. Of course, it will not be possible to incorporate all of the skills identified earlier. However, by becoming intentional research-active teachers, we will ensure that student employability is part of our teacher practice.

4. Challenges in connecting students with the real world

Any teacher committed to implementing the above changes will necessarily engage in a difficult task. There are several elements that need to be accounted for, such as teachers' understanding of non-academic workplaces, student diversity and supply and demand in the labour market. Here, I will discuss five points that I consider to be the most essential in successfully implementing research-based teaching for the purpose of enhancing students' employability skills.

Let us start with the students, and more precisely the issue of convincing students. This is particularly true for certain degrees that do not necessarily include academic research work, whether teacher-led or student-led. It is very important to present the value of research to students, and signpost them to resources and the actual steps towards performing research. It is not all about learning how to do a job, but it is also about understanding and addressing the inherent complexities of any job, which is possible through the development of research skills such as critical inquiry and problem-solving. Moreover, the changes should come gradually and consistently so that students are not scared off. This involves reflecting on timing and implementation of these teaching methods across classes. Students have, after all, high expectations of what they will gain after a three-year-long and expensive investment (Woodall et al. 2014). If they do not see the (immediate) benefit of engaging in innovative teaching and learning, they might not respond to the material and study format presented to them nor realise the usefulness of their research skills beyond academia.

Another challenge is related to opportunities to gain work experience or engage in the research activity of departmental staff, which can be higher in 'hard' disciplines than in 'soft' ones. For example, a chemistry student might get a chance to work in their teacher's laboratory, whereas a sociology student would not necessarily be able to conduct semi-structured interviews with/for their teacher. Interdisciplinary collaboration across departments or institutions might be an answer to this challenge. Building stronger partnerships with local businesses, government and NGOs can also contribute to minimising the 'disadvantages' associated with certain disciplines' study format (especially those which are not applied disciplines).

Similarly, departmental culture and even the university's policy can very strongly influence the research–teaching nexus. For example, in universities focused on teaching excellence, priority is given to student learning, leaving less time for staff to conduct research. To further complicate the situation, university staff also need to consider government policies such as the introduction of the Research Excellence Framework (REF) and the more recently announced Teaching Excellence Framework (TEF). Since 2008, the REF exercises have shifted the priority from teaching to research in the majority of

HE institutions in the UK. Arguably then, research-active teaching staff might not be able to devote the time and effort necessary for the provision of quality teaching and learning. This is an issue that is often raised by students (i.e. the availability of research-active academics). Likewise, questions are often raised about their research-active academic competencies and whether or not they are 'good' teachers. With the implementation of TEF exercises, HE institutions will need to consider excellence equally in both teaching and research, thus ensuring that teaching and research remain mutually productive.

Another important question is who can initiate change? As an early career academic, can I be the strongest in implementing change or in suggesting new ideas to often more experienced and senior colleagues? Or to a department well set in its pedagogy? I do not think so. Teamwork (between newly qualified and experienced staff) can provide a platform for collaborations and a voice to (new) student-turned-academic enthusiasts (like me!).

The final point of reflection is on the actual study format and context. When should students engage in research? During their first or second year? This decision will of course vary according to disciplines. For example, in education studies, Year 1 is dedicated to imparting knowledge. This foundation is deemed important as the work in Year 2 is built upon the Year 1 work. Yet, inquiry-based learning needs to be implemented as early as possible so that students can be familiar with this learning approach and see the benefits for their future employment. This acknowledges that it takes times for students to become familiar with a mode of learning and master the required skills. An important point to remember is that the research process can be lengthy and is non-linear. Skills are built gradually and strengthened over time; a reality that further advocates implementing research-based teaching as early as possible.

As stated earlier, these are only a few of the many challenges that academic staff may face while engaging in innovative research-based teaching and learning. Although it will take time to alter a whole institution's culture, small changes within a department, course or even from an individual teacher can be a great step forward.

5. Getting ready for an ever-changing economy: rethinking learning in higher education

In discussing all the benefits and challenges associated with including research in teaching for the sake of students' employability, I made one significant assumption: Higher Education Institutions (HEIs) should prepare students for the labour market (especially students in non-professional degrees). Let's admit it: the UK government has long removed itself from any duties towards young people (deemed irresponsible and blamed for their struggle and failure, especially if they do not buy into the myth of the knowledge economy) (Tomlinson 2008). So is it really the role of HEIs to solve all these issues for young people in a world ruled by individualisation? Are educational institutions not supposed to uphold, and therefore exclusively be responsible for, the role of nurturing knowledge? At the same time, in a world where young people (and graduates) are required to become resilient, show flexibility and adaptability, is it wrong to raise our expectations of what HEIs can deliver? Education should not be limited to formal education. Several of the transferable research skills and personal attributes referred to earlier are indeed lifelong skills (such as critical thinking, social skills, the ability to be resourceful). So how do we re-envision HEIs?

Reshaping pedagogy in all disciplines, so that there is a greater emphasis on active and inquiry-based learning, will make university education move beyond the current instrumental use. This starts with making degrees interdisciplinary, and providing students with a sound foundation in lifelong learning education. This new vision, although ambitious, would build a learning environment suited for non-linear life trajectories (Aspin et al. 2001).

Interdisciplinary changes should not be limited to just the academic disciplines, but ideally should involve a university-wide opening up of doors to industry, government and charitable organisations for all degree programmes, professional and non-professional. Although effort and decision-making will still lie with students, universities can provide a platform for exchange between the 'real world' and the academy.

Links with other educational institutions should also become the norm rather than a subject-specific requirement. Connecting skills across the educational spectrum is another area where university teachers can be self-reflective of their practice. University teachers should work to build stronger relationships between high school, further education colleges and other universities. This would ensure that skills are developed over a lengthy period of time and more consistently. University and high-school teachers can work together in setting up common practices for recurrent activities throughout a person's student life (e.g. effectively communicating the presentation of findings). This would not only ensure that learning leans towards a lifelong process (at least while in the educational system), but also that students have a longer period of time to master and perfect their skills.

So where does all of this leave me (or us now, since I hope to have triggered avenues of reflections)? Research-based education is a valuable pedagogy that, if implemented intentionally, can contribute to the success of university students within and beyond academia. In the long run, it will provide students with an opportunity to identify and develop skills useful for their future workplace (and with time, for life). Yes, this will require a fundamental re-thinking of the role of the twenty-first-century HE sector and call for the strength of more than one individual and department. All of this is unlikely to happen overnight. To be more realistic, both staff and student motivation are crucial, but it starts with (a team of) teachers who would see the benefit that research-based education can bring to students and the academic community. Self-awareness will therefore be primordial in beginning this journey.

Case study: Object-based teaching and learning as innovative assessment in undergraduate education studies

I joined the Education Department at Middlesex University to teach youth studies to final-year students. Although I had gained previous experience as a postgraduate teaching assistant, this was my first comprehensive teaching role post-PhD. I was very excited to know that I was to work with a very forward-looking module leader who could not stop thinking of different ways to make teaching more interactive to raise student engagement levels. One of the areas we worked on was innovative assessment. Since then, I have implemented this practice in my roles at Birkbeck and now at the University of Birmingham. I will discuss, here, my students' Term 2 assessment (at Middlesex University), a design implemented for the first time in the department: a critical analysis of an artefact related to youth in the form of a presentation. Lost? Let me explain.

For their individual fifteen-minute presentation followed by a short Q/A session with two moderators and me, all students were required to use an artefact (defined as a physical object, visual aid, piece of music and/or film extract) and critically discuss it by bringing in youth-related theoretical frameworks, relevant research work and political debates. This assessment was built on several transferable research skills: innovating, attitude of inquiry, resourcefulness, debating, ability to apply knowledge, and presentation and communication (see Section 3, 'Research-based teaching equals building employability skills', for more information on these skills).

Novelty in teaching can be perceived as a 'no-go' area, especially for final-year students (who have other priorities than engaging in their teacher's experiments!); or it can be completely welcomed by students. There is no middle ground. From my own experience, let me admit: 'no!' and even 'never!' were the overwhelming student reactions.

Yes, my students felt thrown into the unknown (at first). They had other issues to worry about such as their dissertations, and other 'traditional' assessments to prepare for (presumably requiring a known and well-rehearsed intellectual effort applicable to all exams). Nevertheless, I managed to reassure or at least minimise my students' fears by doing the following:

- I modelled the exercise in class; this gave students an opportunity to see exactly what was expected of them (for information, I used a game controller to discuss youth culture and consumption).
- I led several formative sessions where students were able to get peer feedback and also practise their presentation. Many also took advantage of the sessions to brainstorm with their peers.
- I shared a clear set of assessment guidelines with students and also verbally explained and discussed these in class, highlighting the learning outcomes. This allowed students to ask further questions and raise any concerns they had well before the assessment date.
- Most importantly, I signposted the students: I explained in detail all the skills they already had and that were transferable to this particular assessment. These included presentation skills (communication, body language, eye contact), use of presentation software (PowerPoint and Prezi) and engaging in critical discussion of the artefact (akin to writing a critical essay).

Jobs are not for life; students need to be ready to adapt quickly and respond quickly to the demands of the labour market. I believe that the above assessment did exactly that. Innovative research-based assessments build resilience among students, which is crucial in an ever-changing world. It breaks the routine by setting up new challenges, calling for students to think (or in this case act) 'differently'.

Note

1. These were a series of major reports that looked into the future of higher education in the UK and were published in 1997. They constituted the second largest inquiry on HE commissioned by the then Conservative Government. The major recommendation was related to funding of undergraduate degrees, which led to the introduction of tuition fees by the then Labour Government in 1998.
2. See Gee (2014) for an introduction to discourse analysis.

References

Allen, D., Donham, R. and Bernhardt, S. 2011. Problem-based learning. *New Directions for Teaching and Learning*, Winter 2011, 21–9.

Andrews, J. and Higson, H. 2008. Graduate employability, 'soft skills' versus 'hard' business knowledge: A European study. *Higher Education in Europe* 33, 411–22.

Aspin, D.N., Chapman, J. D., Hatton, M., Sawano, Y. (eds). 2001. *International Handbook of Lifelong Learning*. New York: Springer.

Biggs, J. and Tang, C. 2011. *Teaching for Quality Learning at University*. Maidenhead: McGraw-Hill Education.

Brew, A. 2010. Imperatives and challenges in integrating teaching and research. *Higher Education Research & Development* 29, 139–50.

Brown, P., Hesketh, A. and Williams, S. 2003. Employability in a knowledge driven economy. *Journal of Education and Work* 16, 107–26.

Dearing, R. 1997. Higher Education in the Learning Society. London. Available at: http://www.educationengland.org.uk/documents/dearing1997/dearing1997.html. [Accessed 1 July 2016].

The Economist. 2017. *Growing Competition Between Universities is Changing Student Life*. Available at: https://www.economist.com/news/britain/21717402-universities-must-now-battle-each-other-attract-students-how-changing-them-growing. [Accessed 2 August 2017].

Foley, B. and Brinkley, I. 2015. *Unemployed and Overqualified?: Graduates in the UK Labour Market*. London: Work Foundation.

Furedi, F. 2011. Introduction to the marketisation of higher education and the student as consumer. In Molesworth, M., Scullion, R. and Nixon, E. (eds) *The Marketisation of Higher Education*. London: Routledge.

Gee, J.P. 2014. *How to Do Discourse Analysis: A Toolkit*. Abingdon: Routledge.

Gill, R. 2014. Academics, cultural workers and critical labour studies. *Journal of Cultural Economy* 7, 12–30.

Grasha, A. 2002. The dynamics of one-on-one teaching. *College Teaching*, 50, 139–46.

Hannafin M. J., Hill, J. R., Land, S. M. and Lee, E. 2013. Student-centered, open learning environments: Research, theory, and practice. In Spector J., Merrill, M., Elen, J. and Bishop, M. (eds) *Handbook of Research on Educational Communications and Technology*. New York: Springer.

Hannan, L., Duhs, R. and Chatterjee, H. 2016. Object-based learning: A powerful pedagogy for higher education. In Boys, J. (ed.) *Museums and Higher Education Working Together: Challenges and Opportunities*. London: Routledge.

Healey, M. 2005. Linking research and teaching to benefit student learning. *Journal of Geography in Higher Education* 29, 183–201.

Heinz, Walter R. (2004). From work trajectories to negotiated careers: The contingent work life course. In Mortimer, Jeylan T. and Shanahan, Michael J. (eds) *Handbook of the Life Course*. New York: Springer.

Lauder, H., Young, M., Daniels, H., Balarin, M. and Lowe, J. 2012. *Educating for the Knowledge Economy?* London: Routledge.

McDonald, S. and Thompson, A. 2016. What happens if you graduate in a recession? HEFCE. Available at: http://blog.hefce.ac.uk/2016/08/25/what-happens-if-you-graduate-in-a-recession/ [Accessed 2 August 2017].

McGrath, W. 1978. Relationships between hard/soft, pure/applied, and life/nonlife disciplines and subject book use in a university library. *Information Processing & Management* 14, 17–28.

McLinden, M., Edwards, C., Garfield, J. and Moron-Garcia, S. 2015. Strengthening the links between research and teaching: Cultivating student expectations of research-informed teaching approaches'. *Education in Practice* 2, 24–9.

Molesworth, M., Scullion, R. and Nixon, E. (eds). 2011. *The Marketisation of Higher Education*. London: Routledge.

Murray, J., Lachowsky, N. and Green, N. 2017. Enquiry-based learning online: Course development and student experience of a first-year enquiry-based learning seminar. *CELT* 10, 129–42.

OECD. 1996. *The Knowledge-Based Economy*. Paris: OECD.

Schapper, J. and Mayson. S. 2010. Research-led teaching: moving from a fractured engagement to a marriage of convenience. *Higher Education Research & Development*, 29, 641–51.

Tomlinson, M. 2008. 'The degree is not enough': Students' perceptions of the role of higher education credentials for graduate work and employability. *British Journal of Sociology of Education* 29, 49–61.

Woodall, T., Hiller, A. and Resnick, S. 2014. Making sense of higher education: Students as consumers and the value of the university experience. *Studies in Higher Education* 39, 48–67.

Ziniel, Curtis E. and Ghalib, Asad K. 2016. *Research Informed Teaching – A Mixed Methods Approach to Assessing Perception and Practice Within a Higher Education Setting*. Sage, Sage Case Studies Online. Available at: http://hira.hope.ac.uk/id/eprint/1820/. [Accessed 2 August 2017].

Links to the R=T Framework

Danny Garside

Department of Civil, Environmental and Geomatic Engineering, UCL

- Educators generally agree that 'preparing students for the workplace' is a valid priority. There is no consensus on what exactly this should look like. Jawiria suggests that 'research skills' might fit this gap.

  The skills required for research share a great deal of similarity with the skills required for a productive career in the future workplace. Skills such as: being able to question critically, to plan an approach to solving a problem, and to present ideas and findings. The value of these skills often overshadows the value of knowledge of specific facts, particularly when careers are more likely to span a wider range of professions than they were previously.

  From the perspective of an educator, research-based education should be more than just a lecturer presenting their own research, although this can be a good place to start. It can encompass a wide gamut of practices which can be described as taking an active, innovative, experimental approach to the provision of education. Due to its experimental nature, research-based education is not easy, for students or educators, as for both groups it is a departure from the known and trusted. The educator has to devote more time and effort to plan modules from the ground up, rather than relying on traditional models, and the students have to take time to understand exactly what it being asked of them.

- For students, this type of education sounds decidedly more enjoyable (never mind more valuable) than education dominated by exams and lectures. It requires students to think as well as to respond to tasks in active and novel ways. This will undoubtedly prepare students better for future challenges, where confidence (previously undervalued in education) is immensely valuable.

Judged in the cold light of a 'return on investment', in a labour marketplace where a large number of students depart from their subject, an aptitude for flexibility should allow a graduate to fare better in roles that they may not have considered prior to university.

However, departing from the traditional rule book of education takes time and effort, and those most inclined to be active researchers are not necessarily one and the same as those willing to devote time and energy to pedagogical innovation. A balance between the two is desirable at a societal level, but at a more micro level there is often a bias towards research.

It is inherently more difficult to assess flexible education, where rubrics are necessarily looser and, while summative assessment remains the norm, this is a fundamental difficulty.

- The best way to teach a subject will constantly change, and in order to provide valuable education a progressive and experimental approach is required. With transparency and honesty, students can be engaged in the development of their own education, and can assist in the ongoing development of courses. Currently, where broad skill sets seem the most likely to allow graduates to succeed in non-academic environments, educators should strive to push syllabi to provide this. Rather usefully, these broad skill sets can be provided by encouraging students to be active researchers, and this serves the double purpose of preparing them well for a future in academia, should this be their aim.

2.11

Can research-based education be a tool to help students prepare for the world of work?

Joseph Telfer
School of Management, UCL

with Professor Martin Oliver
UCL Institute of Education

Joseph's chapter provides a clear and valuable discussion of the relationship between universities and employers. There are many debates about what universities are for; this chapter provides a careful account of what is distinctive about higher education, and offers the possibility of increasing the relevance of higher education to work, without positioning universities simply as training departments for industry. A particularly important part of this account is the focus on double-loop learning. This involves moving beyond competent performance to ask more critical questions, redesigning systems or reframing experiences. Students have always needed to be creative and resilient if they are to thrive in higher education; this perspective will help recognise and reward that.

Professor Martin Oliver

1. Introduction

Research-based education as an approach to teaching is not a completely new concept. Research academics have taught their research 'as it happens' to students for centuries. Professor David D'Avray of UCL's Department of History states that it is a crucial part of his research process, allowing him to test ideas and theories on a live audience before committing to publishing (R=T Launch Event).

For students, working on the cusp of knowledge is exciting and pioneering and it can increase engagement and motivation. As they explore the limitations of their own understanding in a real-world and live research setting, students are encouraged to acquire knowledge suitable to their research needs. The concept of this skill – being able to not just learn what you need to operate now but being able to learn *how to learn to operate* – is vital in a fast-paced and competitive world. Research-based education is about how knowledge is created – the process behind innovation.

So while the idea of research-based education is not new, by naming it and formalising it into our teaching and syllabi we are better able to harness its benefits in a number of areas. One such area is in the preparedness of students for the workplace following the completion of their studies. Research-based education allows us to analyse not just what our students need now in their professional practice but also what they will need in the future, and to work this into our study programmes. Research-based education also creates the opportunity for greater partnerships between universities and external organisations, which enriches the student experience. It offers students greater exposure to workplace culture and helps improve preparedness.

However, research-based education should be contextualised and appropriate for your programme of study. It should be part of a blended curriculum and used to enrich elements of programmes of study. Pedagogical rigour must still be applied to research-based education and one must be conscious that it should provide *higher* education and not simply *more* education. Used effectively, research-based education can be beneficial to researchers/academics, students and a wider base of external stakeholder organisations.

Research-based education encourages students to engage in 'double-loop learning' (Argyris and Schön 1978), whereby they are able to learn from their errors: not simply to 'do better next time' but to structurally change the approach that created the error. This is a core feature of academic research but is less often applied to the learning process both at university and in the workplace. The rate of change now present in our ever faster-paced society means that previous norms of knowledge acquisition and application are no longer valid for long-term skill and resource planning. In short, what we know and learn today will not be what we need to know for long.

To apply this to workplace preparedness we, as teachers and facilitators, must recognise and understand the skills that our students need to thrive in today's professional environment. We must balance what they need as individuals – confidence, resilience, self-belief, entrepreneurialism, etc. – with what their employers expect of them: loyalty, commitment, passion, innovation, etc. Striking this balance, while maintaining a commitment to the core values of higher education, is a challenging exercise, but research-based education gives us tools that can help.

2. What do employers think now?

To understand the impact that research-based education can have on preparing students for their professional careers it is important to contextualise it for their programme of study. Depending on the area of study, employers will have differing views on the general preparedness of students joining at entry level. What is for certain is that right now we are seeing that employers are not satisfied with the preparedness of their new recruits (Jaschik 2015).

Increasingly, employers are turning away from traditional recruitment practices. In 2015 the international accounting and consultancy firm EY (Ernst & Young) removed the minimum requirement of an upper-second honours degree from their application process. This was after internal EY research found that there was no correlation between university grades and workplace performance (Sherriff 2016). What this shows is that however we are grading and assessing our students (at least specifically in accountancy and consultancy feeder programmes) is not helping employers to choose the best long-term staff to join their organisations.

The nature of work is changing: agile teams self-form and move fluidly to quickly and efficiently innovate. This occurs both on an internal and external basis within organisations. Collaboration and leadership are qualities most highly prized by employers but under-delivered by newly graduated students. This day-to-day model means that the long-term, focused and independent work that a student applies to a dissertation or lengthy report is largely obsolete.

To utilise research-based education to its greatest effect, it is up to our institutions, our departments and us, with our teaching colleagues, to do more to attract greater partnerships and liaisons with our professional and industry counterparts. This activity needs to be as large and as broad as the career pool that attracts students from their area of study.

Careful consideration should also be put into forging relationships with other departments and, indeed, institutions that give students opportunities to collaborate with people wildly different from their own narrow base of colleagues. As educators we must build these networks and use them to create programmes that recognise the needs of industry not just now but in the future. This means using our critical-thinking skills and our proximity to research to recognise trends in society, technology, finance and science so that we can be 'ahead' of the needs gap, not behind it.

We must, however, be vigilant against blindly accepting exactly what employers tell us they need without working with our colleagues to independently assess future needs. Doing so runs the very real risk of simply transferring corporate training budgets to universities and diluting the higher education experience.

Research-based education is a very effective model here because it makes students participants and has an emphasis on processes and problems over rote learning. This means it offers greater capacity for teamwork and collaboration. This approach can be utilised to put students in almost real-life research scenarios, or in some circumstances combine their academic studies with real-life projects. Cases have been seen where students are encouraged to find a problem in their communities and set out to solve it using a combination of the university's resources and their own enterprise.

One such case study worthy of note is the cross-university Mobile Business Ventures programme run by UCL's School of Management Technology Entrepreneurship programme. In this course students are drawn from three different institutions and three different programmes: UCL (Management), Makers Academy (Programming) and Central Saint Martins (Fine Art). These disparate groups attend an intensive twelve-session training programme over four weeks where they are taught by leading industry professionals about cutting-edge management, design, business and technology methods and approaches. Individuals are encouraged to come up with designs for smartphone applications and by a democratic process form teams. For the remainder of the programme the teams must research, design, build and launch their apps to market. Students have the support of the university and its network but are otherwise left to complete the work almost entirely independently. They must do this all on a shoestring budget and thus mimic 'start-up' business conditions. This research-based approach puts students in the driving seat: almost independently they are forced to acquire the knowledge they need to complete tasks. It also teaches them deep lessons about softer skills like teamwork, people management, budgeting and problem-solving – the kinds of skills that employers are increasingly searching for in their employees.

3. What are universities really good at?

As we have discussed above we must be careful when bringing research-based education into our programmes and syllabi, particularly when using it as a tool to increase workplace preparedness. It is important to remember what we are good at as a university – and what we are *not* good at. To try to be all things to all people simply dilutes the quality and experience of higher education. It is our responsibility as educators and facilitators to instil in our students a number of qualities that are somewhat unique to higher education: a thirst for knowledge; an ability to think and analyse critically; a systematic approach to learning and knowledge acquisition; a boldness and confidence in the face of the unknown.

Improving these qualities should be the focus of using a research-based education approach in university programmes of study and should be made explicit to external third-party partners in the design, development and delivery of any initiatives. It is not appropriate, for example, that a university delivers a purely vocational module within its programme where that module does not promote the values of higher education, regardless of how much an external partner or sponsor supports its inclusion.

This brings us back to the single-loop/double-loop learning models. Research-based education in its design allows for participants to adjust their approach to learning to change the *rules* by which decisions are made, not simply using feedback data to make more decisions (Figure 2.11.1).

Students are encouraged to become the architects of *how* they will go about achieving their learning objectives – their approach to the learning – instead of just undertaking the learning itself. This causes students to innovate and create new, efficient, personalised and independent approaches to overcoming challenges. It also helps students to learn from their mistakes, to pursue improvement and increase resilience as part of their process, thus responding to many modern management standards and norms.

As educators we are responsible for educating the next generation of workers, innovators and managers and so it is important to understand what the future holds in terms of employment and economics. In an increasingly

Process of learning

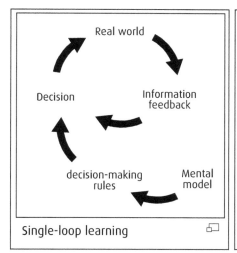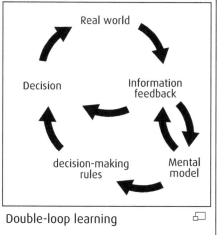

Figure 2.11.1   Single-loop and double-loop learning

automated world, even formally protected areas like accountancy are being squeezed by more sophisticated technologies. So what kinds of people are we creating, and into what kind of world are we sending them?

Computers are very good at a single-loop model but not so good at double-loop learning. Machines can easily and quickly gather data and feedback to make their decisions but they cannot easily change the protocols by which the system is governed. Almost always this is the task of a human, and it is this critical thinking which is developed and nurtured by research-based education. The workers of the future who pass through our halls of learning must have the skills needed to understand the systems they operate in, not merely the operations themselves. Because research-based education is on the fringes and frontiers of knowledge and understanding, those protocols and rules are still to be written. Thus research-based education gives us the opportunity to equip our students with greater analytical abilities to add additional value to their prospective employers and industries.

4. Where does research-based education really help?

If we are to adopt a more research-based education approach in the design and delivery of our programmes then it is important to consider the prominent areas in which it improves the higher education experience and ultimately the outcomes for students. Research-based education has the ability to increase students' abilities to acquire and retain their core knowledge through the double-loop learning model and the act of designing one's own approach to learning. However, 'soft' and transferable skills are an additional outcome of a research-based education approach and if considered properly can be systematically achieved, as opposed to simply being a happy accident.

It is important, however, that we understand what 'key transferable skills' are, as far too often they can be used to describe skills that are neither 'key' nor 'transferable'. It will be up to you as an educator to determine what these skills might be and how they might be specific to your discipline. But looking at it through the lens of 'is this skill a *key* skill?' and 'is this skill truly *transferable*?' will help us to whittle down our lists and focus on the outcomes of our programmes.

Through experience and consultation with colleagues and students I have found that three key transferable skills that are positively impacted by research-based education are: confidence, resilience and innovation.

4.1 Confidence

Research-based education takes the typical student experience of rote learning (or of 'watch and learn') and turns it into 'do and learn'. It encourages – indeed demands – that mistakes are made and methodologies adjusted accordingly. Whereas a researcher builds their confidence in their undergraduate years through learning, assessment and feedback, a student participating in a research-based education programme is already doing that: continually learning and using a combination of feedforward and feedback to hone and harness their academic knowledge and abilities. A growth in confidence is a necessary part of this process.

When a student then passes into their professional career, whatever this may be, they have already been exposed to things they did not know how to do but were encouraged to find a way to achieve. It is almost a shame that in the most traditional approaches to education a student can expect an almost identical approach from their teachers and institutions – from their early teens to their final-year dissertations and even sometimes beyond. Research-based education flips this approach and puts the student in the driver's seat and makes them the architect of their learning. As a result it creates students who are more confident.

4.2 Resilience

Entering into the workplace, students need to be resilient in the face of challenges and setbacks. In the years immediately following university, twenty-somethings increasingly face testing times – emotionally, psychologically and financially – and this is in part due to the fairness and support that universities pride themselves on providing while so many employers do not. It would be remiss to suggest that universities should in some way renege on these noble pursuits. But anything that we can do as educators to prepare students for the rigours of work and the 'real world' should be welcomed.

Research-based education in its design provides students with a growing sense of resilience due to the pioneering, independent and mistake-driven learning process at its core. The model of 'listen, learn, repeat and assess' means that students have only one chance to get it right. Pass or fail remains largely detached from the actual process of learning itself. This is a process that almost entirely vanishes in the workplace, with challenges and expectations a daily occurrence. Research-based education's design means that mistakes can be made and approaches adjusted accordingly. It better mimics the way that challenges really work 'out there' and better prepares students to be ready when they occur.

4.3 Innovation

Innovation does not happen by following the rules. It does not happen by repeating what has already been said or by doing what has already been done. It happens when we rewrite the rulebook, and to do that we need to know how the rulebook has been written and how to rewrite it.

Research-based education teaches students not only to look at the results of their study and learning but also to look at the process by which they do it – the mechanisms by which they acquire and create knowledge. Research-based education helps us create future workers who do not just repeat wasteful and inefficient processes but that rather look at the whole system and ask questions that have not been previously asked. Questions that sometimes we can be blinded to by years of conditioning.

Research-based education does not just say 'this is how we do it now'. Instead it teaches us how to understand *why* we do it like this now and *how* we might in the future. It is not just about how to follow protocol but also how to write it.

There is a risk that a research-based education approach could create students who are too pioneering for the workplaces of today, but in a world full of big and urgent problems I think this is a good problem for society to have as a whole.

5. Partnerships and sponsorship with business using research-based education

To maximise the benefit that research-based education can offer students in terms of workplace preparedness, it will be important to encourage greater partnerships and collaboration with businesses and external organisations. Research-based education is a good facilitator and proposition for these relationships as it comes from the position of innovation. Increasingly business is finding that the skills students acquire at university are sometimes already out of date by the time they emerge from their studies. The pace of change is such that business innovators need real-time access to universities, programme directors, teachers and students. To take advantage of this, our syllabi-planning practices, both design and approval, have to be able to be flexible and respond as our industry partners offer their input.

Universities are 're-establishing their role in society and re-evaluating their relationships with communities and stakeholders' (Berbegal-Mirabent et al. 2015) by expanding their influence in ever more knowledge-focused work. Human capital and the value of knowledge and innovation are essential to businesses in the highly competitive private sector. The interplay between businesses' need and universities' power to take advantage of this need is reshaping the way that these two parties interact. If we get this right, then we can use research-based education as a lever to earn ultimate benefit for our students while providing a return to our partners from industry.

To attract businesses to participate in a research-based education programme within your university programme it will be vital to understand what is in it for the business/external partner – what is their return on investment? Gone are the days when partnerships with universities were a simple box-ticking exercise helping the organisation make a positive statement in their annual corporate social responsibility report. Nowadays everything must be measured and maximised, and this includes the time and energy that an external organisation will put into contributing to a programme of study.

However, as educators and university staff, we enter into a challenging space as we seek these partnerships based on a return on investment to our partners. If we are to take financial or non-financial assistance from outside sources we must cede some influence over design and deliverables to our partners to satisfy their needs. On the other hand, it is our ethical and institutional responsibility to ensure that high standards of learning are maintained and that students are undertaking *higher* education and not simply *more* education.

We must also acknowledge that it is far easier to attract financial partnership to a nanotechnology programme than, say, medieval history. That is not to say that one offers more value than the other, but when value is viewed through the narrow lens of commercial potential some programmes will naturally have an easier time of it. It is therefore important to consider the 'true' value of the potential research-based education partnerships that you wish to form and present these alongside any commercial benefit. Fortunately, there are many different forms of funding and grants available for innovative partnerships and programmes, particularly those that feature research-based education. If partnerships based on research-based education allow us as universities, academics and students to ask more questions and enrich the learning experience, then it is something that we should pursue. Most universities have a structure in place to enable commercial projects to operate, called the knowledge transfer department. They will be able to assist you if you are looking to build a research-based education partnership programme that you think might have commercial potential.

6. How to bring research-based education to your teaching

By approaching my teaching with a view to increasing workplace preparedness, I find research-based education can offer a number of helpful facets. I am able to work with my students to set the parameters of the work we are going to do – in essence, set the rules of engagement with the students. Through being the architects, not only of the project outcomes but also the actual design of the project, engagement and motivation increases. It is a good opportunity to be humble in front of one's students as you, the co-researcher, may not have the answers to the questions that will be asked in the research-based education process. While it is sometimes nerve-wracking and intimidating, it can show students that learning is a lifelong experience and that answers are found in collaboration with colleagues, not simply gifted from an all-knowing teacher.

Research-based education speeds up knowledge acquisition through time pressure and design: adopting documented improvement methodologies in the programme allows for all stakeholders to play an active role in the design and improvement of the programme. This process itself, built into the design of your research-based education programme, increases motivation. By increasing motivation, you improve knowledge acquisition and retention.

Embarking on research-based education projects with students where it is clear to them that there is no known outcome – that they are working in new territory, on the frontiers of knowledge – invites their confidence to grow. The desirable outcome that research-based education offers in this regard is having students who do not know the answer but are excited by that absence of knowledge and understand what to do to, who have mastered the processes to go through to find an answer. And thus, they are more prepared for daily life in the workplace setting.

We must be cautious and mindful, however, of the limitations of research-based education. While it offers great advantages in a number of fields for delivering more engaging learning with improved outcomes, it cannot completely replace all other forms of education. One such area is where a base of knowledge is essential before embarking on new, research-based education programmes. This may be due to safety conditions, as in a lab, or perhaps hardware or software training modules. Research-based education cannot replace other forms of learning in these areas but we would encourage some thought into how facets of research-based education can also be used to improve and enhance learning programmes even in these early modules.

Research-based education works fantastically well as the basis for partnerships with external organisations. However, as we have seen, when accepting support or influence from outside forces we must ensure that this adheres to the strict rigour and standards of higher education institutions. Almost all areas of study could benefit from a research-based education partnership programme, and this can be sourced from as broad a field as the career pool of your programmes' alumni. The best place to begin in designing your own research-based education programme is with your heads of department. Ensuring that the outcomes of any programme are aligned with the syllabus is the first most important step and these should also be clearly presented to any external sponsor as essential to the programme. Next, speak with your knowledge transfer department if you believe that there may be some commercial application of your programme. They will be able to ensure that the programme is set up correctly, resourced and financed and will offer you the value of their networks. Lastly, engage your student body, explain the basis of research-based education and partnerships to build workplace preparedness and see what they can come up with. It is often more insightful than an afternoon meeting with colleagues.

Research-based education also encourages cross-disciplinary, even cross-institutional, study. This is something that should be embraced and celebrated within research-based education but it is important when doing this that standards don't slip for any of the disciplines and/or institutions involved. To cite the example above from Mobile Business Ventures, it is very hard to find assessment criteria and standards that can satisfy three disciplines and three institutions and moreover feed into the overall degree allocations for the participants. While it is an enriching experience for students that helps prepare them for the realities of working in the outside world, it is also a complex and demanding exercise to undertake from an administrative perspective.

Overall, research-based education offers fantastic new opportunities to educators and to students to enrich the learning experience. It provides us with the possibility to help students increase some of their 'softer' skills that will set them apart in the competitive world. It gives them the confidence to close the gaps in their own knowledge and teaches them how to go about acquiring answers to challenging questions. In a world with ever more automation it simply is not good enough to create a generation of automatons. Our future societies, economies and world need people who can write a new protocol, not just follow what we have always done.

References

Argyris, C. and Schön, D. 1978. *Organisational Learning: A Theory of Action Perspective.* Reading, MA: Addison Wesley.

Berbegal-Mirabent, J., García, J. L. S., Ribeiro-Soriano, D. E. 2015. University–industry partnerships for the provision of R&D services. *Journal of Business Research* 68, 1407–13.

Jaschik, S. 2015. Well prepared in their own eyes. *Inside Higher Education.* 20 January. https://www.insidehighered.com/news/2015/01/20/study-finds-big-gaps-between-student-and-employer-perceptions [Accessed 29 April 2016].

Sherriff, Lucy. 2016. Ernst & Young removes degree classification from entry criteria as there's 'no evidence' university equals success. *Huffington Post*, 18 January. http://www.huffington-post.co.uk/2016/01/07/ernst-and-young-removes-degree-classification-entry-criteria_n_7932590.html. [Accessed 29 April 2016].

Links to the R=T Framework

Tobias Buschel
Department of Computer Science, UCL

- Joseph's key message is that research-based education can prepare students better for future work environments. More and more, employers are recognising the lack of soft skills in new student recruits and so, by collaborating with industry, universities can ensure students are able to gain more practical experiences.

  Within this setting, the emphasis is on learning by doing as opposed to familiar theoretical learning environments. Through trial and error, students gain core knowledge and soft skills but also have the ability to challenge conventional methods by becoming architects of their own learning experiences.

  While research-based education can be a new experience for all parties involved, bringing with it a handful of challenges, educators and students alike will benefit from an enriched learning experience by challenging the status quo and engaging with external organisations.

- Joseph's argument alludes to student engagement in the scope of industry projects: he states that research-based education should foster practical applications of academic and vocational experiences for students by collaborating with industry partners. A third party is thus added to the equation, one which who brings its own challenges and opportunities that will affect the success of student and staff efforts within research-based education.

  Fostering more industry projects would entail a substantial time investment for staff, as clients have to be obtained, projects have to be coordinated, and correspondence has to be managed. It may also become more difficult to measure the success of projects and quantify the result as a grade. Projects will be different across student groups, with some perceived to be 'better', more interesting, relevant or challenging. Therefore, a collaboration between all parties (including the client) is required. Clients might want to change details of the project – and the academics and students will need to be able to react dynamically to such changes.

• A potential pitfall is that students and researchers alike may feel compelled to participate in an artificial situation of collaboration. Some students might feel that they would rather gain more fundamental and theoretical knowledge at a research-intensive university as opposed to an institution that is focused on applied sciences. For staff, the involvement of industry can be appealing but only when outweighed by the time commitment and financial investment for all parties.

My key recommendation is thus that we need to find a way to spark the ambition and excitement of both students and staff to work on meaningful and impactful projects together.

Section 3
Research-Based Education Through Student–Staff Partnership in Action

3.0
R=T in action
*Making connections to support
transitions and develop identities*

Alex Standen and Mina Sotiriou

In this final section of the volume we present a series of eight short case studies on research-based education through student–staff partnership. In the true spirit of our initiative, the case studies are all co-authored (and in the majority of cases were projects that were co-designed and co-implemented) by academics and students, underlining the importance of working in a consortium setting (see **Introduction).** The eight projects are diverse in aims and approaches, from digital innovations in research dissemination (**3.1**) to exploiting students' linguistic diversity to foster an inclusive learning community (**3.6**). The case studies extol the many and varied benefits of participating in such projects. We learn, for example, of a project in science communication that seeks to provide students with an immediate connection to research and researchers, and increase their sense of belonging to a department (**3.7**). We also see how student feedback can be elicited, which draws on the benefit of hindsight for reflection and evaluation (**3.2**). Read together, the case studies offer a compelling portrait of how research-based education through student–staff partnership can be taken forward by individuals, teams and departments to help shape higher education.

In this short introductory chapter we highlight two particular ways in which these examples of R=T 'in action' present a persuasive argument for the relevance of research-based education through student–staff partnership in the contemporary higher education landscape: how it can be employed to enhance the student experience during challenging transitionary phases, and how it can foster the formation of communities of practice and new 'researcher' identities.

Navigating the transitions into higher education, between phases of study, and out of study into the workplace are inherently challenging. Students undertaking any one of these shifts may find themselves in a 'liminal state', or requiring 'transformations, ontological and epistemological' (Barkess and Tierney 2015, 1). The challenges facing the newly arrived undergraduate have been well documented (see, for example, Briggs et al. 2012; Leese 2010). But so too must the student moving from undergraduate to postgraduate education (or from the relative safety net of the university into the professional world) cross thresholds in understanding, knowledge and skills, autonomy, self-perception and social and cultural integration.

Modules, programmes of study, departments and institutions can do much to support students as they negotiate their way through these states of liminality. For students moving into higher education for the first time, gaining experience of its realities via summer schools, for example, or presenting school curriculum topics in the style of higher education, can help to prepare students for independent learning (Rowley et al. 2008, 410). The development of a higher education 'learner identity' is essential to student achievement and is initially encouraged where schools, colleges and universities adopt integrated systems of transition (Brigg et al. 2012). Likewise, institutional support, tailored supervisory interventions and an inclusive research culture are all proposed as strategies to support learners in their transition to postgraduate education (Kiley 2009).

What place does R=T hold in this landscape? Crisan et al (**3.3**) interrogate the ways in which targeted student–staff partnership projects can enhance transitionary phases in mathematics and engineering, in particular that of undergraduate to postgraduate education. As one of the student authors explains, as an undergraduate what is often felt to be missing is learning how to see the discipline as a 'unified field of interconnected knowledge', rather than a set of discrete skills and topic areas. The authors thus advocate close and early collaboration between students and academics, both to raise awareness of what it is that researchers *do*, and what research in the discipline indeed means.

For Marjanovic-Halburd and Bobrova (**3.4**) it is support from students in the next phase of study that can similarly enrich transitionary phases (and indeed be mutually beneficial to the student at that next level). While the case study focuses specifically on student–student supervision, it is a model which can be adapted to numerous contexts and to foster a learning environment that is inherently 'collegial' and 'relaxed' – fertile terrain, in other words, for the requisite shifts in learner identity and autonomy.

In their exploration of the role of digital tools in the transition into university-level mathematics, Geraniou, Mavrikis and Margeti (**3.5**) comment that, 'the transition from school to university requires a shift from an external locus of control to an internal one'. To a certain extent this is true of all such transitions: after all, as a student moves from one phase to another – both within education and beyond – there is an ever-greater call for independence and self-motivation. For Evans et al. (**3.8**), whose project also targets first-year undergraduates, learning communities underpin a successful academic experience for students – and certainly strengthen transitionary phases. The authors emphasise that learning communities should encompass both academic staff and students from all years of the programme, and that there is a method for sharing knowledge within that learning community.

All eight case studies bring together groups of people who share a common interest to learn by research and engage with each other to create a shared output to promote learning. Such social participation in learning echoes Lave and Wenger's (1991) communities of practice, defined as groups of people with shared concerns, interests or passions for something they do, who learn collaboratively how to do it better.

Miller et al.'s chapter (**3.1**) clearly demonstrates the development of such a community of practice in which students and staff, over a period of time, actively interact, participate, collaborate and share ideas to build a shared repertoire of resources – in this instance books and a MOOC (Massive Online Open Course).

The concept of social participation, however, does not exist by itself. It also affects the way in which participants think and experience learning as the production of social structure, which as a result affects their identity. Identity, as Wenger defines it, is 'a way of talking about how learning changes who we are and creates personal histories of becoming in the context of our communities' (1999, 5).

Learning can be viewed as a journey that results in the production of a new identity. Such journeys are evident both in Crisan et al. (**3.3**) and in Gombrich et al.'s (**3.2**) chapters. The evolution of students' identity – from school-leaver to undergraduate to researcher – shapes their experience of themselves and it also shapes the way they see learning.

In such a view, communities of practice can be seen as the nexus of implementing R=T, referring to a process in which learners are not only participating (student–staff partnership) in learning (research-based education) but also shaping and defining their identity.

The words 'collaboration' and 'community' recur repeatedly in the eight case studies (**1.0**). To varying extents, all of the projects are born of the concept of learning as a social experience. Already, Fung's UCL Connected Curriculum (2017) foregrounds the importance of students connecting with both researchers (Dimension One) and each other, across phases and with alumni (Dimension Six) to enhance their sense of belonging and to ensure they feel part of a learning community. Through the R=T initiative, we can see how such projects can be transformative for both students and their academic partners. At the same time we see the development of communities of practice and, potentially, the formation of new identities.

References

Barkess, G. and Tierney, A. 2015. Transition to Research: Experiencing new paradigms. http://www.enhancementthemes.ac.uk/docs/paper/transition-to-research-experiencing-new-paradigms.pdf?sfvrsn=6 [Accessed 12 March 2017].

Briggs, A. R. J., Clark, J. and Hall, I. 2012. Building bridges: Understanding student transition to university. *Quality in Higher Education* 18, 3–21.

Fung, D. 2017. *A Connected Curriculum for Higher Education*. London: UCL Press.

Kiley, M. 2009. Identifying threshold concepts and proposing strategies to support doctoral candidates. *Innovations in Education and Teaching International* 46, 293–304.

Lave, J. and Wenger, E. 1991. *Situated Learning: Legitimate Peripheral Participation*. Cambridge: Cambridge University Press.

Leese, M. 2010. Bridging the gap: supporting student transitions into higher education.' *Journal of Further and Higher Education* 34, 239–51.

Rowley, M., Hartley J. and Larkin, D. 2008. Learning from experience: The expectations and experiences of first-year undergraduate psychology students. *Journal of Further and Higher Education* 32, 399–413.

Wenger, E. 1999. *Communities of Practice: Learning, Meaning, and Identity.* Cambridge: Cambridge University Press.

3.1
Why We Post – a team approach to research dissemination

Daniel Miller, Elisabetta Costa, Laura Haapio-Kirk, Nell Haynes, Tom McDonald, Razvan Nicolescu, Jolynna Sinanan, Juliano Spyer, Shriram Venkatraman and Xinyuan Wang

Department of Anthropology, UCL

This chapter discusses the way that nine anthropologists formed a team that disavowed our differences as staff or students. It shows how we collaborated equally to create a strategy for research dissemination that recognised the huge audience for a project on the use and consequences of social media. All aspects of research and writing were conducted in direct collaboration and much of what has resulted has been collectively authored.

To try and reach as diverse an audience as possible, we reconceptualised research dissemination as a spectrum. We started by writing journal articles for academic consumption, and then moved to eleven open-access books written in a highly accessible style. Following this we created a massive open online course (MOOC) on the FutureLearn platform and then, for the widest appeal, we created a website called 'Why We Post' that includes over 100 films, many stories and announces our results as 'discoveries'. Apart from the books, all our materials are translated into all the languages of our fieldsites. All of this was possible only through combining the skills and language knowledge of our team as a whole.

1. Introduction

Discussing what has flashed across our smartphone screens may have finally surpassed the weather as our favourite topic of conversation. Items on the social and cultural consequences of social media appear daily in our newspapers. So it would be a great pity if the academic contribution to the understanding of this topic did not at least attempt to reach the vast audiences who might be interested in the result. In this study, we consider the results of nine anthropologists, each of whom spent 15 months on fieldsites all around the world to study the use and consequences of social media in a project funded by the European Research Council ERC grant 2011-AdG-295486 Socnet.

In this instance, our ambition was closely connected to a method of research and engagement that may be more common in the natural sciences but is quite rare in social science: collaborative team effort. Although our group consisted of researchers at different stages of their academic careers – postgraduates, postdoctoral staff and a professor – we only ever changed our collective ideas about what to research and how to research based on a simple discussion and vote. Very unusually we decided that the PhD students would write their books before writing their PhDs, so as to be synchronised with the rest of the team. During the fieldwork all nine researchers focused on the same topic each month, exchanging extensive notes before moving on to the next topic. The writing-up of the nine monographs followed the same procedure, with all but one book chapter being written simultaneously under the same heading. Much of what was produced for the MOOC and website were created collectively and anonymously. This commitment to a genuinely collaborative and comparative project was essential to the subsequent dissemination of our findings.

2. Connecting with our audiences

Once we accept that this research is of interest to an extremely diverse audience, we need to see research dissemination not as a single thing, but as a spectrum that can span that diversity. At the most academic end are the journal articles, which we expect to be read only by academics and so made no concessions in their writing style. However, we provide the core of our results in 11 open-access volumes being published by UCL Press. This is where we can exploit the rich stories and poignant instances of personal engagement that make up so much of an ethnographic study. For this reason, citations and discussions of other academics are mainly found in footnotes. The first three books of the series were launched on 29 February 2016. The fact that there have already been over 320,000 downloads from our books worldwide (as of December 2017) suggests that our desire to connect with a wider readership was warranted.

In recent years, traditional forms of lecturing have been challenged by the rise of free e-learning courses known as MOOCs. Recently the Open University developed its own initiative through a platform called FutureLearn. For various reasons this was our preferred platform. We were fortunate that at just the right moment UCL signed an arrangement with FutureLearn, and so we were chosen to create the first UCL FutureLearn course. Rather than using traditional lectures, the steps of a MOOC typically consist of short videos of the kind that we were producing.

The English-language version of the course will repeat three times in 2016: in February, June and October. As is common for such courses, the 13,000 people who registered reduced to some 5,000 'learners' during the course, but, unlike most classes that we teach, these people are voluntarily undertaking education in their spare time. The degree of participation on every step of the course has been impressive: one of the more theoretical components, an argument for a new definition of social media as 'scalable sociality,' received over 1,000 comments from participants by the end of the course's first delivery. The course was produced entirely in-house with the infographics created by Xinyuan Wang (one of the team) and most of the films made by Cassie Quarless, a student on the UCL MSc in Digital Anthropology, who had also produced the films for our Trinidad fieldsite. In a way, a MOOC is itself a form of interactive social media, and all the team enjoyed the direct participation of taking part in these conversations that followed from comments by those taking the course.

The audience for this course was clearly global, as the map in Figure 3.1.1 shows. There were more than a hundred registered students from places as diverse as Ukraine, Mexico, Indonesia and Russia. Typical students are people studying social media, or anthropology, around the world.

Such e-learning courses often tend to attract older audiences who may already have a university degree, as this is clearly a university/college-level format. To reach still wider audiences, we also created a website called 'Why We Post' (www.ucl.ac.uk/why-we-post), where we announce our results as 'discoveries' with comments from each of the fieldsites. The site also includes over a hundred short films and many stories to enhance the popular appeal.

Figure 3.1.1 Numbers of learners who enrolled in the first offering of our FutureLearn MOOC, and where they are based

3. Spreading the word across languages

One critical limitation to all of this would be language. Most of our informants, like most of the world's population, do not speak English. We therefore used some of our funding to translate the entirety of the MOOC and website into the seven languages of our fieldsites in addition to English. This required subtitling 130 films in English and then managing the subsequent 910 individual pieces of translation, all of which was managed by Laura Happio-Kirk, who had also to ensure that what was said in the films did not thereby lose any of its anthropological inflection. At present, FutureLearn does not support multiple languages and we do not have the long-term resources for our own online engagement in these languages, so the foreign language MOOCs sit on an alternative platform developed by UCL called UCLeXtend. Our Portuguese site already has over 1,300 followers and we have barely begun the publicity.

Finally, we have two more strategies to attempt to engage still more widely. One is to integrate our material into the National Curriculum in schools, for example within the A-level (i.e. university entrance examinations offered in England, Wales and Northern Ireland) courses for anthropology and sociology. The other has been to reach low-income colleges in South Asia with poor internet access through distributed DVD copies of the course in Tamil. When distributing these individual copies, we always explain to educators that since all our material is under a Creative Commons licence, they are free to incorporate it under their own local certification schemes. Once again, we have benefited from a team approach that exploits our combined languages and skills to do so much more than any one of us could have accomplished alone.

3.2

Challenges of interdisciplinary courses containing research-based learning components

Carl Gombrich, Virginia Alonso Navarro, Isabelle Blackmore, Jacopo Blumberg, Emily Cox, Graham Hodges-Smikle, Jiaqi Lin and Charles Orr

BASc Programme, UCL

1. Introduction and background

Provision of interdisciplinary (ID) modules and full ID degree programmes is expected to rise in the UK and indeed in global higher education (HE) (Kirby and van der Wende 2016; Lyall et al. 2016). Contemporaneously, there are drives to increase the amount of research-based learning (RBL) in HE (HEA 2014, Healey 2015, University of Leeds 2016). Yet both ID courses and RBL are challenging to deliver and present challenges to students. ID courses can be problematic due to issues of administration (e.g. teaching loads and interdepartmental funding), and also of conceptualisation (Morrison 2015; Lyall et al. 2016); RBL makes demands, among other things, upon student expectations, and can have cost implications.

Students are vital partners in understanding this landscape. However, student course evaluations can be a blunt instrument. Perceptions change over time and what might seem a good (or a bad) idea at one point in a learning journey may, with hindsight, be perceived differently (see e.g. Rice 1988; Taylor 2014). As teachers and students interested in progressive moves in, and benefits arising from, both ID courses and RBL, we wish to disentangle some of these themes to better understand the student experience and to deliver the most interesting courses.

2. Method

To research these issues a call was put out to Arts and Sciences students via Facebook (approximately 300 student followers) asking for volunteers from years 2 and 3 who would be happy to state that they had some serious reservations about key aspects of these Year 1 ID/RBL courses at the time they took them (resulting in not fully positive evaluations) but after one to three years' further study and experience, would now evaluate these courses differently.

Ten students replied and seven eventually agreed to be co-authors in the research. An email containing eight open questions relating to ID learning and RBL was sent to each student and a short email exchange in the form of a dialogue followed.

3. Evolution of perceptions and evaluations

When discussing the content of an ID course, one author comments: '[Regarding] Approaches To Knowledge, [at the time] I disliked the . . . vagueness of the course. I was never really sure what the course was . . . about, whether it fell under education studies, or philosophy . . . or something else entirely.' However, from the vantage point of two subsequent years of study, the same author notes: 'I still would not be able to put a finger on what the course exactly was, but in hindsight I can say that the topics covered during [this course] have been surprisingly useful in other subjects, and have resulted in transferable skills and topics I did not foresee.'

And, with regard to RBL, one of us comments: 'my initial reaction towards the . . . research projects was one of resentment'. But two years later and after graduation:

> . . . my initial reservations . . . are perhaps more a reflection of a naivety . . . about what a university education . . . involved than of the . . . value of the course itself. Furthermore, as an impressionable first-year, my sentiments were perhaps more affected by the reactions of my peers than I would care to admit. Nevertheless, as I progressed through university, becoming more independent and confident with my own academic work, the more I came to realise the benefits of undertaking those initial assignments.

Another author comments that being asked to do research projects affected her initial evaluation of the course greatly: 'I did fantastically in my [first assignment], [the] podcast. However, in the first Approaches To Knowledge [research] essay I did terribly; it really brought down my morale and I hated [the topic of "superconcepts" we were studying], I thought they were stupid and that [the degree] was trying [too] hard to be special.'

Reflecting on the challenges of delivering RBL, one author notes:

> I think there is a . . . fine balance between a research assignment that is broad, yet relevant [to] the course and an assignment that is undirected and confusing. This means that a lecturer has to take great care . . . to make sure that their course material is clearly presented and that what they want to be included in their undergraduates' research is clearly stated. I also think there is an issue with assuming that undergraduates know more about research than they actually do.

However, although perceptions and evaluations of ID learning and RBL can become entangled and change markedly over time, other authors who, at the time they studied them, were negative about the *content* of ID courses, remark that it was the RBL component that redeemed the courses for them and led to more positive feelings on exiting them:

> . . . undertaking a research project was the only useful part of the entire experience of Interdisciplinary Research Methods (IRM) and would have been the only part of the course I evaluated favourably.

And:

> It was a trying process to make sense of the course material and the nature of the research project. However, overall, while each brings is own challenges, the two facilitate the understanding of one another.

And:

> I surely preferred the IRM [RBL] assessments to the lectures.

Finally, as one author comments: 'I was very glad to be doing research projects, as they gave me a chance to investigate a topic I was interested in.' Might we then use RBL productively to mitigate any of the more negative perceptions about ID courses?

4. Next steps

We are proponents of both RBL and ID courses. We have seen these ideas and approaches work well both in our personal study experiences and in terms of the overall outputs of a degree programme. Nevertheless, we should not accept the value of RBL uncritically. On the trendiness curve it is perhaps a little behind ID itself, but catching up fast. RBL should therefore be subject to the same scrutiny as ID education or any other practices that claim to be necessary innovations in an otherwise fusty academy.

Despite the wealth of literature on student evaluations, RBL and problem-based learning (see e.g. Dochy et al. 2003; RICE 2015) there are, we propose, rich seams of qualitative research involving student experiences of RBL, ID learning, learning journeys and adult development still to explore.

Are there ways to highlight some advantages of ID learning to younger and more sceptical undergraduates? Can we motivate and substantiate earlier the advantages of RBL? Can we build narratives, perhaps using the experience of peers or slightly older students to enable less experienced students to grasp opportunities earlier in their learning journeys? Can RBL help in making sense of ID courses? Or might it hinder?

It is vital, we suggest, to continue to investigate an evidence base for the value of both RBL and ID courses if universities wish to develop these learning initiatives.

References

Dochy, F., Segers, M., Van de Bossche, P. and Gijbels, D. 2003. Effects of problem-based learning: A meta-analysis. *Learning and Instruction* 13, 533–68.

Healey, M. 2015. Research-based Curricula in College-based Higher Education: A selected bibliography. Available at: www.mickhealey.co.uk/resources. [Accessed 5 July 2016].

Higher Education Academy (HEA). 2014. Developing research-based curricula in college-based higher education. https://www.heacademy.ac.uk/sites/default/files/resources/developing_research-based_curricula_in_cbhe_14.pdf [Accessed 24 October 2017].

Kirby, W. C. and van der Wende, M. (eds). 2016. *Experiences in Liberal Arts and Science Education from America, Europe, and Asia: A Dialogue across Continents.* New York: Palgrave Macmillan.

Lyall, C., Meagher, L., Bandola, J. and Kettle, A. 2016. Interdisciplinary provision in higher education. https://www.heacademy.ac.uk/sites/default/files/interdisciplinary_provision_in_he.pdf [Accessed 24 October 2017].

Morrison, D. 2015. The underdetermination of interdisciplinarity: theory and curriculum design in undergraduate higher education. PhD. University of Glasgow.

Rice, R. E. 1988. Extending the domain of teaching effectiveness assessment. http://www.comm.ucsb.edu/faculty/rrice/teachpap.htm#allen. [Accessed 5 July 2016].

RICE Centre for Teaching Excellence. 2015. Student Ratings of Instruction: A literature review. http://cte.rice.edu/blogarchive/2015/02/01/studentratings. [Accessed 5 July 2016].

Taylor, S. 2014. How useful are teaching evaluation scores? http://www.simontaylorsblog.com/2014/05/21/how-useful-are-teaching-evaluations-scores/. [Accessed 5 July 2016].

University of Leeds. 2016. Research-based Learning. http://curriculum.leeds.ac.uk/rbl. [Accessed 5 July 2016].

3.3

Learning about what research is and how researchers do it

Supporting the pursuit of and transition to postgraduate studies

Cosette Crisan and Eirini Geraniou
UCL Institute of Education

Adam Townsend
Department of Mathematics, UCL

Sebastian Seriani
Deptartment of Civil, Environmental & Geomatic Engineering, UCL

Pedro I. O. Filho
Department of Chemical Engineering, UCL

1. Introduction

This chapter is the result of conversations between the various authors about how to raise awareness among undergraduates about what research entails, and what support could be put in place to facilitate the development of those skills needed by researchers in mathematics and maths-related fields. We carry out a brief review of non-subject-specific research about transitioning to postgraduate education. We then suggest some strategies for engaging undergraduates, postgraduates and academics in a partnership intended to develop their subject-based research and enquiry skills, grounding their understanding about what research is and what researchers do from early on in their studies.

2. The current postgraduate transition landscape

Research suggests that the transition to postgraduate study deserves the same attention as that of the transition to undergraduate. In their project involving focus groups with 30 members of staff and 41 postgraduate students, and five in-depth individual interviews with postgraduate students (one PGCE, one MA, one MBA and two PhDs) at Greenwich University, Alsford and Smith (2013) found that postgraduate students want recognition that their study level is different and that their transitional needs are as valid as those of undergraduates. Indeed, there is a growing body of research into Masters and doctoral students' that acknowledges that these students have particular transitional needs. Preparedness for postgraduate life and study, communication and socialisation skills, staff and student training – these various issues are now being acknowledged by research, with some institutions starting to improve their policy and practice around postgraduate transition (Alsford and Smith 2013).

Researchers have suggested that a lack of focus on the transitional needs of postgraduate students reflected an assumption that students were (a) somehow already prepared for postgraduate study since postgraduate-level study is simply 'more of the same . . . taken to the next level' (O'Donnell et al. 2009, 27) or (b) already experts in the realm of higher education and learning, and so would not even acknowledge moving on to the next level of study as being a transition issue (Tobbell et al. 2010). Indeed, it was only when working on his Masters project that Adam, one of the PhD students contributing to this chapter, formed a clearer idea about what his PhD research was going to be like. Many students who decide not to complete a Masters degree would graduate with no insight or experience about the research process, and therefore unprepared for a workplace that requires them to confidently tackle and solve problems.

3. Making the transition: the student experience

Through interviews and focus groups, Symons (2001) found that students had a desire for more information about the course they were going to be studying and wanted to know what would be expected of them in terms of academic requirement. Approaching a taught undergraduate degree versus a research degree requires significant changes on the part of the students in terms of how they deal with the subject. At undergraduate level, one accumulates a solid foundation of discrete knowledge, mainly through the understanding and reproduction of lecture notes. Adam recalls his undergraduate years when he was given a problem to work on, which most of the time was already broken down into 'bits and pieces' for him. Understanding the statement of a theorem, being able to reproduce its proof and applying it were skills and knowledge Adam developed through regularly assigned homework, which tended to focus on the techniques and applications of maths results introduced in the lectures. These skills were invaluable for Adam in carrying out his PhD research. However, Adam came to realise that he was missing the big picture, of how the different maths topics he had studied fitted together in the maths landscape that he is now – through much of his own individual and lengthy pursuit – aware of. In his view, undergraduates would benefit from being able to see maths as a unified field of interconnected knowledge, rather than a collection of disjointed subtopics.

Both Sebastian and Pedro, PhD students in Engineering, reflect on their undergraduate experience and how it contributed to and supported their development as engineers. Pedro works with optimisation under uncertainty, which has applications in many fields, for example modelling and design of processes. He believes that the knowledge and skills he developed through studying pure mathematics for the first two years of his engineering degree developed his enquiring mind, paying attention to details and asking lots of 'what if' questions. These skills and knowledge empowered him not only to understand the 'theory behind the models out there' but also 'to go inside' those models and adapt them for the problem at hand. In his view, current engineering undergraduates would benefit from being made aware that understanding the principles behind how models work can enable them to modify, adapt and customise the models 'to work for them'.

Sebastian thinks that undergraduates' learning could be made more exciting. In his opinion, undergraduate engineers find it difficult to engage with mathematics. They find it 'dry' and as a result are not really motivated to know more than the final equation that is needed for the application of a model. For this reason, Sebastian suggests that undergraduates could be shown what research entails: engaging creatively with the 'dry maths' to create and improve the models.

4. The importance of doing research

In this chapter we propose that engaging students in research and inquiry could and should be supported from early on in their undergraduate studies. In their report for the Higher Education Academy, Healey and Jenkins (2009) argue that all undergraduates students in all higher education institutions should come as close as possible to the experience of academic staff in carrying out disciplinary research. Indeed, the UCL Connected Curriculum aims to ensure that all students are able to learn through participating in research and enquiry at all levels of their programme of study. Moreover, Hathaway et al. (2002) found that those undergraduates involved in research were more likely to pursue graduate education and postgraduate research activity than students who did not participate in undergraduate research.

Through exposure to disciplinary research, all students will benefit from asking the right questions in the right way, conducting experiments, and collating and evaluating information. In the UK, most undergraduate students experience research as part of their final-year dissertation. For their dissertation, students choose a topic of interest to them, and such interest is mainly shared with the supervisor and the second marker, with no further dissemination of the outcomes of their work. Adam recounted his near struggle at the beginning of his postgraduate degree with reading maths papers. These papers tend to be quite technical and difficult to understand. But once understanding was achieved, Adam found that he needed to develop a habit of sitting back and trying to see the bigger picture, rising above the maths propositions, lemmas, theorems, etc., and understanding where the ideas fit in the maths landscape. Adam's view is that this skill should and could be learned early on, at undergraduate level, through collaboration with peers and researchers.

Although academic mathematicians are well aware of the role of intuition in mathematics (Burton 2004), they may not address it explicitly in their teaching beyond linking it with problem-solving. Just as Burton (1999) pleaded with anyone who has responsibility for the learning of mathematics to model their own intuitive processes, to create the conditions in which learners are encouraged to value and explore their own and colleagues' intuitions, Adam too thinks that 'intuition needs to be explicitly taught'. He tries to develop intuition in the tutorials he teaches to undergraduates, as intuition could then be used and developed further in acquiring new knowledge.

5. Recommendation

We thus propose a collaboration between staff and students at undergraduate and postgraduate levels aimed at raising awareness among undergraduates about what research is and what researchers do. Undergraduates could be brought into the world of research by enabling them to learn in ways that parallel and reflect how academic staff and postgraduates research and learn their discipline.

References

Alsford, S. and Smith, K. 2013. Transition into Postgraduate Study. Case Study 23 in Learning from International Practice – Taught Postgraduate Student Experience. SHEEC Enhancement Themes. http://www.enhancementthemes.ac.uk/sheec/learning-from-international-practice/taught-postgraduate-student-experience [Accessed 24 October 2017].

Burton, L. 1999. Why is intuition so important to mathematicians but missing from mathematics education? *For the Learning of Mathematics* 19(3), 27–32.

Burton, L. 2004. *Mathematicians as Enquirers: Learning about Learning Mathematics*. Dordrecht: Kluwer.

Hathaway, R. S., Nagda, B. and Gregerman, S. 2002. The relationship of undergraduate research participation to graduate and professional education pursuit: An empirical study. *Journal of College Student Development* 43, 614–31.

Healey, M. and Jenkins, A. 2009. Developing undergraduate research and inquiry. Higher Education Academy. https://www.heacademy.ac.uk/resource/developing-undergraduate-research-and-inquiry [Accessed 24 October 2017].

O'Donnell, V. L., Tobboll, J., Lawthom, R. and Zammit, M. 2009. Transition to postgraduate study: Practice, participation, and the wider participation agenda. *Active Learning in Higher Education* 10, 26–40.

Symons, M. 2001. Starting a coursework postgraduate degree: The neglected transition. Paper presented at the Changing Identities: Language and Academic Skills Conference. University of Wollongong, 29–30 November.

Tobbell, J., O'Donnell, V. and Zammit, M. 2010. Exploring transition to postgraduate study: Shifting identities in interaction with communities, practice and participation. *Educational Research Journal* 36, 261–78.

3.4
Final-year projects as a vehicle for delivering research-based education

Ljiljana Marjanovic-Halburd and Yekaterina Bobrova
The UCL Bartlett Faculty of the Built Environment

1. Introduction

The final project for the MSc Facility and Environment Management (FEM) programme is designed to give students the opportunity to conduct independent research relevant to facility management practice, and, in the case of part-time students, the needs of their employer and sponsor. The quality of the work across the board is generally high and the research design robust, which is independently confirmed year on year by external examiners' comments. If the student takes a further step and writes up their dissertation in the format of a research paper, it gives him or her the chance to further reflect on the importance of well-defined research design, work towards a deadline with the co-authors in a team environment and, ultimately, communicate their new learning to audiences in both the UK and overseas. The importance of all these extra dimensions are clearly identified within the UCL Connected Curriculum framework.

2. The case for student–student supervision

Over the course of my 25-year-long lecturing career, I have co-authored about 18 papers, initially with my undergraduates and now with my MSc students. As I began to engage with the surrounding educational literature, I recognised that my relationship with my students had always been collegial. It is therefore not surprising that I am still in contact with most of these students with whom I co-authored papers, or that the majority of them have remained active researchers either in academia or in their various professional settings. This is possibly best described in some feedback sent to the then course director from one of the students I supervised in 2015, published at an international conference in 2016: 'I am especially happy with the grade awarded to my dissertation, and for that please extend a special thank you to Dr. Ljiljana who was really a very knowledgeable and encouraging supervisor. Her unique style of supervision helped me to focus on my research in a way that enhanced my innovation and passion to explore.'

However, the effort of involving students at research level, including helping them produce refereed publications, is time-consuming for academic staff, who are already under pressure trying to meet the high-level expectations for their own work. To address this, in 2015 I involved one of the PhD students from my institute in supervising one of my MSc students. At the time, Yekatherina had just started the third year of her PhD, so I had confidence in her as a researcher. While supervision is something I do routinely, for Yekatherina it was the first time she had ever supervised anyone, and so she was extremely enthusiastic and excited about it. That enthusiasm almost certainly transferred to Claire, the MSc student, as well. Yekatherina generally also had fewer work commitments than me, and so was able to allocate more time and resources to Claire's supervision, creating the potential for Claire to grow from a B-grade student to someone who eventually achieved a commendation for her dissertation.

Having one student, albeit more experienced, supervise another contributes to a collegial atmosphere in which an MSc student can feel more relaxed – for instance, not ashamed to tell her peer that she didn't understand something. An MSc student might feel uncomfortable admitting this to her lecturer, as she might have a perception that she was expected to know that 'something' already. In other words, the MSc student might feel more comfortable asking her peer for repeated feedback rather than a busy superior.

As for Yekatherina, this is what she has to say about the experience:

It was an amazing opportunity for me to structure my thoughts on how to do research. At the time of the dissertation I was already in the beginning of the third year of my PhD, so I already knew how to do research. However, the best way to learn about the topic is to explain it to somebody else. It was the first time for me that I [had] ever explained [to] somebody else how to do research. It was also an amazing opportunity to get some teaching experience. I got to experience a difference between doing research myself and guiding somebody else to do it. When reflecting now on the process, I come to [the] conclusion that I probably imposed too much of my thoughts on her, and next time I should make sure that I rather create an atmosphere for thoughts to grow, rather then impose my own. However, it was a valuable experience and a valuable lesson to learn and next time I will do it differently – and probably learn something new as well. I was supervising on a topic different to . . . my PhD. I had knowledge in some aspects of the topic and an interest in others. However, I did not have time to explore those topics within my PhD. Through Claire's work it was possible for me to explore a new and interesting topic, which I would not have been able to do within the scope of my PhD.

The rapport and mutual respect Yekatherina and Claire had for each other are best described in the following email exchange:

Claire hi,

I just want to say thank you! You are my first master dissertation student and it was a pleasure supervising you, talking to you and reading your work!

I am glad you pushed it so far. We would still need to work on it, but it is a really good dissertation.

Best,
Katya

Hi Katya,

I should be thanking you!! You gave me so much help and direction that I would never have achieved on my own.

Your future students will be very lucky.

Kind Regards,
Claire

3. Conclusion

To summarise, by involving a student (PhD) from a neighbouring field in the supervision side of a teaching process (MSc dissertation supervision), we created an amazing learning experience for the taught student (MSc student). The result, an MSc dissertation that adopted innovative research design, was singled out in the external examiner's report as something 'he learned from' and was the basis for the joint journal paper currently under review.

3.5

Digital tools for bridging the knowledge gap to university mathematics

Eirini Geraniou
UCL Institute of Education

Manolis Mavrikis and Maria Margeti
UCL Knowledge Lab

1. Introduction

According to the Organisation for Economic Cooperation and Development (OECD), England has three times more low-skilled people among sixteen- to nineteen-year-olds than the best-performing countries (Kuczera et al. 2016). Anecdotally, researchers and university teaching staff seem more concerned than ever with the evident problem of the growing deficiency in mathematical skills among undergraduate students in science, engineering and other applied sciences. While most of these problems have their origins at school, universities have to cope with several challenges, such as students' diverse backgrounds and levels, and that students often fail to recognise the importance of mathematics for their main degree. All these problems make additional support (tutorials, formative assessment and feedback, etc.) difficult and, in conjunction with the increased intake of students, time-consuming. Additionally, most undergraduate courses require a higher foundation in mathematics than that provided by GCSE (UK school examinations taken at the age of around 16). And so it often falls to universities to deal with this poor level of prior knowledge that can have a negative impact on students' progress.

We advocate that to help students to transition from school to university mathematics, higher education should look into the vast research of digital education. It should consider innovative technologies and associated pedagogies that can help students bridge the gap to university mathematics and achieve their full potential on their degrees.

Without endorsing specific tools, we provide below a brief description of some digital technologies that could transform higher education pedagogy. We also make a call to arms to the teaching community to: consider such technologies; engage with research in mathematics education that aims to understand better how learners interact with emerging technologies; identify ways to support the learners; and provide meaningful information about their interaction to instructors.

2. Digital technologies supporting university mathematics learning

There are a huge variety of systems for learning and teaching that can be used at undergraduate level. Comprehensive reviews include Engelbrecht and Harding (2005), Lavicza (2006) and, more recently, Kissane et al. (2015). Readers may also be interested in a broader review on the impact of technological change on science, technology, engineering and mathematics education (Davies et al. 2013) that, despite its focus on schools, can inform undergraduate teaching practice as well. In brief, such systems include: computer algebra systems (CAS), graph plotters, automatic assessment, and adaptive and intelligent systems. The above-mentioned reviews also show that the different functions of these systems are often combined. Going beyond the direct use of CAS, which is well reviewed (e.g. Marshall et al. 2012), we highlight two key types of digital technologies on which we and colleagues have undertaken research, and which we have noticed are underutilised despite their potential.

2.1 Computer-aided assessment

Automatic formative and summative assessment has important teaching and learning implications. Readers may be interested in a comprehensive review of the field and the practical suggestions discussed in Sangwin (2013). Among successful examples in mathematics is the STACK project (www.stack.bham.ac.uk/) that has evolved over years of research (see Sangwin and Grove (2006) and previous related work in Mavrikis and Maciocia (2003) and Mavrikis and González-Palomo (2004)). This work recognises that mathematically rich assessment requires the use of CAS in the background to automate the assessment of pedagogically valid questions. Unlike the traditional use of CAS, systems like STACK utilise the power of CAS to accurately compare mathematical expressions, automate graphical representations and perform rapid re-calculation to facilitate assessment (Sangwin and Grove 2006).

2.2 Adaptive and intelligent systems

Adaptive systems equipped with artificial intelligence can provide students with individualised learning based on their abilities, knowledge and skills. This is possible through recommendation algorithms underpinned by pedagogical models that can adapt task selection, taking into account difficulty and previous performance of students in a previous cohort (see a short review in Davies et al. 2013). Similarly, intelligent tutoring systems provide a degree of intelligent support during problem-solving. An actively maintained research-oriented example is the ActiveMath project (now MathBridge – see www.math-bridge.org/). A variety of commercial tools are also beginning to emerge from well-known educational publishers in the field.

3. Pedagogical considerations

Although today's students are technologically literate – many students entering university in 2017 will have never known a life without the internet and will have experience of social networking technologies – using technology for learning requires 'learning how to learn' with the new medium. Research in mathematics education has long demonstrated the potential challenges – in, for example, exposing students' limited understanding of computer algebra systems (Lavicza 2007). In our research, we have noticed that the design of a system can have an impact on students' approach to learning, including triggering curiosity and interest (Margeti and Mavrikis 2015).

There are still several questions about the pedagogy of digital technologies for university mathematics that need addressing. For example, the transition from school to university requires a shift from an external locus of control to an internal one. Even though interacting with digital tools can be engaging, how can we promote engagement with the actual mathematics? How can we support students' interactions with the tool in hand and ensure the focus is on the mathematics by addressing any technical difficulties that could potentially lead to disengagement? How do students collaborate and support each other through digital tools, online communities or collaborative digital platforms? How can we promote resilience, mathematical 'habits of mind' and inquiry-based learning that equip students to tackle the 'harder' mathematics and apply them where needed? Considering the wide range of digital literacy skills of today's university students, there needs to be a clear distinction between technical competence and mathematical competence. We need to identify strategies to facilitate the appropriate use of digital tools for teaching and learning mathematics at university.

4. Join the community

We are seeking to form a 'community of interest' (Henri and Pudelko 2003) to host a close collaboration between researchers, university lecturers of mathematics and students, with the aim of utilising our expertise and plethora of research prototypes to produce supporting material and integrate digital tools in mathematics teaching across UCL.

The inclusion of researchers, lecturers and students in the design of supporting materials is critical, with respect to both lecturers' development processes and for supporting students' transition to higher education. In another area of educational digital technology, namely learning analytics, we are beginning to observe how the availability of data showing learners' engagement with digital environments can be used for both real-time monitoring and post-interaction reflection (Mavrikis et al. 2016). This requires bringing together the expertise of different stakeholders, including computer scientists, developers, educators and students.

Our aspiration is to harness teaching expertise in mathematics across our university, which, combined with research in computer science and digital education, can act as a springboard for spreading excellent practice even more widely. This won't just help the study of mathematics, but will benefit all students and teaching staff from different departments, at both UCL and other universities.

References

Davies, P., Kent, G., Laurillard, D., Lieben, C., Mavrikis, M., Noss, R., Price, S. and Pratt, D. 2013. *The Royal Society Vision: The Impact of Technological Change on STEM Education*. London: Institute of Education. https://royalsociety.org/~/media/education/policy/vision/reports/ev-6-vision-research-report-20140624.pdf?la=en-GB [Accessed 24 October 2017].

Engelbrecht, J. and Harding, A. 2005. Teaching Undergraduate Mathematics on the Internet Part 1: Technologies and Taxonomy. *Educational Studies in Mathematics* 58, 235–52.

Henri, F. and Pudelko, B. 2003. Understanding and analysing activity and learning in virtual communities. *Journal of Computer Assisted Learning* 19, 474–87.

Kissane, B., McConney, A. and Ho, K. F. 2015. *Review of the Use of Technology in Mathematics Education and the Related Use of CAS Calculators in External Examinations and in Post School Tertiary Education Settings*. Perth, WA: School Curriculum and Standards Authority.

Kuczera, M., Field, S. and Windisch, H. C. 2016. Building skills for all: a review of England. OECD Skills Studies. https://www.oecd.org/unitedkingdom/building-skills-for-all-review-of-england.pdf [Accessed 24 October 2017].

Lavicza, Z. 2006. The examination of Computer Algebra Systems (CAS) integration into university-level mathematics teaching. In *Online Proceedings for the 17th ICMI study conference*, edited by C. Hoyles, J. B. Lagrange, L. H. Son, and N. Sinclair, pp. 37–44. Hanoi, Vietnam: Hanoi University of Technology.

Lavicza, Z. 2007. Factors influencing the integration of Computer Algebra Systems into university-level mathematics education. *International Journal for Technology in Mathematics Education* 14, 121–9.

Margeti, M. and Mavrikis, M. 2015. Students' deep and surface approach: Links to interaction in learning environments. In *Design for Teaching and Learning in a Networked World*, pp. 435–40. Cham, Switzerland: Springer International Publishing.

Marshall, N., Buteau, C., Jarvis, D. H. and Lavicza, Z. 2012. Do mathematicians integrate computer algebra systems in university teaching? Comparing a literature review to an international survey study. *Computers & Education* 58, 423–34.

Mavrikis, M. and González-Palomo, A. 2004. Mathematical, interactive exercise generation from static documents. *Electronic Notes in Theoretical Computer Science* 93, 183–201.

Mavrikis, M. and Maciocia, A. 2003. WaLLiS: a Web-based ILE for Science and Engineering Students Studying Mathematics. In *Workshop of Advanced Technologies for Mathematics Education in 11th International Conference on Artificial Intelligence in Education*. Sydney, Australia.

Mavrikis, M., Gutierrez-Santos, S. and Poulovassilis, A. 2016. Design and evaluation of teacher assistance tools for exploratory learning environments. In *Proceedings of the Sixth International Conference on Learning Analytics & Knowledge*, pp. 168–72. ACM.

Sangwin, C. J. 2013. *Computer Aided Assessment of Mathematics*. Oxford: Oxford University Press.

Sangwin, C. J. and Grove, M. J. 2006. STACK: Addressing the needs of the 'neglected learners'. In *Proceedings of the First WebALT Conference and Exhibition January 5–6, Technical University of Eindhoven*, pp. 81–95. Oy WebALT Inc, University of Helsinki.

3.6

Examining linguistic diversity as a resource for higher education in the anglophone world

Siân Preece, Arnaldo Griffin, Yu Hao and Gozzal Utemuratova
UCL Institute of Education

1. The ChangeMakers Multilingual University project

Our ChangeMakers project arose from the UK's Economic and Social Research Council (ESRC) seminar series *The Multilingual University* (Preece et al. 2016b). The seminar series examined the notion of the multilingual university within the anglophone world and in non-English dominant settings where English is used as a medium of instruction (EMI). Research shows that while higher education institutions in anglophone settings have welcomed the cultural diversification of the student population, they are less certain about how to approach the linguistic diversity that accompanies a culturally diverse body of students. While welcoming cultural diversity, universities tend to treat linguistic diversity in terms of language deficit and a problem to be fixed (see, e.g., Preece 2009, 2010; Marshall 2010; Martin 2010). The seminar series set out to put forward alternative perspectives to linguistic diversity, in which the varied linguistic repertoires of bilingual and multilingual students are viewed as resources and assets for the institution to develop and in which higher education space is viewed as a site of multilingualism. To this end, the UCL ChangeMakers project aimed to illustrate ways in which postgraduate students drew on their own and each other's linguistic diversity as a resource. In the process, we hoped to strengthen the link between research and teaching.

The project was located in the Applied Linguistics and TESOL (ALT) group at the UCL Institute of Education (IOE). Our team consisted of a member of academic staff with specialist interest in multilingual learners and higher education, and three postgraduate international students who were interested in bi/multilingualism and participating in a collaborative staff–student partnership. The team agreed that a case study examining the phenomenon of linguistic diversity among the ALT cohort was rich with possibilities as among the 120 (or so) students, bi/multilingualism was the norm; very few monolingual English speakers were in evidence. Additionally, the project was a good opportunity for fostering research-based education, as second-language and bilingual learners/education are key areas of interest in our field. The main aims of the project (and associated research questions) were to document linguistic diversity in the ALT cohort and investigate how bi/multilingual students made use of linguistic diversity in higher education in an anglophone setting.

The team met regularly to design the study, devise data collection tools, analyse the data and prepare for the dissemination of the findings. We adopted a mixed-method methodology commonly used in applied linguistics (Dörnyei 2007). This methodology enabled the students to contribute to a range of data collection tools, namely: an online survey, reflective journals and video-recorded campus observations. Given the short time frame for the project, we eventually focused on the survey and journals and agreed to pursue video-recorded observations in a future project. The online survey was devised to document the linguistic repertoires of ALT students and ascertain their attitudes towards linguistic diversity. The student members of the project team took the lead in developing the questions, which were refined at project meetings, piloting the survey in paper format before administering it via Google Docs. In all, 45 surveys were completed. The journals were designed to gather more in-depth qualitative data about linguistic practices in the ALT cohort. Student members of the project team recruited sub teams of student participants to keep a reflective journal for three weeks during the spring term. To guide the journal reflections, participants were given prompts and the student team members collected the journals via email attachment. In total, 11 three-week journals were submitted, ranging from 2 to 15 pages in length. Following the data collection, the team engaged in two rounds of preliminary analysis, the findings of which were disseminated by poster at the UCL Teaching and Learning Conference and by a Panel presentation at the final conference in the ESRC seminar series[1] (Preece et al. 2016a).

In sum, the project facilitated a staff–student collaboration that enabled the student members to theorise their experiential knowledge of linguistic diversity and contribute to thinking about linguistic diversity in applied linguistics by enquiring into the perceptions and practices of their bi/multilingual peers. This is illustrated in the following section, in which the student team members reflect on their experiences of research-based education.

2. The student experience of research-based education

2.1 The lead student

Collaborating on the project has indelibly enriched my graduate experience. It has meant putting theory into practice and working closely with experienced researchers. The joint faculty–student project has made me aware of how important it is to allow your research to lead your opinions versus personal expectations shaping data. I became aware of this at the initial data-collecting stage when many times I felt as if I was walking in the dark with only a question: How do multilingual UCL students use their multilingual repertoires in higher education? The team leader encouraged us to trust the process and in the end we were able to analyse our data, and the findings pointed us in directions we had not foreseen at its onset. For example, how students' multilingual abilities can help create, influence and substantiate UCL classroom discussions. Our research showed that on a fact-checking level, students' multilingual abilities help to correct misinformation. Additionally, our research displayed how encouraging multilingual students to read and prepare for classroom discussions using sources in different languages allowed them to re-enter the classroom with perspectives and opinions that were being informed by their multilingual abilities. In essence, UCL has a Pangaea-sized pool of linguistic diversity, and its ability to contribute to UCL as a global university has yet to be taken advantage of. The ChangeMakers project has imbued me with a greater sense of leadership. I no longer feel like a student in a classroom, but an active participant connected to a wider UCL IOE community working towards innovation, change and answers.

2.2 The supporting students

Doing this project has definitely been one of the most unforgettable and rewarding experiences. The key things I learnt about research were planning and methodology. I became more aware of the time frame of doing research while taking into consideration different approaches. We were involved in multiple types of data collection and this experience broadened my knowledge of different data collection processes and their pros and cons. Most importantly, being able to work in a staff–student collaborative group was truly a privilege, as the academic environment in my undergraduate study at a UK university was one in which individuals worked alone. I felt very supported doing research on the UCL ChangeMakers project, as there was clear guidance and support from the academic staff member in the team, while the student members contributed to the project with their different backgrounds and expertise. Our findings show that it is beneficial to create spaces that encourage students to make use of their diverse linguistic repertoires. We found that students benefitted from using literature written in the range of languages that they speak and that their linguistic diversity could be brought to bear by collecting data in different languages that could inform academia in the anglophone world.

The UCL ChangeMakers project has been inspiring for various reasons, such as working in collaboration with the tutor and peers, finding out about MA students' learning experience and collecting and analysing data. For me, analysing the data from different perspectives has been the most exciting part, as it gave us the chance to explore more about linguistic diversity and bi/multilingualism. Before doing my Masters, I supported an English-only language policy in the classroom, because in my country, in most cases, the classroom is the only place to practise English. But getting to know the benefit of the native language in the second-language learning process, I realised that linguistic diversity is key to second-language learning and learning subject content. This project helped me to validate this experience and enhanced my knowledge about sociocultural perspectives of learning that view language as a symbolic tool for mediating knowledge. I also gained valuable insights into the ways in which students use their linguistic repertoires to internalise academic knowledge. The project also illustrated the important role of language in developing intercultural relationships and learning at university. The most important thing is that this project reinforced the positive feeling about doing research. As a result, I realised that research is an interesting activity to engage in, even though it requires a lot of knowledge, effort and passion. Consequently, this project contributed to making my Masters of Arts journey more interesting and inspiring. The key words to highlight my experiences are learning community, collaboration and best practice.

3. Recommendations for other academics

There are a number of recommendations for academics arising from the project. The first relates to the pedagogical implications of the research. We found that bi/multilingual students drew on linguistic diversity in a number of ways for their studies as well as to develop their social networks in the university. It is important for students to know that tutors see their bi/multilingualism as a resource for teaching and learning and that they are encouraged to make use of it. We would recommend that tutors find out about students' linguistic repertoires and share their own experiences of bi/multilingualism. The data from this study suggest that students benefit from drawing on their linguistic diversity in the areas of library-based research, data collection, group work and in preparation for taught sessions.

The other recommendations relate to collaborative staff–student research projects in facilitating the teaching–research link. A key issue is the nature of the relationship between the academic and student members of the team. A strength of our project was the decision to adopt a 'research with' or empowerment model (Cameron 1992), in which the student participants quickly came to realise that their own definitions, experiences and agendas were central to the research process and the research team. As the accounts of their experiences illustrate, this approach enabled them to take control of disciplinary knowledge and use it for their own ends. This facilitated their passion for the research and their desire to contribute to enlivening the link between teaching and research.

Second, academics need to give careful thought to compiling a team that is ready and willing to take up the challenges posed by the research project within the allocated time span and resources. As these projects are generally undertaken on top of already heavy workloads for students and staff, it is important that team meetings energise team members. Spending time on developing and maintaining social relations that are conducive to collaborative staff–student projects is central to the process.

While academics may facilitate this process, our experience showed that students are vital to maintaining team relations.

Finally, academics need to be able to scaffold the process of research-based education for students. To do this effectively requires knowledge of and expertise in how to assist and support members of the project team in accomplishing tasks that they would not be able to achieve on their own. Drawing on Wood, Bruner and Ross's (1976) seminal article on scaffolding, this involves thinking through how to interest intended participants in the project, what interventions will be needed as the project leader at different stages of the project, how to maintain focus among team members on the task at hand, which features of the research process to bring to the participants' attention, how to manage frustration and difficulties that arise, and what processes and practices to model for group members. Depending on level of experience, it may be necessary to enlist the support of other colleagues in assisting with this process.

Note

1. An audio recording of the presentation is available at https://mediacentral.ucl.ac.uk/Play/2165. The abstract and PowerPoint slides can be found on the ESRC seminar website at https://multilingualuniversity.wordpress.com/sian-preece-arnaldo-bernabe-griffin-yu-hao-gozzal-utemuratova/ [Both accessed 24 October 2017].

References

Cameron, D. 1992. *Researching Language: Issues of Power and Method.* London: Routledge.

Dörnyei, Z. 2007. *Research Methods in Applied Linguistics.* Oxford: Oxford University Press.

Marshall, S. 2010. Re-becoming ESL: Multilingual university students and a deficit identity. *Language and Education* 24, 41–56.

Martin, P. 2010. 'They have lost their identity but not gained a British one': non-traditional multilingual students in higher education in the United Kingdom. *Language and Education* 24, 9–20.

Preece, S. 2009. *Posh Talk: Language and Identity in Higher Education.* Basingstoke: Palgrave Macmillan.

Preece, S. 2010. Multilingual identities in higher education: negotiating the 'mother tongue', 'posh' and 'slang'. *Language and Education* 24, 21–40.

Preece, S., Griffin, A., Hao, Y. and Utemuratova, G. 2016a. Making the most of linguistic diversity: The views and practices of bi/multilingual postgraduate students. Panel at 'The linguistic landscape in higher education in English-dominant and EMI settings: Future directions.' Final conference ESRC seminar series: *The Multilingual University*, 8–9 July 2016, UCL Institute of Education.

Preece, S., Li, W., Creese, A., Blackledge, A., McPake, J. and Block, D. 2016b. 'The multilingual university: The impact of linguistic diversity on higher education in English-dominant and English-medium instructional contexts. ESRC seminar series. Available at https://multilingualuniversity.wordpress.com [Accessed 24 October 2017].

Wood, D., Bruner, J.S. and Ross, G. 1976. The role of tutoring in problem solving. *Journal of Child Psychology and Psychiatry* 17(2), 89–100.

3.7
Phys FilmMakers

Connecting Physics students and researchers through the production of YouTube videos

Laura K. McKemmish, Rebecca L. Coates, Frazina S. Botelho, Alvina Kuhai, Katherine V. C. Marshall and Laurence Z. J. Turlej

Department of Physics and Astronomy, UCL

1. Introduction

The pilot version of the Phys FilmMakers programme ran from January to June 2016 with funding from the UCL ChangeMakers programme. The course taught eleven undergraduate physicists how to produce YouTube-style videos on physics research. Lecturing, workshop and technical support was provided by science communicator and YouTube expert Rebecca Coates, while Laura McKemmish managed the course and provided subject expertise. The major project of the course involved groups of three students each producing a short video based on research by a UCL Physics & Astronomy group. A PhD or postdoc in the research group (the 'science consultant') took students on a laboratory tour and explained their research. The students then planned and produced a related YouTube video.

The Phys FilmMakers course directly connects undergraduate Physics students with cutting-edge research, with significant benefits to both students and the research groups. Students agree that the transferable and employability skills obtained from the programme are invaluable. Skills can be divided into three groups: practical and technical skills; skills required to distil and communicate a story creatively to the audience; and the skills to work successfully within a team with a tight time frame. Students loved the immediate connection that the course facilitated with the research and researchers within UCL, finding this fascinating and motivating. Students highlighted the fact that they gained an increased sense of belonging to the department. The researcher and scientists also benefited from increased exposure to the public and potential collaborators, funders and students.

The YouTube videos themselves provide a legacy 'edutainment' resource that educate and inspire young people. The involvement of females and other underrepresented groups in physics is encouraged by the inclusion of successful and enthusiastic role-model scientists.

The Phys FilmMakers pilot involved teaching 11 second-year undergraduate Physics students how to produce YouTube-style videos on research done within the UCL Physics & Astronomy department. During this experience, students witnessed the experiments and research process first-hand and spoke directly to the scientists. In this way, the Phys FilmMakers programme increased links between teaching and research in the UCL Physics & Astronomy department. Here, we discuss and explore the benefits to both the students and research groups.

Phys FilmMakers is a course with elements of project-based (Thomas 2000; Krajcik and Blumenfeld 2006) and inquiry-based (Weaver et al. 2008; Spronken-Smith and Walker 2010) learning. Many of the benefits we discuss here are also reported by participants in citizen science (Raddick et al. 2009), undergraduate research (Hunter et al. 2007; Healey and Jenkins 2009), video-making assignments (Smith 2014) and the PhD student–staff partnership. There are, however, three particularly notable and unusual aspects of this course: (i) inclusion of an arts/creativity element into science teaching; (ii) teaching of physics students jointly by a physicist and science communicator; and (iii) the use of YouTube videos as a central component of the course. This is a reproducible teaching model that can be applied in many different science and non-science subject areas. The course probably works best with groups of around 15. However, the course could be replicated on a larger scale with reasonable adjustments, for example by including a large number of PhD students as expert consultants.

The Phys FilmMakers programme represents an innovative way of learning, both for the students producing the videos and the much larger number of students viewing the videos. The film-makers engage in independent research, gain further scientific knowledge and explore more complex physics concepts. They become active participants in knowledge transfer from universities, a key 'scholarly activity' as defined by Clegg (2004). For all students, the videos give a direct link with cutting-edge research, with these potential applications and career options allowing students to contextualise and motivate (Hannover 1998) their study and course content. As Jenkins (2004, 29) summarises: 'There is clear evidence from a range of studies in different types of institutions of students valuing learning in a research-based environment'. The exposure to current research is also 'just great fun', reminding students why they love and are studying physics.

2. Gaining technical proficiency

Students highlight that they obtained the practical and technical skills required to film and edit a short video successfully. For example, students learnt to use the camera and microphone effectively and create three-point lighting. The Phys FilmMakers training and experience gave students the skills to address common sound problems usually caused by bad placement of the microphone or insufficiently accounting for external noise. Students gained confidence in front of the camera while narrating. They learnt how to interview effectively, recognising the need for enthusiasm and making the interviewee feel comfortable. Students also gained a variety of budget techniques for producing creative B-roll footage, such as: computationally speeding up hand-drawn animations; illustrating concepts via direct experiment or an appropriate metaphor through practical demonstrations using people or props; preparing and then filming experiments and demonstrations. Students improved their computer skills, for example by using the Adobe Premiere Elements package for video editing and Google Docs for group collaboration. Students encountered and then solved significant computer memory issues when editing using large video files, usually of many gigabytes; the storage of data on their physical computer hard drive (i.e. not the student's remote storage on campus) or a fast external hard drive was essential. The knowledge and problem-solving techniques gained by the students (e.g. 'Googling' for solutions, isolating different components, etc.) will be useful to debug many other computer-related issues in the future.

3. Communication and teamwork

All aspects of the conception and execution of a Phys FilmMakers YouTube video involve students communicating science to a scientifically literate but non-specialist audience. The methods of communication used within Phys FilmMakers were diverse: written (script), verbal (narration, interviewing) and visual (editing, B-roll, presentational aspects of narration). The demands for this communication were high; it needed to not only be scientifically accurate, but be understandable, creative, interesting and entertaining. The simplification of conceptions and their depiction through words and film rather than mathematics was difficult, but rewarding. Students gained the ability to filter a diverse range of information, often quite technical, and distil the essential elements required for understanding the science. They also learnt to identify a 'hook' and/or story (Bik et al. 2015) to make viewers interested in the science and motivated to continue watching the video. In producing an independent video, students displayed creativity and vision for a cohesive output. This course bridges science and art, developing the 'artistic ears and eyes' of the students and putting the 'Art' into 'STEM' (Science, Technology, Engineering and Mathematics): often called STEAM (Wilkinson and Weitkamp 2016, 5). Looking into the twenty-first century, we want to produce diverse graduates with a variety of skills (Hunter et al. 2007; Healey and Jenkins 2009); this course is a way to encourage science students to bring out their creativity. Even in the hard sciences, most academics agree that creativity is essential to making intuitive leaps, conceiving of new ideas and ultimately making scientific progress. Communication skills (Brownell et al. 2013) are critical in allowing scientists to bring others along with their creative scientific vision.

To make a video in a group, significant organisational, teamwork and internal group communication skills are required; this is typical of group projects (Bell 2010). Judging by the initial reports from staff and students from the pilot course, these aspects of the project were the most difficult. The project and deadlines forced students to test new methods and develop new skills for achieving team cohesion, coordination that resulted in the final product: a video. As in project-based learning, planning, organisation, collaboration and communication were essential. Communication within the student group, between students and lecturers, and between students and researchers was more difficult than initially envisaged. We found that a Facebook group, as discussed by De Villiers (2010), was quite successful in addressing this problem. We particularly noted that it was easy to check that everyone had seen the post, while 'likes' could be used to indicate agreement or attendance rather than an explicit reply. Students also gained the ability and confidence to write emails to senior people, to organise meetings and interviews and ask scientific questions, for example. This skill is perhaps underestimated by university teachers who do this sort of task everyday, usually without a thought.

Internal group dynamics were also difficult and definitely caused the most tension within the class. Students identified the importance of dividing workloads, helping each other out, finishing the task given and, especially, patience! Time management and organising the logistics of getting a team ready to film with the necessary equipment, props and people were consistently difficult, given the other demands on students (e.g. coursework, external employment). Students were thus forced to develop these skills, establishing and maintaining group communication channels and regularly updating one another on their progress. Another important issue faced by students within their group was how to ensure all team members contributed sufficiently to the group, and as they had previously agreed to. As an unassessed, voluntary course, there was no formal mechanism or enticement for this except each student's own dedication, ethics, commitment to learning and, to some extent, peer-pressure and an impending deadline.

Beyond the skills gained, our pilot set of students reported that one of the most valuable outcomes of the first programme was an increased sense of belonging in the UCL Physics & Astronomy department. This will be enhanced as the FilmMakers community grows, with links established between different year groups and with alumni Phys FilmMakers students. For example, for the next academic year, we are running Phys FilmMakers courses for both second-year undergraduates and PhD students. Some aspects will be co-taught, which will build connections between PhD students and the second-year students. The alumni from previous Phys FilmMakers courses will become mentors, guest lecturers and even tutors in future courses. Phys FilmMakers alumni will also continue to produce videos with UCL Physics & Astronomy equipment, enhancing the sense of a Phys FilmMakers community and continuity.

4. Making connections

The other key element emphasised by students is the access that this course provided them to UCL researchers and their science. The interaction took place at a level appropriate to the students' scientific understanding (unlike, e.g., papers and many departmental talks) and in an environment where the students were actively encouraged, even required, to ask questions and make their own contributions via the methods they suggested to communicate the science. The interaction also enabled students to understand and become familiar with the day-to-day life of researchers; what they do when they are not teaching, typical career progression, what a PhD is like, how funding is utilised, etc. This informal education allowed students to understand the life of an academic and their many competing responsibilities much more deeply, encouraging mutual respect and engagement.

Both the scientists and their research can prosper from the process through which the video is constructed. Being questioned by a curious and intelligent student can help streamline and focus a scientist's thoughts. It might remind them of the importance and strength of their work, impassion them further (Wilkinson and Weitkamp 2016, 17) and ultimately may inspire them to take a new approach or make connections across different research areas. The opportunity for enhancing skills and scientific understanding is particularly relevant for PhD and other early-career researchers who have acted as scientific consultants for the Phys FilmMakers YouTube video. The career prospects of these junior researchers can also be enhanced by the resulting publicity of themselves and their research. Their participation and the tangible video output can contribute positively to their CV, demonstrating enthusiasm, passion and skills in communication, outreach and teaching. The opportunity also helps early-career researchers make connections with promising future Masters or PhD students, essential for advancing their careers.

5. Wider benefits

The researchers, specific research topic, science and society as a whole can all benefit from the Phys FilmMakers approach. The videos generate increased interest from the public, students and other scientists about a particular research topic and group. The accessibility of the video format, combined with good science communication, can assist researchers in gaining funding, particularly from sources other than the usual academic streams. Social media metrics (Haran and Poliakoff 2011a; Thelwall et al. 2012), such as the number of YouTube views, can provide a quantitative measure of impact for academics and departments (for example, in grant applications or in the UK Research Excellence Framework and/or Teaching Excellence Framework). The videos serve as great advertisements of the research group to other academics (expanding scientific networks and promoting collaboration opportunities) and future students (enhancing quality recruitment), particularly if a great internal group dynamic is highlighted and celebrated. On a broad scale, increased interest in science increases the number and quality of STEM graduates. The computational, mathematical, scientific and reasoning skills of these graduates provides an important driver of economic progress. From a social perspective, discussion of research with the general public is vital to establish the risks and fears associated with new research. This is essential in eventually accepting the science and its applications or meanings to everyday life. It is in the cultural sphere that the science production process is completed. The more people are involved in science, the stronger it becomes. All these factors mean that the videos act to enhance the research's impact on scientific understanding, the economy and society.

The videos are important legacy resources available online globally via YouTube. Our chosen format incorporates authentic research and scientists, sharing many similarities (Haran and Poliakoff 2011b) with the very successful Brady Haran (Nottingham University) YouTube channels,[1] which collectively have millions of views and subscribers. By using YouTube, the Phys FilmMakers videos can help achieve many of the broader science communication objectives, such as widening participation and interest in the subject (Atkins and Ebdon 2014; UCL 2014), particularly if they are strong videos with appropriate gender and ethical representation, and are viewed by many. The videos can serve to promote UCL as a vibrant, evolving powerhouse of research and teaching innovation, where young students come face to face with the research. The choice of YouTube can also help to ensure that UCL maintains its relevancy in the modern world, complementing the university's rich history. UCL, proudly, was the first university in the UK to admit students of any race, religion and gender. This ideology is important in addressing the much broader and well-documented reduced female interest in physics in the western world (Archer et al. 2013). This is an issue that Phys FilmMakers can help to address by providing positive representation of talented and passionate female researchers (Evans et al. 1995; Sandberg 2013; Young et al. 2013). Similar strong representations of underrepresented groups, for example black and minority ethnicities, can also be made to help counter implicit bias (Kessels et al. 2006). We do not aim to make this an explicit feature of the videos, but rather something implicit (and impactful) through the diverse choice of interviewees and narrators. The aim is for young people and the wider public to understand and embrace (Taconis and Kessels 2009) the idea that physicists are just normal people of all genders, ages and ethnicities, who are fascinated (Kessels and Hannover 2007) by the world in which we live.

To other educators looking to initiate a FilmMakers-type course (both within and external to the sciences), we give strong encouragement linked with counsel on the importance of communication.

Communication forms the heart of this course: it is the communication between students and teachers, between students and scientists, and within the student group that work in concert to allow students to produce the final video communicating science to the general public. Communication is challenging, time-consuming and continually evolving. But, done well, communication is the key ingredient enabling the advancement of humanity by science.

Note

1. See http://www.bradyharan.com/ for a full list of videos; relevant very influential channels include Sixty Symbols (Physics), Periodic Table of Videos (Chemistry) and Numberphile (Mathematics).

References

Archer, Louise, DeWitt, Jennifer, Osborne, Jonathan, Dillon, Justin, Willis, Beatrice and Wong, Billy. 2013. 'Not girly, not sexy, not glamorous': primary school girls' and parents' constructions of science aspirations 1. *Pedagogy, Culture & Society* 21, 171–94.

Atkins, Madeleine and Ebdon, Les. 2014. *National Strategy for Access and Student Success in Higher Education*. London: Department for Business, Innovation and Skills.

Bell, Stephanie. 2010. Project-based learning for the 21st century: Skills for the future. *The Clearing House* 83, 39–43.

Bik, Holly M., Dove, Alistair D. M., Goldstein, Miriam C., Helm, Rebecca R., MacPherson, Rick, Martini, Kim, Warneke, Alexandria and McClain, Craig. 2015. Ten Simple Rules for Effective Online Outreach. *PLoS Comput Biol* 11, e1003906.

Brownell, Sara E., Price, Jordan V. and Steinman, Lawrence. 2013. Science communication to the general public: Why we need to teach undergraduate and graduate students this skill as part of their formal scientific training. *Journal of Undergraduate Neuroscience Education* 12, E6.

Clegg, Andrew. 2004. Reflections on Embedding Scholarly Activity in Teaching and Learning Strategies. *Planet* 12, 3–5.

De Villiers, M. R. 2010. Academic use of a group on Facebook: Initial findings and perceptions. *Proceedings of Informing Science & IT Education Conference (InSITE) 2010*.

Evans, Mary Ann, Whigham, Myrna and Wang, Morgan C. 1995. The effect of a role model project upon the attitudes of ninth-grade science students. *Journal of Research in Science Teaching* 32, 195–204.

Hannover, B. 1998. The development of self-concept and interests. In Hoffmann, L., Krapp, A., Renninger, K. and Baumert, J. (eds) *Interest and Learning*, pp. 105–25. Kiel: IPN.

Haran, Brady and Poliakoff, Martyn. 2011a. How to measure the impact of chemistry on the small screen. *Nature Chemistry* 3, 180–2.

Haran, Brady and Poliakoff, Martyn. 2011b. The periodic table of videos. *Science* 332, 1046–7.

Healey, Mick and Jenkins, Alan. 2009. *Developing Undergraduate Research and Inquiry*. York: Higher Education Academy.

Hunter, Anne-Barrie, Laursen, Sandra L. and Seymour, Elaine. 2007. Becoming a scientist: The role of undergraduate research in students' cognitive, personal, and professional development. *Science Education* 91, 36–74.

Jenkins, Alan. 2004. *A Guide to the Research Evidence on Teachig--Research Relations*. York: Higher Education Academy.

Kessels, Ursula and Hannover, Bettina. 2007. How the image of math and science affects the development of academic interests. *Studies on the Educational Quality of Schools. The Final Report on the DFG Priority Programme*, pp. 283–97. Munster: Waxmann Verlag.

Kessels, Ursula, Rau, Melanie and Hannover, Bettina. 2006. What goes well with physics? Measuring and altering the image of science. *British Journal of Educational Psychology* 76, 761–80.

Krajcik, Joseph S. and Blumenfeld, Phyllis C. 2006. Project-based learning. In Sawyer, R. Keith (ed.) *The Cambridge Handbook of the Learning Sciences*. Cambridge: Cambridge University Press.

Raddick, M. Jordan, Bracey, Georgia, Carney, Karen, Gyuk, Geza, Borne, Kirk, Wallin, John, Jacoby, Suzanne and Adler Planetarium. 2009. Citizen science: Status and research directions for the coming decade. *AGB Stars and Related Phenomenastro 2010: The Astronomy and Astrophysics Decadal Survey* 2010, 46.

Sandberg, Sheryl. 2013. *Lean in: Women, Work, and the Will to Lead*. New York: Random House.

Smith, David K. 2014. iTube, YouTube, WeTube: Social media videos in chemistry education and outreach. *Journal of Chemical Education* 91, 1594–9.

Spronken-Smith, Rachel and Walker, Rebecca. 2010. Can inquiry-based learning strengthen the links between teaching and disciplinary research? *Studies in Higher Education* 35, 723–40.

Taconis, Ruurd and Kessels, Ursula. 2009. How choosing science depends on students' individual fit to 'science culture'. *International Journal of Science Education* 31, 1115–32.

Thelwall, Mike, Kousha, Kayvan, Weller, Katrin, and Puschmann, Cornelius. 2012. Chapter 9 Assessing the Impact of Online Academic Videos. In Widén, Gunilla and Holmberg, Kim (eds) *Social Information Research (Library and Information Science, Volume 5)*, pp. 195–213. Bingley: Emerald Group Publishing Limited.

Thomas, John W. 2000. A review of research on project-based learning.. http://www.bobpearlman.org/BestPractices/PBL_Research.pdf.

UCL. 2014. *UCL 2034 Strategy*. https://www.ucl.ac.uk/ucl-2034.

Weaver, Gabriela C., Russell, Cianán B., and Wink, Donald J. 2008. Inquiry-based and research-based laboratory pedagogies in undergraduate science. *Nature Chemical Biology* 4, 577–80.

Wilkinson, Clare and Weitkamp, Emma. 2016. *Creative Research Communication: Theory and Practice*. Oxford: Oxford University Press.

Young, Danielle M., Rudman, Laurie A., Buettner, Helen M., and C. McLean, Meghan. 2013. The influence of female role models on women's implicit science cognitions. *Psychology of Women Quarterly* 37, 283–92.

3.8
Meet the researcher

The use of interviews to connect first-year undergraduate students to research staff at UCL

Julie Evans, Alex Standen, Alastair McClelland and Siir Saydam
Faculty of Brain Sciences, UCL

1. Introduction

There is considerable international interest in the relationship between teaching and research in the higher education sector (for a review, see Malcolm 2014) and, in particular, the concept of strengthening the link between them as a way of enhancing the student experience and improving learning outcomes (e.g. Healey et al. 2010; Healey 2005).

UCL offers an intensive research-embedded education that expects students not just passively to receive the wisdom of scholarly activity conducted by our academic staff, but to be actively involved in their own research as part of our larger institutional research community. The first dimension of the UCL Connected Curriculum is on 'Students connect with researchers at UCL and have an opportunity to learn about the institution's research' (Fung and Carnell 2016, 4). On both the BSc Psychology and BSc Psychology and Language Sciences programmes in the Faculty of Brain Sciences there is a clear 'research throughline' from Year 1 through to the project in Year 3 which is a piece of empirical research conducted by each student under the supervision of a member of staff. Research methods teaching and the opportunity to participate in empirical studies starts in Year 1, but students have not had the opportunity to engage with members of the research staff in the faculty. The aim of the 'meet the researcher' initiative was to give first-year students some exposure to the research community within the faculty in the first term of their degree programme by getting small groups of students to interview a researcher in the faculty.

An important concept underpinning the initiative is that of learning communities (Lave and Wenger 1991), and the relationship between such communities and a successful academic experience for students. The general framework was outlined by Belaczyc and Collins (1999) and expanded upon by later authors (e.g. Stassen 2003; Hafferty and Watson 2007; Rosenbaum et al. 2007). Key developments pertinent to an enhanced student experience are: (i) members of learning communities can include students enrolled in several common programmes; (ii) learning communities can include academic staff and students from all years of the programme; and (iii) there is a method for sharing knowledge within that learning community (Moser et al. 2015).

2. Methodology

2.1 Researchers

The Faculty of Brain Sciences consists of four institutes (Ear Institute, Institute of Cognitive Neuroscience, Institute of Neurology and Institute of Ophthalmology) and two divisions (Psychology & Language Sciences and Psychiatry). A call to participate in the scheme was sent out to all staff, and 42 researchers volunteered to take part. Each of these researchers was filmed while they answered three key questions: what is your major research question? why is this important? and what have you found? The videos can be viewed at http://www.ucl.ac.uk/brain-sciences/videos.

2.2 Students

Each year, approximately 150 new students are recruited onto the BSc Psychology and BSc Psychology and Language Sciences programmes, and are allocated to seminar groups of 6–10 students which meet on a regular basis. For the purposes of the 'meet the researcher' scheme, each seminar group was divided in half to create two smaller 'meet the researcher' groups of students.

2.3 Procedure

The first author met with the students during Induction Week to explain the initiative, and further detailed information about the scheme was provided to the students via the Moodle Virtual Learning Environment. This included guidance about how to prepare for their interview (e.g. gathering information on the staff member, suggestions for the sort of questions that they might ask) and how to structure a PowerPoint presentation about the interview which would be shown to the other half of their seminar group later in the term.

The students in their 'meet the researcher' groups were required to watch the videos, rank order three researchers they would like to interview, and then contact the Faculty Education Officer via email with their choices. The Education Officer had information about the researcher's availability and was able to allocate students a time to meet and interview the staff member. Each group then met with their allocated researcher and interviewed him or her for a minimum of 30 minutes (although some interviews lasted up to an hour).

Finally, each 'meet the researcher' group gave a short PowerPoint presentation to the other half of their seminar group in the presence of their personal tutor. The tutors provided feedback to their students on their presentations and facilitated discussions about the research that had been presented.

3. Feedback

3.1 Quantitative Feedback

Students were asked to complete a 10-item questionnaire to provide feedback about the initiative, with an option to add additional comments, and complete data was obtained from 47 students. The results are presented in Table 3.8.1.

3.2 Qualitative feedback

There were some very positive and useful comments from students, researchers and personal tutors.

Comments from the students:

Excellent experience, and I would very much like to take part in more initiatives like this.

A fantastic idea and overwhelmingly positive experience! I hope you roll it out widely for years to come.

Table 3.8.1 Responses to the 'meet the researcher' questionnaire

Question	Percentage endorsement		
	Strongly agree/Agree	Neutral	Disagree/ Strongly disagree
The 'meet the researcher' project was overall a good experience for me	94	6	0
Guidelines were clear and helpful	77	17	6
I enjoyed watching the videos	43	34	23
I enjoyed meeting my allocated Researcher	90	10	0
I was encouraged by my Personal Tutor to take part	77	17	6
My Personal Tutor gave me feedback on my presentation	72	13	10
Taking part in this initiative has helped me understand better the research culture at UCL	85	15	0
I developed my skills in interviewing, presenting and peer evaluation	66	23	10
Working as part of a team was an effective way for me to get to know other students	79	13	8
It was helpful to get comments about our presentations from other students	60	17	15

Notes: Percentages are rounded. Some students responded 'N/A'.

Our researcher was very keen to talk about many aspects and interesting topics of his field.

It was not only a brilliant opportunity to gain some additional knowledge, but also we could make connections and see how the career of a researcher develops.

I loved meeting the researchers because it was really interesting and inspiring to meet those I hope to emulate one day. Researchers gave such good advice and insight and I'm very thankful.

A short summary of their research to be provided along with the videos to help determine whether students are interested in the topic would've been nice - rather than having to spend time watching every single video

Comments from the researchers:

I really enjoyed participating in this project. I thought this was an interesting initiative and every step of it was well organised and enjoyable. I would love to participate again. I found it very interesting and well organised. I've used the short film as teaching material so it's been useful to me. Happy to participate next year.

The two interviews that I had were both good. The students had prepared good questions and seemed engaged when we discussed it. The videos look good and I was pleased to see a lot of variability in the way people chose to do them – I think that worked well. I'd certainly be happy to be involved in future versions.

I found it a pleasure to take part and very well organised. The students seemed very engaged and enthusiastic. The video is great and showcased on my website!

Comments from personal tutors:

I think the scheme helped the students with interviewing skills and it gave them an experience of presenting as a group which is a nice introduction to presenting.

Yes, I think it helped students understand the research culture at UCL.

I think the students were really motivated and enthused about studying psychology by speaking to real academics about their research, I think it is worth doing in future years.

They felt especially engaged in research and 'being part of something bigger'.

From my perspective the presentations were fantastic, and the students were really engaged in discussing each other's presentations as well (including relating the research themes and approaches to their module content).

4. Discussion

The quantitative findings strongly suggest that the main aims of the initiative have been met; the majority of students felt that meeting a researcher had been a positive experience, and had given them insight into the research culture at UCL. There were also other perceived benefits concerning skill development, getting to know other students and receiving feedback from peers. The comments made by students echo these findings and in addition, there was clearly a very positive response to the initiative from both the researchers involved and the personal tutors.

One aspect of the scheme which appeared to be less successful was the use of videos. It was evident that the students found watching all 42 videos in order to select three researchers they wished to interview rather demanding. In response to this feedback, we asked the participating researchers this year to provide a 50-word description of their research in addition to the video, as an aid to the students when making their selection. Here are the thoughts of Siir Saydam, a first-year BSc Psychology student in 2015–16 and the fourth author of this chapter:

> As a new undergraduate student, getting accustomed to the methods of teaching and different ways of learning at university can be disorienting, and I think it is very important for students to be in contact with those who can provide them with an insight into and greater knowledge of the academic world. I was initially unsure about what was expected from me as a first-year psychology student, and I also felt that I needed assistance to plan how best to make use of my education at UCL. One of the projects that helped me through this process was 'meet the researcher'. I was able to meet with someone who had once been occupied with similar questions and had gone on to become an academic researcher. The information I received was very valuable to me, and made me feel confident about what was expected if I were to pursue a career in academia. Although I had an idea about what being a researcher might entail (in terms of possessing a certain set of skills and a specific work ethic) I was not sure about the process of developing these skills. Therefore, the experience of meeting a researcher at UCL is one of the most useful things that can be offered to first-year students who are yet to discover the nature of their chosen field of study.
>
> As I browsed through the names of the researchers, the descriptions of their research and their videos, I felt intrigued about their subjects and I was also very impressed by the knowledge they demonstrated in their respective fields. This led me to formulate questions that I was genuinely interested in, as I was preparing for the interview with my group mates. I did not just want to know about the content of their research, but also about the process that led the researchers to focus on their specific subject areas. I think my questions also helped my group mates to think more about the researchers as people and colleagues who can be approached – rather than just names on academic papers. That, I believe, was the most important aspect of the project; not only to provide subject knowledge but to make

the researchers approachable to the students. There are still some aspects of the project that could be changed. For instance, some of my peers were unsure about the type of information they were expected to deliver in their presentations about the researcher. Most of them focused on the content of their research which I believe resulted in a limited interaction with the researcher. Therefore, the project could be improved by clearly informing the students that the interviews should be about the process of becoming a researcher and the researchers' personal experiences in the academic field as well as the content knowledge of the research area.

The project is also useful as it develops the students' learning skills via group work and in the preparation of a presentation, plus students are given feedback from their personal tutors. Personally, at the end of the project I felt more prepared and confident about presenting in front of my peers as well as starting to consider a career in academic research as a result of the interview. Lastly, my experience of 'meet the researcher' allowed me to be more conscientious about the process of preparing, conducting, and writing up the experiments I encountered through the first year of the BSc Psychology programme at UCL.

5. Meet the Researcher at UCL and future directions

It is interesting to note that the use of student-led interviews of research staff as a means of connecting the teaching and research was pioneered at UCL within the Department of Geography in the 1980s (Dwyer 2001). A survey by the third author revealed that 'meet the researcher' schemes are operating in a relative small number of undergraduate degree programmes in the University (e.g. Linguistics: https://www.ucl.ac.uk/teaching-learning/case-studies-news/research-basedlearning/meet-researcher-linguistics [Accessed 20 September 2017]). All have two things in common: (i) a small group of first-year students meet and interview a researcher – typically for 30 minutes and produce some form of output, and (ii) all the schemes have received extremely positive feedback from students, researchers and tutors.

However, these interview projects do vary somewhat across a number of dimensions: some are incorporated into the tutorial teaching whereas others are a component of a module. In some schemes, students are able to choose a researcher but on others they are allocated a member of staff to interview. The nature of the questions varies: on some schemes students are given the questions to ask, on others they formulate the questions themselves within a guidance framework. This means that some interviews have a relatively narrow focus on the research being undertaken, but others are broader so that the students get an idea of what it is like to work as an academic researcher in a research-intensive university. Finally, they differ in the output produced by the students: commonly this takes the form of an oral presentation, but on some schemes the students produce a piece of written work which carries a percentage of marks for that module.

In his role as a Connected Curriculum Fellow, the third author has been actively promoting 'meet the researcher' across UCL. Ideally, we would like to see some version of the scheme on every undergraduate programme as a first-year activity – and clearly there is the potential to extend the initiative to postgraduate taught programmes.

References

Belaczyc, K. and Collins, A. 1999. Learning communities in classrooms. A reconceptualization of educational practice. In C. M. Reigeluth (ed.) *Instructional design theories and models, Vol. II*, pp. 271–92. Mahwah NJ: Lawrence Erlbaum Associates.

Dwyer, C. 2001. Linking research and teaching: A staff–student interview project. *Journal of Geography in Higher Education* 25(3), 357–66.

Fung, D. and Carnell, B. 2016. *UCL Connected Curriculum: A Guide for Educators and Programme Teams*. London: University College London, UK. Available online: www.ucl.ac.uk/connectedcurriculum

Hafferty, F. W. and Watson, K. V. 2007. The rise of learning communities in medical education: A socio-structural analysis. *Journal of Cancer Education* 22(1), 6–9.

Healey, M. 2005. Linking research and teaching to benefit student learning. *Journal of Geography in Higher Education*, 29(2), 183–201.

Healey, M., Jordan, F., Pell, B. and Short, C. 2010. The research–teaching nexus: A case study of students' awareness, experiences and perceptions of research. *Innovations in Education and Teaching International* 47(2), 235–46.

Lave, J. and Wenger, E. 1991. *Situated Learning. Legitimate Peripheral Participation*. Cambridge: University Press.

Malcolm, M. 2014. A critical evaluation of recent progress in understanding the role of the research-teaching link in higher education. *Higher Education* 67(3), 289–301.

Moser, L, Berlie, H, Salitric, F, McCuiston, M. and Slaughter, R. 2015. Enhancing academic success by creating a community of learners. *American Journal of Pharmaceutical Education* 79(5), 70.

Rosenbaum, M. E., Schwabbauer, M., Kreiter, C. and Ferguson, K. J. 2007. Medical students' perception of emerging learning communities at one medical school. *Academic Medicine* 82(5), 508–15.

Stassen, M. L. A. 2003. Student outcomes: The impact of varying living-learning community models. *Research in Higher Education* 44(5), 581–613.

Acknowledgements

This work was supported by two small grants from CALT to the first author.

We would also like to acknowledge the support of all the UCL researchers who made this initiative possible, their names, titles and research areas can be found at http://www.ucl.ac.uk/brain-sciences/videos

Epilogue

Inspiring Change

Advancing student–staff partnership and research-based education together

Vincent C. H. Tong, Lauren Clark, Alex Standen and Mina Sotiriou

This book is the result of our ambitious attempts at bringing together a diverse group of students and academics for a pedagogical 'experiment' in the UCL setting. It is not just about testing new ways to engage students and staff from across UCL with learning and teaching. Our hope has been to inspire and develop a novel collaborative approach to influencing and shaping higher education pedagogy beyond the local contexts that students and staff find themselves in. Despite the complex logistics behind the scenes, our R=T initiative has always been clearly underpinned by two key ideas that have attracted significant attention in higher education: student–staff partnership and research-based education. Both ideas are about making connections in specific ways. Student–staff partnership is about linking up two main groups of people in higher education, whereas research-based education is about bringing together two main functions of higher education institutions. It is evident from the introductory chapters of the book that we are connecting up the people and the functions in these exciting collaborative contexts (**1.0, 2.0, 3.0**). With the student and staff authors showing how these connections can be made in different ways and through a variety of perspectives, what are the emerging relationships between research-based education and student–staff partnership beyond the UCL contexts? What can we now say about 'shaping higher education with students', the title of our book, in the light of research-based education *and* student–staff partnership?

First, student–staff partnership and research-based education can both serve as an effective platform for inspiring change in the other domain. Let us start with student–staff partnership as a vehicle for facilitating change in research-based education. Students can work with staff as partners in a variety of ways to inspire new ideas about 'learning' and 'learning communities' in research-based education from their perspectives, thereby changing how research and teaching may be linked. The universality of learning (**2.1**) and the significance of learning through mistakes (**2.2**), dialogue (**2.3**) and cross-disciplinary interactions (**2.4**) in research-based education provide the background for introducing changes to pedagogical practices (**2.6**, **2.7**, **2.8**) and for building learning communities (**2.5**, **2.9**). The findings from the focus groups (**1.5–1.9**) and the critical reflections on the links between research-based education and the workplace (**2.10**, **2.11**) highlight the complexity of the interlinked factors and perspectives that need to be considered when introducing change in research-based education.

Despite the interplay of the complex considerations, the eight case studies in Section 3 of the book (**3.1–3.8**) as a whole demonstrate that student–staff partnership is a flexible way to effect change in connecting research and teaching for student education. As its name clearly proclaims, UCL ChangeMakers, the institutional initiative to facilitate student–staff partnerships in learning and teaching (Marie et al. 2016), underscores the power of the partnerships in conceiving and implementing changes in pedagogical practices. It is no coincidence that the R=T initiative has adopted the ChangeMakers' way of working with students, from providing research ethics training and agreeing how they will be supported by the R=T initiative, to deciding together the aims and scope of the project and what individual responsibilities will be.

Student–staff partnership has therefore been instrumental in inspiring change when approaching research-based education in the R=T initiative. Has research-based education played a role in driving innovation in student–staff partnerships? With its development based on the findings from the student-led focus groups on themes linked to research-based education (see **Introduction**), the R=T Framework highlights the challenges, opportunities and principles in student–staff partnerships. These challenges, opportunities and principles, which are applicable to contexts other than research-based education, are fundamental to understanding how to bring about changes to the dynamics between students and staff. Being the editorial reference point for the critical reflection chapters in Section 2, the R=T Framework can be used more widely as a lens for looking at 'inspiring change' in student–staff partnerships.

In any kind of change, especially institution-wide change, communication is a huge challenge, but also presents an opportunity for reflection and evaluation of the changes being made. Discussing changes to pedagogy, curriculum and university ethos is a sensitive exercise, and one that should be undertaken at all levels: in classes, programmes, departments and institutions. This is particularly important because sometimes staff can feel that initiatives that are imposed upon them in a top-down manner have been instrumentalised and are less authentic, which can lead to more resistance, as pointed out in **1.6**. This also highlights a tension that can exist between the theory that underpins partnership and partnership policies at the institutional level (Healey et al. 2014).

Providing staff and students with guidelines that focus heavily on outcomes or the development of skills through research-based education and student–staff partnership can be antithetical to the openness that is at the core of research-based education and student–staff partnership (Healey et al. 2014, 9). This focus on being open allows students and staff to co-create and explore and discover new ways of thinking and working together. At UCL, although the research-based education initiative is institution-wide, departments and programmes are encouraged to explore how they implement student–staff partnership and research-based education in their programmes, because there is not a one-size-fits-all approach to research-based education. Although we believe that it can be implemented in different contexts and in different disciplines, part of the reason we can make this claim is because we know that research-based education and student–staff partnership are flexible enough to work in a range of situations.

1. Both students and staff must change

Implementing student–staff partnership does come with challenges – most challenging among them being resistance to change. This resistance comes on several different levels – resistance to different kinds of pedagogy, curriculum and institutional organisation – but ultimately resistance to changing the staff–student relationship. This was something that was mentioned in almost every chapter in the book and represents a fundamental change that needs to take place if student–staff partnership is going to work. Other research around student–staff partnership and research-based education have similarly recognised this is as a significant obstacle to successful and beneficial partnership (Cousin 2010; Cook-Sather 2014; Cook-Sather et al. 2014; Bovill et al. 2016). This challenge is an issue for students as much as for staff, as it poses a threat to the 'taken-for-granted' way of approaching education, which sees the teacher as expert and the student as inexperienced listener. A move from authoritative styles of teaching to student–staff partnership requires 'a rupture of the ordinary and this demands as much of teachers as it does of students' (Fielding 2004).

Although several critical reflection chapters (**2.1**, **2.3**, **2.4**, **2.6**, **2.10**) mentioned that the use of student–staff partnership and research-based education made the power dynamic between staff and students seem more equal, they also recognised that if this had not happened it would have made working together in a partnership very difficult. But more than that, unless this dynamic changes, it is not a true partnership. Cook-Sather et al. (2014, 6–7) define partnership as 'a collaborative, reciprocal process through which all participants have the opportunity to contribute equally, although not necessarily in the same ways, to curricular or pedagogical conceptualisation, decision making, implementation, investigation, or analysis'. This presents a fundamental challenge to traditional staff–student dynamics, and we would argue that if this is not part of the programme, it is not true partnership. We can see the potential of student–staff partnership to change radically the way that students, staff, institutions and society think about higher education. Of course, this may seem like a very idealistic position, but we think it is possible at both a macro- and micro-level. Where institution-wide initiatives such as the UCL Connected Curriculum and UCL ChangeMakers provide the frameworks, resources and strategic direction to drive change at a macro level, micro-changes, the small changes that staff and students make in one course, can spread to an entire programme, then to an entire department, and then maybe even the whole university (Cook-Sather et al. 2014). These small changes allow for low cost, low-risk adjustments to existing pedagogy and curriculum that can end up revolutionising higher education.

1.1 Would making micro-changes work?

Again, at the risk of sounding naïve and overly optimistic, we believe it can – and have seen the evidence of such at other institutions. At the University of Lincoln in the UK, for example, Students as Producers, a project that started small ended up changing the way the university functioned (Neary 2014). In the USA, Cook-Sather (2014) started a small programme where students acted as pedagogical consultants in the teacher-training programme at Bryn Mawr College, which ended up spreading to the rest of the university and completely changing its ethos. Although staff are not required to take part in the scheme, as of 2014, 158 staff members have participated (Cook-Sather 2014). Both of these projects demonstrate that small changes that start at a micro-level can gain momentum and make radical changes to the way universities function.

1.2 Would students be competent enough to facilitate change?

One of the key obstacles to a more equal power dynamic between staff and students is the idea that students do not have enough experience or knowledge to contribute meaningfully to the project. This is a view that is often held by staff who have not worked with students, and have not witnessed the innovative ideas and different perspective they bring to projects. Students may also feel anxious about working with staff, believing that they are not smart enough or experienced enough to contribute to the project. However, as discussed in **2.1**, involving students in research not only teaches them how to do research and create new knowledge, but it also benefits researchers because students often provide a fresh perspective that can lead to innovative projects and ideas. Miller and his group (**3.1**) overcame their different levels of experience and worked together to deliver and disseminate their research findings and experiences using social media while working on a research project. Their team consisted of postgraduate students, postdocs, and academic staff, who all contributed to a series of books and online resources about their ethnographic research. There is also some research showing that students who are involved in student–staff partnership are more likely to get involved in changing the university and society (Kincheloe and Steinberg, 1998) – the transformative potential of student–staff partnership (**2.0**).

1.3 Do we need a lot of resources to introduce change?

Another important challenge to implementing student–staff partnership and research-based education is the availability of resources and the plausibility of allowing all students to access and experience both domains. Although this could be an issue in science or more lab-based disciplines, in many cases the resources needed to engage with staff in research are already available due to existing projects, courses and programme structures (see for example **3.8**). In the majority of the projects mentioned in this book, the only extra resource needed was time. Perhaps if we change the way we think about the purpose of higher education, with more of a focus on students producing knowledge rather than consuming it, we could change the curriculum to better utilise staff time by focusing on student–staff partnership and research-based education for all (Bovill et al. 2016). As pointed out by Standen (**1.3**), giving PhD students the opportunity to teach and work with other students might be another way to address some of the resourcing problems around student–staff partnership and research-based education. For example, Marjanovic-Halburd and Bobrova (**3.4**) addressed the challenge of supervision being time demanding by enlisting the help of a PhD student – this allowed both the PhD student and the MSc student to benefit from supervision.

With the advent of external quality indicators (e.g. National Student Survey and the Teaching Excellence Framework in the UK), student–staff partnership and research-based education might be even more welcome as it seems to improve student engagement and satisfaction (**1.2**; Healey and Jenkins 2009; Cook-Sather et al. 2014). Research-based education could also help academics get more research, as students often have innovative and exciting ideas leading to publications (e.g. Walkington 2015). Students collaborating with academics on innovative new projects can also be beneficial for students, as they have the opportunity to learn about the process of doing research by working with a more experienced researcher (whether a PhD student, postdoctoral researcher, or academic).

2. Student–staff partnership as a form of research-based education

Inspiring change is therefore a two-way process between research-based education and student–staff partnership. It can be seen as a chicken-and-egg phenomenon, but the 'positive feedback mechanisms' in inspiring change as explored in this epilogue may eventually lead to some desirable snowball effects. Any bottom-up micro-changes may be a trigger to kick start the whole process of how the functions of higher education are viewed differently *and* how the people in higher education work with each other. Some academics may claim that they have always been linking research and teaching, and that they have always been working closely with and listening to their students. Inspiring change may also be important to those who are 'already doing it' in these scenarios where nothing *apparently* needs to change – the inspired changes are not (merely) about complying with top-down policies with all the associated obligations. The inspired changes are ultimately about the enacting of creativity and innovation that higher education holds dear. The opportunities and possibilities between research-based education and student–staff partnership represent such a space for inspiring change.

The consortium approach we have developed in the R=T initiative is one way of making use of this space for inspiring change in approaching higher education pedagogy. Are the students and staff themselves inspired? Chapters **1.3** and **1.4** discuss how our initiative has influenced the students who participated. How about the academics? All 11 critical reflection chapters in Section 2 start with a quote from the partner R=T Professors. It is evident from the Prof Fleming's quote (**2.10**) that she was inspired:

> Coming from a research-intensive and non-reflective tradition of 'see one, do one, teach one', it is a thought-provoking pleasure to read and ponder Jawiria's reflections on the opportunities and challenges of incorporating research into teaching to better prepare students in Higher Education for jobs in all walks of life. I also find it very humbling but also comforting that pedagogic techniques, which I thought I had developed carefully and creatively over 30-plus years of interacting with students around research-intensive learning, are part of Jawiria's established 'toolkit' as an early-career teacher and researcher!

The quote also echoes the idea of praxis, the cycle of theory, action and reflection, in research-based education (**2.0**). How do we encourage students and staff to engage in praxis through the R=T initiative?

- The students are linked up with exemplary teaching practices and outstanding practitioners in the teaching community.
- We have designed a joined-up programme of activities, from the Masterclasses and focus groups to the editorial work of the chapters and development of the R=T Framework.
- Students from 24 Departments in 10 UCL Faculties worked alongside academics from different disciplines on the book chapters and case studies, which look at pedagogy within and beyond the institutional contexts.
- Apart from hosting the Masterclasses for staff and students, the R=T students have more recently hosted an international workshop on research-based education and staff development workshops at UCL – effectively taking on the role as 'teachers' in a 'workplace'.
- Their book chapters and co-hosted international workshop on research-based education are external-facing.

- The R=T students come from different years of study, from undergraduate to postgraduate research levels. Students who have graduated (and got permanent academic positions) – our R=T alumni – have returned to work with those who are still studying at UCL as they hosted the workshop on research-based education for academics from around the world.

Although the R=T initiative is not an academic programme of study, these six bullet points correspond very nicely to the six dimensions of the UCL Connected Curriculum Framework (Fung 2017). Perhaps it is therefore not too much of an exaggeration that our student–staff partnership initiative can itself be regarded as a form of research-based education. Identities resulting from community practice (**3.0**) may also emerge, develop and evolve – as student–staff partnership and research-based education *together* inspire and shape changes in higher education.

References

Bovill, C., Cook-Sather, A., Felten, P., Millard, L. and Moore-Cherry, N. 2016. Addressing potential challenges in co-creating learning and teaching: Overcoming resistance, navigating institutional norms and ensuring inclusivity in staff-student partnerships, *Higher Education* 71(2), 195–208.

Carey, P. 2013. Student as co-producer in a marketised higher education system: A case study of students' experience of participation in curriculum design. *Innovations in Education and Teaching International* 50(3), 250–60.

Cook-Sather, A. 2014. Student–faculty partnership in explorations of pedagogical practice: A threshold concept in academic development. *International Journal for Academic Development* 19(3), 186–98.

Cook-Sather, A., Bovill, C. and Felten, P. 2014. *Engaging Students as Partners in Learning and Teaching: A Guide For Faculty*. San Francisco: Jossey-Bass.

Cousin, G. 2010. Neither teacher-centred nor student-centred: Threshold concepts and research partnerships. *Journal of Learning Development in Higher Education* 2, 1–9.

Fielding, M. 2004. Transformative approaches to student voice: theoretical underpinnings, recalcitrant realities. *British Educational Research Journal* 30, 295–311.

Fung, D. 2017. *A Connected Curriculum for Higher Education*. London: UCL Press.

Healey, M. and Jenkins, A. 2009. *Developing Undergraduate Research and Enquiry*. York: The Higher Education Academy.

Healey, M., Flint, A. and Harrington, K. 2014. *Engagement through Partnership: Students as Partners in Learning and Teaching in Higher Education*. York: The Higher Education Academy.

Kincheloe, J. and Steinberg, S. 1998. Students as researchers: Critical visions, emancipatory insights. *Students-as-researchers: Creating classrooms that matter*, pp. 2–19. London: The Falmer Press Teachers' Library.

Marie, J., Arif, M. and Joshi, T. 2016. UCL ChangeMakers projects: Supporting staff/student partnership on educational enhancement projects. *Student Engagement in Higher Education Journal* 1(1).

Neary, M. 2014. Student as producer: Research-engaged teaching frames university-wide curriculum development, *Council on Undergraduate Research Quarterly* 35(2), 28–34.

Walkington, H. 2015. *Students as Researchers: Supporting Undergraduates in the Disciplines in Higher Education*. York: The Higher Education Academy.

Index

'Fulfilling our Potential' (green paper, 2015) 179
fun in learning 162
Fung, Dilly 4, 36, 38, 264
FutureLearn 267

Gallou, Eirini 89, 165–6, 176; *co-author of Chapter 2.6*
Garside, Danny *co-author of Chapter 2.10*
geography, study of 154, 157
Geraniou, Eirini 19; *co-author of Chapters 3.3 and 3.5*
Gibbons, W. 197
Gombrich, Carl *co-author of Chapter 3.2*
grading 197
graduate teaching assistants (GTAs) 41–51, 147–8, 160
  and research-based education 42–7
Grasha, A. 232
Greatbatch, Wilson 117
Greenall, Annjo 133
Greenwich University 276
Griffin, Arnaldo *co-author of Chapter 3.6*
Griffiths, R. 179
group dynamics 298–9

Haapio-Kirk, Laura *co-author of Chapter 3.1*
Hammerness, K. 180–1
Happio-Kirk, Laura 268
'hard' disciplines 145, 147, 222, 227, 235, 297
Harrington, K. 18–20, 59–60
Hathaway, R.S. 278
Hattie, J. 179
Havnes, A. 180–1
Haynes, Nell *co-author of Chapter 3.1*
Healey, M. 18–21, 30–1, 38–9, 55–60, 90, 179, 278; *co-author of Chapter 1.1*
health and safety issues 156
heteroglossia 133
higher education
  aims of 191–4, 199
    fragmentation of 193
    general expectations of 185
  purpose of 90, 317–18
Higher Education Academy (HEA) 55, 59, 179
  Associate Fellowship of (AFHEA) 48, 51
Hodges-Smikle, Graham *co-author of Chapter 3.2*
holistic education 102
humanities, study of 129, 145, 147
Humboldt, Wilhelm von 102
Hupy, J. 158

identity of the student 156, 163, 262–3
independent knowing 103
innovation 251–2
inquiry-based learning 179, 227–30, 236–7
inspiring change 318–19
institutional culture 4, 236
instruction as distinct from *teaching* 198–9
instrumentalist approach to education 95
intelligent support for problem-solving 285
interactive research activities 176
interactive teaching 174
interdepartmental collaboration in universities 73–4, 148–9, 188
interdisciplinarity 60, 70–3, 107, 122–3, 139, 146–8, 150–4, 163, 169, 172, 188, 232, 235–7, 270–3

interdisciplinary research methods (IRM) 272
internet resources 95, 200
intrinsic rewards 34
intuition 278
irrelevance of certain disciplines, perceived 222–3

Jenkins, Alan 30–1, 44, 90, 179, 184, 278, 296
Jones, F. 193
Joshi, Tejas *co-author of Chapter 2.3*
journal articles 266

Killen, C. 58–9
Kincheloe, J. 91–2, 95
Kinman, G. 193
knowledge
  heterogeneous and *integrated* nature of 181
  social construction of 87–8
  see also subject knowledge
knowledge creation 125
'knowledge curators' 200, 206
knowledge development 158
'knowledge economy', myth of 225–7, 237
knowledge-sharing 173
'knowledge society' 192–3, 199–200
knowledge transfer 295
knowledge transfer departments 253–4
knowledge transfer partnerships (KTPs) 219–20, 222–3
Knowles, Malcolm 33–4
Kotonya, Neema 20; *author of Chapter 1.6*
Kuhai, Alvina *co-author of Chapter 3.7*

Laoutaris, Chris 173
large-group teaching 78–80, 190–207
  definition of 195–6
  reality and casualties of 194–8
Lave, Jean 19, 45–6, 263
leadership skills 215–16
league tables 185
learning
  link with research 110
  as a social experience 264
learning analytics 286
'learning by doing' 170, 256
learning communities 263–4, 304, 314
learning environments 113, 154, 157, 201, 234, 237, 262–3
'learning how to learn' 285
lecture theatres 79
lectures and lecturing 153, 200, 207, 231–2, 267
Lee, Ann 41
'legacy' concept 50
Levesley, Jeremy 61, 82, 103, 178, 182; *co-author of Chapter 2.7*
Levy, Philippa 45, 55
lifelong learning and lifelong skills 237, 253
Light, G. 91
Lin, Jiaqi *co-author of Chapter 3.2*
Lincoln University 316
linguistic diversity 288–92
Locke, William 193
locus of control, *external* and *internal* 263, 285
lunch-hour lectures 72–3

Lightning Source UK Ltd.
Milton Keynes UK
UKHW051015310122
397962UK00002B/17